SM 18628

Charles Olson's *Maximus*

Charles Olson's *Maximus*

DON BYRD

UNIVERSITY OF ILLINOIS PRESS

Urbana Chicago London

Library of Congress Cataloging in Publication Data

Byrd, Don, 1944–
  Charles Olson's Maximus.

  Includes index.
  1. Olson, Charles, 1910–1970. Maximus poems.
I. Title.
PS3529.L655M3325   811'.5'4   79–21788
ISBN 0–252–00779–4

Contents

Acknowledgments

When I first began reading Charles Olson's *Maximus*, I could find little to guide my way: Robert Duncan's "Notes on Poetics Regarding Olson's *Maximus*" in the *Black Mountain Review*, Edward Dorn's "What I see in *The Maximus Poems*" in *Kulchur*, and Robert Creeley's scattered notes and reviews. Taken together, these would not make a very substantial pamphlet, but they probably still offer the most reliable introductions to the poem. I am indebted to them for getting me started on the right track; to Jack Morgan, with whom I spent many enjoyable and useful hours talking about Olson; and to Edward Grier, Haskell Springer, and Elizabeth Schultz, who patiently directed my first attempts to write about the *Maximus*.

To George F. Butterick, curator of the Olson Archives at the University of Connecticut, I owe a special debt. He not only took time from his own work to answer my questions and to help locate the papers I needed but he also lent me the manuscript of his massive annotated index to the *Maximus*, which is now available from the University of California Press. As some measure of its value to readers of the *Maximus*, I can say that, had it been available to me at an earlier stage in my research, it would have saved me months, if not years, of work. I have made such heavy use of it and the dissertation on which it is based that footnotes are too frail to bear the burden. I have assumed throughout that it will be available to my readers.

Parts of Chapter II appeared in earlier versions in *Boundary 2* and *Athanor*, and in Chapter V I have borrowed liberally from a long review of *The Maximus Poems, Volume III*, which appeared in *Credences*. I appreciate the opportunity which the editors of these journals, Matthew Corrigan, Douglas Calhoun, and Robert Bertholf, have allowed me, to get some initial response to my work.

I also thank the Research Foundation of the State University of New York, which supported my work with a grant.

The unpublished works of Charles Olson are quoted by permission of the University of Connecticut Library.

Albany, N.Y.
December 14, 1978

Introduction   The Work

> Poets as such, that is disciplined lives
> not history or for any "art" reason.
>   Olson, "A Curriculum of the Soul"

Olson was naive, innocent, or sought to be:

> He left him naked,
> the man said, and
> nakedness
> is what one means
>
> that all start up
> to the eye and soul
> as though it had never
> happened before.
>
>   (*Maximus* I, 107)[1]

He made the simplest mistakes: he read stories which would seem to sophisticated adults "made up" and believed them to be true. Stories about a great white whale, about the founding of Gloucester, about Odysseus and a Diorite Stone which grew from the bottom of the ocean, about William Stevens and Enyalion, about the migrations of peoples and the wars of gods, all seemed to him equally plausible. He believed that the cultural traditions which had their origins in ancient Athens were exhausted, and he tried to imagine himself a Mayan or a

---

[1]Reference to the currently available texts of the *Maximus* is inevitably somewhat confusing. In fact, it is not clear what the work as a whole should be called. Presumably, it is *The Maximus Poems*, but with currents texts such a designation would seem to apply only to the first volume. I have called the poem, as Olson himself most frequently did, the *Maximus*.

Citations are by the following abbreviations: *Maximus* I—*The Maximus Poems* (New York, 1960); *Maximus* II—*Maximus Poems IV, V, VI*, numbering the page on which "Letter 41" appears as 1 and counting consecutively, including the several blank pages, to 203 (New York, 1968); *Maximus* III—*The Maximus Poems, Volume III* (New York, 1975).

This system of abbreviations unfortunately introduces another set of

Sumerian or a Pleistocene man, in order to find some vantage from which to begin again. This time, he hoped, we could avoid the mistakes we had made, if we could seize the opportunity which the New World still barely offered.

I follow Olson closely, trying to see his major poem with eyes as fresh as his own and to understand the discipline of the life of which it is the product. In doing so, I have found myself confronted with my own education. I seemed always to know both too much and not nearly, nearly enough. I felt at times that I was falling prey to a cult leader, a man who was insidiously subverting my knowledge in order to replace it with a mystery of his own. I suspect that it is this feeling which makes some readers resist Olson's work. It is easy to believe that he turned his attention to the least known parts of human history just to make the incautious reader feel his own inadequacy and that

---

confusions, but they seem unavoidable. Olson also referred to the individual books—such as those marked in *Maximus Poems IV, V, VI*—with Roman numerals. As I have occasion to refer to the books as significant features of the form, they are indicated by quotation marks, as follows: "Maximus I"—*Maximus* I, 1–47; "Maximus II"—*Maximus* I, 48–98; "Maximus III"—*Maximus* I, 99–160; "Maximus IV"—*Maximus* II, 1–76; "Maximus V"—*Maximus* II, 77–116; "Maximus VI"—*Maximus* II, 117–203; "Maximus VII"—*Maximus* III, 1–65; "Maximus VIII"—*Maximus* III, 66–176; "Maximus IX"—*Maximus* III, 173–229. The book designations in the third volume are based on my own conjecture; there is no authority in the text for them. See Chapter V for my discussion of their significance.

Reference to Olson's other works is made in the text by the following abbreviated titles: *Archaeologist—Archaeologist of Morning* (New York, 1971), numbering the page on which "Lower Field—Enniscorthy" appears as 1 and counting consecutively to page 239; *Berkeley—Reading at Berkeley*, transcribed by Zoe Brown (San Francisco, 1966); *History—The Special View of History*, ed. Ann Charters (Berkeley, Calif., 1970); *Human—Human Universe and Other Essays*, ed. Donald M. Allen (New York, 1967); *Ishmael—Call Me Ishmael: A Study of Melville* (San Francisco, 1966); *Myth—Causal Mythology*, ed. Donald M. Allen (San Francisco, 1969); *Olson—Olson: The Journal of the Charles Olson Archive*, issue number and page identified in individual citations; *Origin—Letters for Origin, 1950–1956*, ed. Albert Glover (New York, 1970); *Pound—Charles Olson & Ezra Pound: An Encounter at St. Elizabeth's*, ed. Catherine Seelye (New York, 1975); *Pleistocene—Pleistocene Man* (Buffalo, N.Y., 1968); *Poetry—Poetry and Truth: The Beloit Lectures and Poems*, ed. George F. Butterick, (San Francisco, 1971); *Prose—Additional Prose: A Bibliography on America, Proprioception, and Other Notes and Essays*, ed. George F. Butterick (Bolinas, Calif., 1974); *Writings—Selected Writings of Charles Olson*, ed. Robert Creeley (New York, 1967).

he razzle-dazzled the language for some equally self-serving reason.

On New Year's eve, 1970, my wife and I went to Gloucester, where we arrived on the Boston-Maine train in the middle of a blizzard. From my reading of the *Maximus*, however, I could find my way around, and we managed to locate a guest house on Meeting House Green. The next morning, when I got up, the snow lay "indeed about a foot thicke" (*Maximus* I, 102), but the sun was shining and the citizens of Gloucester were digging themselves out. I started down Washington, the street along which Maximus paces off the distances in "Letter, May 2, 1959" (*Maximus* I, 145), and met a tall, thin man in a red-plaid jacket. As he passed, I heard him, under his breath, counting one-hundred-four, one-hundred-five, counting off the distances as Maximus had.

I understood completely what he was doing, had intended to do the same myself, but right there I realized that Maximus is not *that* kind of hero. To me, a Midwesterner, who *still* at that point had never seen the Atlantic Ocean, Gloucester was an utterly foreign and strange place, with an odd smell of fish in the air. I had grown up in the interior, in those vast open spaces Olson had only dreamed of. If I had a ritual to perform, it was in Kansas or Missouri, not in Gloucester.

I conceive of my task in this study as understanding the development of the idiosyncratic and personal image of man which appears in Olson's *Maximus*. Its use as an image is not as a model of behavior or belief. At the Berkeley poetry conference Olson said, "I wouldn't propose what I am proposing to anybody because you end up obviously being eaten by Zeus' eagle only, and you're nobody, you're not even a hero. You're simply stuck with the original visionary experience of having been *you*, which is a hell of a thing." And he added, "I assume that the epigraph that I've offered today is my only way of supporting that, which [he writes on the board]: 'that which exists through itself is what is called meaning,'" (*Myth*, 11). If Olson is a teacher, his pedagogical technique is to present an image so compelling and particular that no one could persist—without massive self-delusion—in seeing him/herself in it. The nation which Olson undertakes to initiate (see *Maximus* III, 228) is one which values, even demands, the idiosyncracy of its citizens. It is a nation, not by virtue of a Whitmanian paradox but by the fact that anything which exists through itself reveals the inherent structure of things, or the biological intelligence which presides over the evolution of forms, perhaps the universal unconscious, which is to say, in Olson's sense of the term, the human body itself (see *Prose*, 17–19).

What interests me in the *Maximus*, then, is the way in which Olson proposes his heroic figure to himself with such force that he can only pursue every possible lead and bit of evidence which bears on the situation. He does not present the poem as an aesthetic object, and the reader looking for aesthetic satisfaction in any usual sense of the term will probably be disappointed. He is so relentless in his pursuit of the usable evidence that the reader cannot find the necessary distance or leisure to contemplate his or her experience dispassionately. Some might reasonably object that the *Maximus* is just like life, and in one sense (but only in one sense) they would be right. The promise of Olson's work is not that life can be escaped in art but that it can be lived with magnificent intensity.

The recent books by Sherman Paul and Paul Christensen provide excellent general introductions to Olson's work and relate it both to the tradition of American poetry and to the important intellectual trends of this century. I have focused more narrowly on the *Maximus*, its sources, and the process which generates it. The underlying argument is that the *Maximus* proposes a kind of action which again allows the possibility of meaningful political life.

Most of the terms I use here need some qualification. The vision at which Olson finally arrives is so removed from common western assumptions that words no longer mean quite what they have traditionally meant. The context in which they were previously reified has disappeared, and so to speak meaningfully of the *Maximus* requires an unusual rigor of language. It is possible for a reader to slip and slide over the surface of the *Maximus* on the ice of language which almost means what he intends.

In common usage, for example, "politics" relates to matters of secular law, zoning ordinances, regulation of commerce, and so forth; "myth" relates almost exclusively to matters of the soul or, in psychologized form, the self. One might be convinced, therefore, that Olson loses the thread of his political argument in the second and most of the third volumes where his overt concerns are largely mythological. In the *Maximus*, however, John Burke, the Gloucester councilman (*Maximus* I, 142–44), and Ptah, the Memphite lord of creation (*Maximus* II, 160–62), are equally political *and* mythic. One of Olson's most significant acts in the *Maximus* is to restore the city, and so politics, to its myths. He opens the theater of the psyche and the figures therein begin to walk the streets.

Similarly, I might confuse both myself and my reader by thinking that the phrase "proposes a kind of action which allows the possibility of meaningful political life" is synonymous with the phrase "proposes a political theory."

Olson is perhaps the first writer to produce a major body of work in full consciousness of the implications of modern totalitarianism. He does not address a situation in which one has choices between this ideology and that one. The contenders in the political struggle are not ideas. Totalitarianism is the organization of perplexed masses who respond to manipulation of their economic vulnerability, their personal confusion, and their spiritual insecurity. Life is organized in the state by accident or whim. Reality itself is called into question; thus the grounds on which ideas might be tested become themselves unreliable. Only by *doing something* does one begin to feel the way concretely through the forms which were so long matters of debate and have been in modern times wholly occluded.

The paradox which the western world has confronted in the emergence of totalitarianism is that programs for social change have failed to establish meaningful forms of political life. Marx could imagine the postrevolutionary state only in negative terms, as a "withering away," freedom from work, etc. Consequently, Marxist revolutions have been idealistic disturbances in fields of life which continue to require totalitarian discipline.

Olson's most radical political gesture is his acceptance of work as the sole, reliable content of reality. He implicitly conceives of work not as a penalty which the unfortunate masses must pay in hopes of opening entrances for themselves into the golden realms of subjectivity but as the basis for participation in the processes of nature. Labor is alienated not because it objectifies the laborer—as Olson understands it—but because it does so partially. It is only to the completely objectified, to the men and women who become objective extensions of themselves as physical beings, that the Lady of Good Voyages ceases to be a symbol or a wooden doll and becomes the goddess of the city.

In the following pages I undertake to make this somewhat unlikely story plausible.

The first chapter is devoted to Olson's relationship with the mod-

ern poets, especially Ezra Pound and William Carlos Williams, and
introduces three terms which will inform the remainder of the study:
space, fact, and stance. It is implicitly an attempt to clarify the distinction between modernism and postmodernism.

The second chapter outlines Olson's theoretical synthesis and argues that it opens a poetic space larger and more useful than any to
be found in its modernist constituents. Olson was not primarily an
innovator. The importance of his work is its confirmation of the wild,
lucky, and inconsistent guesses of his immediate predecessors. Modernism for him was not merely a style to be imitated, as it was for
many of his contemporaries. It was rather a series of discrete discoveries which, taken together, offered the grounds for a poetic practice
which is thoroughly secular, active, and available for use in a democratic context.

The last three chapters are addressed to the three volumes of the
Maximus. In them I attempt to trace the most significant lines of force
in this massive poetic form. Since Whitman, American poets have conceived of a poetry which would be the equivalent of actual, immediate, and on-going experience. The desire has been not to reflect on life
or to realize a theme or even "to tell the truth," but to impress the
literal body and world of the poet upon the language in a consistent,
moving image. One concern of this study is to test Olson's success in
satisfying this desire.

There is, then, no theme: a very large man stands astride Cabot
fault, "one leg upon the Ocean one leg / upon the Westward drifting
continent" (*Maximus* III, 37). The task is to direct the attention to
what happens in this inherently unstable situation which is always
Maximus's condition. What appears is a process, a narrative: the two
halves of the world come together and produce the triune image of a
man who, in turn, gestures to a space which others can share and
where meaningful public life can be conducted. In effect, however,
nothing has changed. The "story" is a temporal revelation of what is
and what always was.

that that which has been found out by work may, by work, be passed on
(without due loss of force)
for use
     USE

                         Charles Olson, "The Praises"

Chapter I   The Terms

1 Olson and the Modernist Masters

Beginning in the 1940s to think seriously about writing poetry, Olson was heir to newly discovered technical resources which had been barely tapped. In a notebook from 1947 he lectures himself, saying, " . . . use language with the freedom of movement that Eliot, Pound, Joyce, and Perse have given us. . . . Have in mind the freest possible extensions in any direction so long as the intensity is achieved, in fact in order that it be achieved, for I think your vision demands a lot of space in which to move" (*Olson 5*, 22). He was doing in middle age (he was already thirty-seven and had a good beginning on a career in politics behind him) what most poets do in their twenties, trying to learn what he could from the masters of the previous generation and to establish their limits, to see what they left undone.

In several of these early notes Olson addresses himself in the second person. It is the man who had already begun to articulate a mature vision, talking to the young writer looking for a form. Despite his life-long interest in Melville, the novel is about the only form which he did not give serious consideration. In the 1940s he wrote poems, short stories, plays. He put a great deal of energy and time into plans for a prose study of the American West, which would have probably had a form something like Williams's *In the American Grain*. He seems to have known, however, that he was too impatient, too mercurial, and too rapaciously curious to commit himself to a form which would not respond to new information and almost daily shifts in attention. The book on the West kept growing and shifting as he learned more about his subject. His problem was simple: how does the writer manage to *finish* a project when every day he discovers information which changes the entire picture? In another undated note from the 1940s he writes, " . . . therefore, better device [devise?] form which can be a sum of days, reading, verse and prose. Now what is the secret of such organization? A view of life, the natural string of a man anyhow. For what a man reads, thinks, values are the things which he is, and thus forms the form" (*Olson 5*, 44).

The only available model of such a form was Pound's *Cantos*. It offered the space he felt he needed, an epic sweep, and still it was a kind of journal, which could contain mythology, Renaissance, Chinese, and American history, almost anything Pound felt to be of interest or value. This is most simply what Olson means by "open form."

Of course, Pound presented problems too. He was a racist and a fascist. If "what a man reads, think, values . . . forms the form," the *Cantos* were necessarily suspect. At the time of Pound's trial, Olson wrote, "I propose that he be . . . examined and tried by the only men who conceivably can recognize and judge him, his fellow writers. It is not as a traitor to the U.S., but as fascist he should be judged. It is not his radio broadcasts, but the whole body of his work that should be the testimony" (*Pound*, 16). Olson, however, was almost alone in putting Pound to the test. The public discussion of Pound's work in the 1940s and early 1950s is a case study in the moral and intellectual laziness and irresponsibility which motivated Olson's withdrawal from government, academia, and established literary circles. Although Olson never wrote a formal piece on Pound's poetry, there is evidence in the notebooks, letters, and poems of an on-going examination of Pound's achievement and his limitations. It was one of his constant concerns from 1946 until 1953, at which time the *Maximus* was finally fully underway.

Before the form suggested by the *Cantos* could be useful to Olson, one distinction was necessary. The *Cantos*, he recognized, was retrospective. Pound's entire career was "built on remembering," as he says. "The lines and passages which stand out, from the start, capture a mood of loss, and bear a beauty of loss" (*Pound*, 98). He knew the past Pound longed for was irretrievably and not unhappily lost. Of Pound he said, "He's no easy man. He has many devices. And he's large. I'm not sure that, precisely because of the use he has put nostalgia to, and the way he has used himself, he has not made of himself the ultimate image of the end of the West" (*Pound*, 99). Olson believed that Americans were still faced with a new beginning, and though it has been burdened with an exhausted European tradition, it is still perhaps barely possible to realize what the New World offered. In *Call Me Ishmael* he writes, "We are the last 'first' people. We forget that. We act big, misuse our land, ourselves" (*Ishmael*, 4). From the beginning he was not interested in aesthetics. His intention was to redeem the American promise which was in danger of being squandered. To turn to the European past for guides is obviously useless; *it* is what America proposes to escape. Only the present and the future count to a first people, and if there is to be history, it must bear immediately on the present beginning. Olson's terms, which distinguish his own use of open form from Pound's, are "projective" and "prospective" (*Human*, 51). In the simplest senses these terms are nothing more than antonyms for "retrospective" and "fascist."

Replying to some nameless writer who had proposed a "scientific" definition of poetry, Pound writes: "The Art of Poetry consists in combining these 'essentials to thought,' these dynamic particles, *si licet*, this radium, with that melody of words which shall most draw the emotions of the hearer toward accord with their import, and with that 'form' which shall most delight the intellect."[1] Of most of the poetry which fills the anthologies, Pound is precisely correct. The poem has traditionally offered a zone of experience which differs from the commonplace in that the poem manages to bring the major tensions which develop to a resolution, so the experience as a *whole* can become the object of a mind temporarily relieved of its involvement in time and space. Line by line the poem promises accord of emotion and import, and when it is successful, it arrives at the unity of experience which is usually called "aesthetic." Its intention is to make manifest a transcendent order which can be known only in these instances of specially prepared consciousness. The impulse is to create forms which lift their content from the flow of experience, where it is liable to the caprice of time, into a context which is static.

Even in the early poetry which derives from Pound, Olson's difference is clearly present. The rough energy of his lines never move with Poundian lyricism:

> Ride'em, and, by the ride, down all night, all
> apocalypse
>
> by the, naked, tide, by

[1]*Selected Prose: 1905–1965* (New York, 1974), p. 360.

> beauty, "is most difficult" But
> for that reason is, at her tips, not, NOT
> to be dum-dummed.
>
> *(Archaeologist,* 21)

Olson is thinking of Pound's use of Beardsley in cantos LXXIV and LXXX ("'beauty is difficult' sd / Mr. Beardsley"). Pound, however, would not have allowed the blatancy of the long "i" sounds or such density of harsh dentals and bi-labials, nor would he have submitted the syntax so ruthlessly to the rhythmic demands of the passage. The way "apocalypse" hangs unresolved until it returns, scrambled, in "at her tips, not," would have offended Pound's ear, to say nothing of his tastes. These lines move forward on a dissonance which does not, as it would in a Pound poem, continually promise resolution. For Olson there is no authority which guarantees a final release from involvement in time and space; there is no prospect of arriving at perfected unity; there is no transcendent order which will make itself manifest. Even in Olson's earliest poetry, the unity and stability which appears is the present. The poem is an instrument by which one attempts to overcome the tendency of life to settle down into ever repeating sets of habit.

The other poet of the modernist generation to whom Olson gave extensive attention was William Carlos Williams. In several respects he seemed Pound's opposite. In "Granpa, Goodbye," Olson's piece about his last visit to Pound, he contrasts the image of light in the *Cantos* with the image of fire in *Paterson*: "Maybe fire is the opposite principle to light, and comes to the use of those who do not go the way of light. Fire has to consume to give all its light. But light gets its knowledge—and has its intelligence and its being—by going over things without the necessity of eating the substance of things in the process of purchasing its truth" (*Pound,* 100). Olson was at first disappointed in *Paterson* because its form was not as malleable or as receptive as the *Cantos*. On more than one occasion he speaks of its failure (see *Olson 5,* 45; *Writings,* 84), but in "Against Wisdom as Such" (1954) he recalls the images of light and fire and sides with fire: "Light is reductive. Fire isn't . . . 'heat, all but heat, is symbolic, and thus all but heat is reductive.'. . . A song is heat. There may be light, but light and beauty is not the *state* of: the state is the grip of" (*Human,* 70–71). From Williams, Olson learned that the local is the place of immediacy, the place of heat, because it is literally what must be engaged first, before the light from any more distant place appears.

Olson was influenced more directly by Williams's *In the American Grain* than by his poetry. Williams's short, tightly disciplined line was not suited to Olson's reckless energies, and in the early poems, when he occasionally tries to use it (in "Lower Field—Enniscorthy," "Pacific Lament," or "Only the Red Fox"), he tends to become rather flat and the tension which he is already able to achieve disappears. What seems to be a case of direct influence of Williams on Olson, the use of a single city as the subject of a long poem, is perhaps only coincidental. Olson had thought of doing a prose book on Gloucester as early as 1945, before the publication of *Paterson* (see *Olson 5*, 6–7), and he had conceived of the *Maximus* in 1947, a year before he read the first book of Williams's poem (see *Olson 5*, 38). Williams's characterization of Sam Houston is perhaps more to the point: "He wants to have the feet of his understanding on the ground, his ground, the ground, the only ground that he knows, that which *is* under his feet. I speak of aesthetic satisfaction. This want, in America, can only be filled by knowledge, a poetic knowledge, of that ground."[2] Aesthetic satisfaction as immediate knowledge, rather than as mediated and deferred stasis, is most directly relevant to Olson's undertaking. In fact, Olson's poetry has more in common with some of Williams's early work, *Kora in Hell*, for example, than with *Paterson*.

Olson himself sums up his debts to Pound and Williams clearly: "if i think EP gave any of us the methodological clue: THE RAG-BAG; bill gave us the lead on the LOCAL" (*Origin*, 129). The *Maximus*, however, is not a case of simple addition: Pound's method plus Williams's subject matter. Paul Christensen in his excellent book seems to hint that he finds in Olson the signs of a transformed and redeemed consciousness which leads toward a new reality.[3] I am inclined to agree with him, or I would be if I did not also sense that the consciousness of which his work is the product is really very ancient and common. Although abstract structures which are cumbersome, inexact, and rigid have long appeared as a feature of consciousness, they have been most obtrusive at moments of heightened self-consciousness, when people have been called upon to write, speak, paint, dance, to present themselves publicly. Perhaps the most valuable demonstration of Ol-

[2]*In the American Grain* (New York, 1956), p. 213.
[3]*Charles Olson: Call Him Ishmael* (Austin, Tex., 1978), pp. 24–68.

son's work is that common consciousness, with its own native intelligence and energy, can make its appearance directly, without reference to the conventions of abstract form. His work is characterized not by beginnings, middles, and ends but by intensity of engagement which informs even the most fragmentary records. It is a test of the proposition, "that which exists through itself is what is called meaning" (*Myth*, 2), that is, the unconscious assumption on which most people conduct their daily lives. Only when we want more than the common, when we want to deny it by appeal to the aesthetic or the absolute, do we doubt it at all.

Olson's work differs from the work of his masters in three crucial ways, all of which relate directly to his fundamental sense that common life in itself is its own sufficiency. The terms I use for the loci of these differences in the next three sections—and throughout the study—are Olson's own: space, fact, and stance. I take them as signs of common knowledge which our learning and our art have long disallowed. In the fragmentary and incoherent record left by the modernist masters, Olson found a useful practice which restores us to ourselves.

2   Space

Olson's work begins in *Call Me Ishmael* with the classic dialectician's gesture: wherever he sees "one," he scratches it out and writes "two." For "God," as it appears in *Moby Dick*, he writes "space" and "fact." For "Man" also, he writes the same. He was not demonstrating, however, that life's multiplicity ultimately resolves into final unity but that the great conjectural unities—God, Man, Beauty—obscure the variety of things. This "two" does not resolve back into one but rather goes on to three and beyond. It is a fundamental assumption of Olson's work that the numerable—anything which can be measured— is as understandable as the unifiable. As he understands Melville's parable, it is multiplicity, not unity, that makes life interesting and valuable. He concludes *Ishmael* with this little story: "The son of the father of Ocean was a prophet Proteus, of the changing shape, who, to evade philistine Aristaeus, worried about bees, became first a fire, then a flood, and last a wild sea beast" (*Ishmael*, 119).

Although he had reason to believe the situation might have been different long ago, now everywhere life is in danger of settling down into habits which endlessly repeat themselves, endlessly demonstrating the unity on which they are formed. The state, the personality, history, all are in danger of losing their Protean ability to change.

In space, the most obvious condition is not unity but difference. Its edges are never clear, and its center is a matter of attention. When Olson writes, "I take SPACE to be the central fact to man born in America, from Folsom cave to now" (*Ishmael*, 11), he means that the American condition is the awareness of differences. He describes American space as "merciless" and "harsh" because it is unsettling to the comfortable sense that man and space are one or, more precisely, that man and God are one and therefore space does not count. As Olson understands it, the tragedy which Melville records is not merely a literary event. Ahab's death is history, and it has real consequences in the real world. After three millennia the imagination of western man had been released from its demonic project of traveling across the earth only to find that there are no differences. If Pound was "the ultimate image of the end of the West," Ahab was was the first sign of it. Olson saw the danger that a Poundian nostalgia would be substituted for the new beginning which had appeared as a result of Melville's work.

A year after his break with Pound, Olson wrote "The Kingfishers" (*Archaeologist*, 44–49). It is a direct response to *The Pisan Cantos*, which is a source of some of its lines, and Eliot's *Four Quartets*, with which it shares the image of the kingfisher and a concern with Heraclitus. The poem addresses the fact that the immense accumulation of knowledge to which Olson and his contemporaries were heir not only had failed to extend the avenues in which life might be conducted but had created blocks, confusions, and wastes, which indicated a thoroughgoing cultural exhaustion. "Melville," Olson writes, "saw his likeness in defeated and exiled heroes, not in successful sons who, by their triumph, became the fathers" (*Ishmael*, 82). "The Kingfishers" is not a poem of Olson's triumph over his poetic fathers—in fact, he finally dismisses that Freudian struggle—but it does record his break from home as he goes off to join the rebellious brotherhood. He identifies not with Pound and Eliot but Rimbaud, who goes off in search of a larger space in which to conduct the essential business of living.

If *Call Me Ishmael* deals with the end of the western tradition, "The Kingfishers" deals with its origins, which Olson traces to the Delphic mysteries. As Olson learned from Jane Ellen Harrison's

Themis, the mystery was originally a celebration of Gaia, the Earth, and the stone which was the most sacred object in the shrine was the *omphalos*, the literal point of contact between Earth and her offspring. It is this stone, which has a symbol (perhaps an epsilon) carved on it, that Olson recalls at the beginning of the second movement of "The Kingfishers." Although the Delphians persisted in the belief that the *omphalos* was the center of the earth, the worship of Gaia, whose presence made mythological sense of the tradition, was replaced first by the worship of Phoibe, the Moon, and finally by Phoibos-Apollo. "The shift of attention, of religious focus, from Earth to Sky," Harrison writes, "tended to remove the gods from man; they were purged [of their chthonic connections] but at the price of remoteness."[4] At least by the end of the first century A.D., when Plutarch, who was himself a Delphic priest, wrote his dialogue on the meaning of the symbol on the omphallic stone, which Olson paraphrases in the first half or so of the fourth movement of "The Kingfishers," the grace of the indwelling beginning had been lost. He either does not know or, on theological grounds, refuses to admit that this place dedicated to Apollo was once Gaia's. The Apollonian intelligence is estranged from Earth, "estranged from that which is most familiar," as Heraclitus said in a fragment to which Olson frequently alludes (see *History*, 14). Harrison writes: "Local primitive tradition knew that the oracle at Delphi was of Earth and Night. . . . But an overdone orthodoxy demanded that about Apollo there should be nothing 'earthy' and no deed or dream of darkness."[5] Some mutation had taken place, and the evolutionary process had produced a form which, in order to realize itself, was required to deny its own origins. It lost touch with the only meaningful paradigm of dynamic process. Change itself, rather than the earth, the source of change, became the central mystery, the most profound and frustrating philosophic problem. That is, at the very origin of Western culture the only meaningful image of difference was lost. Literal, physical space was eclipsed by a purified intellectual space and finally, of course, by the Platonic absolute. All earthliness, consequently, appeared as vain and illusory in comparison to the eternal essences of abstract thought.

[4]*Themis: A Study of the Social Origins of Greek Religion* (Cleveland, 1962), p. xx.
   [5]*Ibid.*, p. 389.

In the context of such thought, "The Kingfishers" begins: "What does not change / is the will to change." Guy Davenport suggests that the line is a subtle mistranslation of Heraclitus's paradox, "Change is at rest" or "Change alone is unchanging,"[6] as it is more commonly rendered, and he shows that an etymological hint in the Greek allows "will to change" as a legitimate translation. Aside from the fact that he probably did not have enough Greek to respond to such nuances, however, Olson uses a parallel term (in a piece written a little more than a year after "The Kingfishers") which implies another reading. He speaks of a "will to cohere," which he uses in this context, speaking of the pre-Delphic heroes: "I have this dream, that just as we cannot now see & say the size of these early HUMAN KINGS, we cannot, by the very lost token of their science, see what size man can be once more capable of, once the turn of the flow of his energies that I speak of as the WILL TO COHERE is admitted, and its energy taken up" (*Human*, 21). In light of the poem as a whole, it seems that the *problem* with the will to change is that it does not change. It should be mentioned that Olson does not value change as such (see *Maximus* I, 5). As we will see in the next chapter, his poetic seeks to join intense action with passivity. To put it simply, but perhaps not too simply, he is not interested in going somewhere; he wants only to engage actively the place where he is. Difference does not come in time but in space; the goal is not change but revelation.

The culture, of which the first movement gives evidence, is an expression of the will to change, as it blocks energy, creates stasis, and finally parodies change. He who wakes in the second line, for whatever purpose, attempts to *use* the kingfishers. It is possibly Eliot himself who seeks to "cage" the kingfishers in his symbol of unchangingness. And in the second half of the movement, Fernand's knowledge, which is "uncaged," will not cohere and so leads to an awkward focus of attention which can be filled only by repetition. The facts, more or less interesting in themselves, are without center, to draw them into meaningful shape. Having lost hold in the world, Fernand slides "along the wall of the night, losing himself / in some crack in the ruins." These anecdotes define a context in which both action and

[6]"Scholia and Conjectures for Olson's 'The Kingfishers,'" *Boundary 2*, 2, nos. 1 & 2 (1973–74), 252. Davenport's essay is a model of Olson criticism, and I rely heavily on his lead in my discussion of this poem.

knowledge have become futile, even impossible. Action is defined in terms of projects with self-limiting goals, and knowledge occurs as isolated, inert information.

In the second movement Olson introduces three possible correctives or at least targets which, if properly understood, might produce correction: the mysterious E on the Delphic stone, Mao's call to revolution, and some gritty encyclopedic information about the kingfisher (i.e. the literal bird, not the symbolic counter in human projects). The relevance of this material to the on-going conjecture of the poem is unstated and unlimited. It is merely identified as existing in the space of the poem.

In the forty lines of the third movement Olson juxtaposes four very different cultural circumstances: Angkor Wat, Delphi, the Mexico of Montezuma, and contemporary America. The passage suggests three kinds of cultural change. The two kinds which are most clearly delineated are both cataclysmic: one caused by the loss of vigilant attention required to sustain a static culture; one caused by random conquest. The other kind of change, which is associated with the Delphic stone and Montezuma's ritual gift-giving, appears to occur with the formality of nature, perhaps even according to dialectical law.

As the passage is being read as a juxtaposition of more or less static images, however, it must also be seen as narrative: Cortez arrives in Mexico, is offered gifts by Montezuma, becomes outraged at evidence of what he considers barbaric immorality, and begins the slaughter. The movement ends with a startling telescoping of time in which the sixteenth and twentieth centuries appear as contemporaneous:

> And all now is war
> where so lately there was peace,
> and the sweet brotherhood, the use
> of tilled fields.

Olson intentionally leaves the temporal referent of "now" unclear in order to underscore the ways in which "that other conqueror . . . so resembles ourselves."

The fourth movement begins with a line which allows the temporal confusion to continue ("Not one death but many"), or it is perceived as confusion until one recognizes the precision with which Olson moves along these lines of force which are shared simultaneously by contexts usually seen as discrete. Most obviously, the reference is to the seige of Mexico City, World War II, and the Chinese Revolution. This line, however, is a paraphrase of Ammonius's speech in Plutarch's dialogue on the Delphic stone, and he in turn is paraphrasing Heraclitus. When it is recognized that Heraclitus and Mao are subject-rhymes, the relationships which are revealed become so dense as to almost defy linear language.

Three closely related questions begin to come into view: an ethical question concerning the proper disposition of the will; a political question concerning the process of social and cultural change; and a metaphysical question concerning man's relationship to space. The ethical question is, of course, the one that Olson begins with, and its answer is beginning to emerge fairly clearly. The other two matters are unresolved and come to the fore in the second half of the poem.

The will to change leads only to "accumulation." Because it is itself unchanging, it cannot respond to the new opportunities for change which its exercise creates; it fails to obey the law of feedback. Consequently, space is atomized in an endless succession of discrete events, each perhaps more violent and destructive than the previous one, and the possibility for learning is lost.

The will to cohere cannot be unchanging because action can only be redeemed by an actor who is responsible for the consequences of his own acts. The seeker of coherence must hear the *message*, which "is a discrete or continuous sequence of measurable events distributed in time," the feedback from his own actions, and stand ready to follow, to cohere in a situation that may be in large measure unlike the one which called forth the original act. Such is the process which "The Kingfishers" details in its fourth movement. It concludes:

> And the too strong grasping of it,
> when it is pressed together and condensed,
> loses it
>
> This very thing you are.

The appearance of a section of the poem headed with a Roman two, despite the lack of a Roman one for it to follow, illustrates in a way, if a relatively insignificant one, Olson's refusal to grasp the process too strongly, precisely for fear of losing the very thing he is, which is, of course, the process coinciding with the poem itself. One arc of energy has arrived at a stasis, at least temporarily, and the poem hooks back—"the feed-back is the law"—to an earlier issue, which suddenly opens in an unexpected direction.

Olson recognizes that the matter of the Aztecs remains in the poem more or less unexplored, and when the burial ritual appears to suggest another meaning for "Not one death but many," he responds to it. The glyphs—"serpent cave razor ray of sun"—obviously suggest that death is a journey to a new life, that death too is an active state, subject to the same Heraclitean laws. First reported in French, Mao is now Englished. The call to revolution has been invested with a new context and becomes literally a recognition of the necessity to raise oneself from the dead.

The Heraclitean material from the previous section and the implicit argument with Eliot continue to exercise a force. In one of the fragments which Olson paraphrases in the fourth movement and which Eliot takes as an epigraph to *Four Quartets*, Heraclitus says, "Although the Logos is common the many live as though they had a private understanding." For Eliot, the Logos carries the authority of an institutional theology. Olson manages to avoid the term altogether: "Around an appearance, one common model, we grow up / many." Olson's "logos" is only a shared space, a place of common action where the will to cohere is exercised. Given this reading, Mao's call to collective action is more to the point than a profession of faith. The distinction between man as an expression of the Logos and man as a party to a common model is carried out in the figures of Cortez, who is the measure of our guilt, and Cabeza de Vaca, who, lost in the interior of North America, discovered a miraculous power to heal.

Although the light is in the East, Mao is only tangentially relevant to the New World. He is present as a reminder that action, not Confucian (or Poundian) decorum, is required. Olson is insistent upon the reality of local forces. It is specific response to the telluric force as it is manifest on this continent that we are in need of:

> hear,
> hear, where the dry blood talks
> where the dry blood talks.

The pun on "hear/here" suggests an alternative to the intense looking which is demanded by the light in the East. It is the ear, "which is so close to the mind that it is the mind's, that it has the mind's speed"

(*Human*, 54), as Olson says in "Projective Verse," not the eye or the images it makes, that opens the poem to the deepest, darkest currents of energy that inhere in a place.

Olson recognizes that the Heraclitean economy implies a kind of cannibalism, and when this dark fact is hidden or exposed by a *false* morality (Cortez's), one sees "in the flesh / chalk"; man's participation in nature is replaced by reflection *on* nature; the conflict, which Heraclitus says issues in justice, becomes violence; justice becomes an unnatural thing which makes gestures awkward and false; "awe, night-rest and neighborhood . . . rot"; procreation produces monsters like Cortez or wasted, hopeless men of intelligence like Fernand; and the healing powers of Cabeza de Vaca remain a mystery.

In "The Kingfishers" and the work which follows from it, form is concrete, Heraclitean: ". . . the Logos was probably conceived by Heraclitus as an actual constituent of things, and in many respects it is co-existensive with the primary cosmic constituent, fire. . . . To put it another way, the arrangement would not be fully distinguished from the thing arranged, but would be be felt to possess the same concreteness and reality as the thing itself."[7]

Olson's intention is to propose habits of mind which are not the opposite of Apollonian—that is, of course, the Dionysian, which seems to him a capitulation to chaos—but its true contrary. Olson's strategy, most simply, is to deny the sham clarity of the Apollonian intelligence, in an act of love, and to allow the forms which move in the fire to have their own voices. In the *Maximus* the fire is space, and it is space as a source of energy that replaces for Olson the tradition of Pound and Eliot.

3 Fact

Fact is the geometric projection of space as it appears in the space of human consciousness. Melville's prose and non-Euclidean geometry, contemporaneous developments in the middle of the nineteenth century, were indications for Olson of the dimensions of the factual in space: "Quantity—the measurable and numerable—was suddenly as shafted in, to any thing, as it was also, as had been obvious, the strik-

[7]Geoffrey S. Kirk and J. E. Raven, *Presocratic Philosophers: A Critical History with a Selection of Texts* (Cambridge, 1957), p. 188.

ing character of the external world, that all things do extend out"
(*Human*, 118). Without getting into the complexities of non-Euclidean geometry, it is clear that, in Olson's understanding of it, this
fact unsettled the fundamental assumptions of Western metaphysics.
Space was no longer rigid. Like speech, it was capable of flow. Consciousness and space were no longer discrete. A landscape now appears as a stretch of rocks, grass, and trees in one of its manifestations,
as an organized structure of light or an image on the retina in other
manifestations, and, if the person does not insist upon intruding his
own personality or some abstract principle, it appears in language in
still another manifestation. In this latter form Olson speaks of the
landscape (which, of course, might be something from a book, something overheard on the street, as well as a postcard view) as fact.

Olson denies the fundamental western premise that art and life
are *qualitatively* distinct. He does not imagine the poet as an artisan
as Pound and Williams do, but as a biological machine, the product
of which is distinguished from "nonpoetic" utterances by the accuracy
of its measurement and, therefore, its intensity: " . . . if man is once
more to possess intent in his life and to take up responsibility implicit
in his life, he has to comprehend his own process as intact, from outside, by way of his skin, in, and by his powers of conversion out
again" (*Human*, 10).

Olson makes a radical departure from the conception of poetic
form as it has been practiced since poetry's compromise with philosophy. After Aristotle reintroduced poetry into the Republic by arguing
that it is more general and, hence, more philosophic than history, poetry has been secondary to abstract thought. The specifically "poetic"
qualities—rhythm, image, story—have been considered organic to
perfected thought, if not mere decoration. The conception of poet as
artisan, rather than as primary producer, is a consistent foundation of
literary thought from Aristotle to Pound and Williams. That is, poetry—apart from theme or meaning—has been exclusively a subjective matter, "style," a personal mark on the public property of
thought, or, as Olson says, "the-private-soul-at-any-public-wall." In
proposing a poetry of "essential use" (*Human*, 51), he demands that
poetic practice be restored to primacy.

The tradition against which Olson defines himself can be called
"lyricism"—for lack of a better term, though a better term would
suggest what a large part of our poetry is in fact personal song. In *The*

Discovery of the Mind, a book which Olson read with great interest, Bruno Snell speaks of the early Greek lyrists as the discoverers "of hiterto unmapped areas of the soul."[8] The experience of self as song was exhilarating, filled with intensity, a sense of powerful self-determination, and intimations of a life created in the permanency of being. Even in the handful of fragments from which the Greek lyrists are known, the modern reader can still recover the pleasures of the interior life. As records of possible psychic conditions, they are no less valid now than they were nearly three millennia ago. The opening of the subjective domain, however, required techniques of reportage, not production, because all of the exciting action was taking place "out of sight." The image, consequently, while obviously central to the lyrist's project because of its power to make things visible, became problematic. The tree or the star in the poem had a different status than it did in life. It took on the color of the soul. In the reading of history which is implicit in Olson's work, the lyric mapping of the soul is seen as synchronous with the literal mapping and settlement of the earth. In *Call Me Ishmael* Olson argues, in effect, that lyric space and physical space were very early confused with one another, and the possibilities for action and discovery were limited by the individual ego, which turned out to be far less capacious than it first seemed.

Now, however, the landscape is known: we *have* the map. The quantum of mystery, which threatened to engulf the lyrist or the explorer of terra incognita in darkness and confusion, is gone. The reasons for lyric exhilaration now seem reasons for despair. After Nietzsche, who recognized that the most profound intuition of the soul "is merely a formulation of our grammatical habit, which posits a doer for what is done,"[9] the spiritual landscape appears as a lonely and incommodious place, a waste land, rather than the garden the lyrics promise, or even altogether illusory, in fact, no place at all. Its forms seem as arbitrary as the form of the sonnet or the rondeau. "In the expression of their private sentiments and demands," Snell writes, "the early lyrists try to reproduce those moments in which the individual is all of a sudden snatched out of the broad stream of life, when he senses that he is cut off from the ever-green tree of universal

[8] *The Discovery of the Mind: The Greek Origins of European Thought*, trans. T. G. Rosenmeyer (New York, 1960), p. 69.
[9] *The Portable Nietzsche*, trans. Walter Kaufmann (New York, 1954), p. 455.

growth."[10] The poet in the mid-twentieth century is confronted with the problem of grafting himself, and us, back to that tree, of "getting rid," as Olson says, "of the individual as ego, of the 'subject' and his soul, that peculiar presumption by which western man has interposed himself between what he is as a creature of nature (with certain instructions to carry out) and those other creations of nature which we may, with no derogrations, call objects" (*Human*, 59–60).

In a passage which Olson first found quoted in Eric Havelock's *Preface to Plato*, R. G. Collingwood says, "The general distinction between imagination and intellect is that imagination presents to itself an object which it experiences as one and indivisible; whereas intellect goes beyond that single object and presents to itself a world with relation of determinate kind between them" (see *Prose*, 53). Both imagination and intelligence are necessary, of course; imagination pushes the story ahead, but in doing so it discovers an object which it takes to be a unity and, thus, a block to intelligence. The lyric tradition has faltered through the excessive value it has placed on the imaginative synthesis (see, for example, Olson's treatment of Pindar, *Maximus* I, 100). If imagination can only proceed by tautology and demonstrate an integration which it has assumed, the intelligence alone is without device by which to contain the chaos its practice creates. Until Maximus, there has been no image of totality large enough to order the massive exercise of intelligence which has been the dominant fact of our history. It is for this reason that poetry becomes in Olson's hands once again of *essential* use. As the discrimination of the spatial dimension of the image allows the body re-entry to the poem, the discrimination of the factual allows the re-entry of intelligence.

The relevant early poem in this connection is "The Praises" (*Archaeologist*, 60–64). In it, facts appear as they inevitably do to the active intelligence, complexly and loosely related. Seldom in Olson's work, however, is the distance between space and fact so great. In the second movement he paraphrases the philosopher Ammonius, as he is reported by Plutarch, on the four epiphanies which lead to the most profound initiation: the first is to be awakened to inquiry; the second is to glimpse a part of the truth; the third is to obtain knowledge; and the last is to go beyond knowledge. At the third epiphany the initiate is allowed to sing. He reaches self-knowledge and has legitimate rights

[10]*Discovery of the Mind*, p. 65.

as a lyrist. It is the "triumphant mode" beyond self-knowledge, however, which is most relevant to Olson's concerns: "when men are active, enjoy thought, that is to say / when they talk, they are LESKENOI. *They rage*" (my italics). The "persona" of the poem has no personality. He is absorbed into information which does not yield to a single "lyric" vision. He is the repository of communal information, and, as an individual, he cannot *know* what he knows. He only participates in the knowledge and retains it in useful form.

In the first line of the poem ("she who was burned more than half her body skipped out of death") we are told of a woman who is not mentioned again, and her relationship to Pythagoras, Antiochus, Bonaci, and Ammonius—all important figures in the first third of the poem—or to the stated "concerns . . . in the present inquiry" is not clear. Even taken alone the line is ambiguous. Did she, despite her disaster, avoid death? Or did she literally skip out on death altogether? It is a fundamental assumption of Olson's work that the use of facts—these nutriments, these cosmic gifts of energy—bears on mortality. To generalize on the facts, to simplify them so they are obedient to rules of thumb, is to create abstract parodies which do not have the *virtu* of the original massed, precise, and admittedly inconvenient facts. Olson demands the greatest possible stretches of attention. If every poet has some excess which he or she is always flirting with, testing himself or herself against, Olson's excess is attention overload. He always pushes himself to that point where one more bit of information would break the sense that the facts at hand can barely be managed. In "The Story of an Olson, and Bad Thing," which was written only four months after "The Praises," he writes, thinking of his father: "I'll not break down by the nerves, as my fellows / do, but by, as he did, the blood vessels, by the breaking of, where / the fragrance is" (*Archaeologist*, 14). By the economy which prevails, to take that chance is repaid by the opportunity to enter eternity in the *present*. And even in a more literal sense, to force oneself to the limits in the careful management of information is to find life-sustaining powers. Unless "that which has been found out by work may, by work, be passed on / (without due loss of force) / for use," the work is wasteful and destructive, it wears and tears on the organism's connective tissues (see "The Resistance," *Human*, 48–49). The choices are between drifting with the inertia or grasping (one of Olson's favorite words) a dangerous and useful energy.

Why, though, does this situation require a secret tradition? It seems in fact, that secretiveness is wasteful, at least of the reader's energy, if not the writer's. The beginning of the final movement— "which is about what we had to say, / the clues, anyhow"—sounds almost cynical. Again, a comparison to "The Story of an Olson" is instructive. There Olson writes:

> It is clews, clews that keep
> sails taut. Drama
> is out of business, tears,
> tears. Ships, ships, it's
> steering now that is, it is
> the biz-i-ness NOW, you
> who care, who can
> endure, it's
> "bring the head 'round, keep
> the wind, citizen!
>
> (is it not the wind we obey, are
> kept by?
>
> as good a word as any is
> the SINGLE INTELLIGENCE.

(*Archaeologist*, 18)

The collection of facts in an Olson poem "add up" not to belief but to action. The clews/clues keep the sails taut and the concern is for the steering.

Robert von Hallberg speaks of Olson as a pedagogical poet and, without doubt, he is. "The Praises" especially thrusts its pedagogical intent upon us. The speaker appears to be a learned but somewhat bumbling lecturer, so excited about his subject matter that he cannot possibly arrive at a few, crisp generalizations for his students to record in their notebooks. Mr. von Hallberg writes: ". . . to a poet-pedagogue like Olson—as not to a poet-maker—subject matter must again be as central as it was to the poet-prophet."[11] He completely mistakes, however, both Olson's pedagogical method and his content. Because he assumes that it is merely a bad lecture, he understands his task as somehow to cut through the muddle. It is a puzzle for him, and, with a single word to key his solution, he arrives at the startling conclusion that the poem is about American Cold War foreign policy!

[11]*Charles Olson: The Scholar's Art* (Cambridge, 1978), p. 22.

The secret of "The Praises," however, is not hidden. The poem like "Every natural action obeys by / the straightest possible process." Even the most informed reading will not discover a "simple" meaning. The secret is the whole poem. It will keep the careful reader engaged, reading back and forth across the multiple connections, investigating sources, looking for cases of pendactylism in the animal kingdom, meditating on the significance of the pentagram, or simply reading aloud, listening to the harsh perfection of the movement of language, the rambunctious and exciting juxtaposition of syllable, and so forth. Insights will certainly arise: what *does* happen when significant truths are popularized? If one, two, and three are the terms of the family, then four is the public, political realm, so what is five? Olson would have been familiar with these numerological questions from his study of tarot. Four is the Emperor; five is the Hierophant. It has to do with magical powers, but magic—at least as far as Olson is concerned, and he is not far from traditional beliefs—is the science of the dynamics of information: "What belongs to art and reason is / the knowledge of consequences."

In "The Praises" Olson is poised at the beginning of the *Maximus*. Without encountering new difficulties, he can no longer write the short, self-contained poem: everything has consequences; every poem invokes more poems. If "The Praises" is frustrating, it is because he does not (perhaps cannot) follow the consequences of what he begins. Meaning in this kind of poetry is grasped not from trying to make the poem resolve into a symbolist formula but from watching the dynamics of the process which it initiates. The Leskenoi rage, and they pursue their raging as meaning. Without doubt, it is an obscure poem. Olson is far ahead of himself, conjecturing about the unknown forces which appear to consciousness in extreme states of attention.

The distinction I have made between space and fact—between "The Kingfishers" and "The Praises"—is, of course, a matter of focus. Olson appears in opposed situations in them because he lacks a figure on which all possibilities bear. In "The Kingfishers" he is one of the fellaheen, a survivor of an exhausted culture, picking among the stones. In "The Praises" he is the extrapersonal repository of the ancient wisdom. This dichotomy was much on Olson's mind when he went to the Yucatan in 1951 to study Mayan culture (see *Writings*, 75 and 81–87). Most simply, how did what he find among the stones have to do with what he read and found valuable? Directly or indirectly this is the question which he addresses again and again in his prose writings from 1951 through 1956. How can the poet establish some more reliable center of attention than his own isolated ego?

4 Stance

When the egocentric territory is stretched toward space and toward fact, the human content reappears not as a thing (ego, soul) but as a relationship. It becomes a question of how one stands as a medium through which space finds its realization as fact: "A poem is energy transferred from where the poet got it (he will have some several causations), by way of the poem itself to, all the way over to, the reader" (*Human*, 52). The poet draws the dispersed energies displayed in space into proximity, where the *intensities* are made manifest as facts, which are themselves no less spatial.

As we will see, it is love that flows through this circuit, as its fundamental causation; it is love that draws related things to related things, syllables to syllables, words to words, poems to poems (in a sequence). Love is the energy of men and women seeking the facts of themselves in space.

Death enters the process not when the organisms break down (that is simply a reality of the process) but when things are ordered in some form *other than* space. This is what Olson means by abstraction. Some of Olson's readers have failed to understand how a poet so distinctly in the imagist lineage can allow himself so many "abstract" words.[12] As far as Olson is concerned, however, no word—scribbles on the page, vibrations in the air—is in itself abstract. Abstraction is a matter of use. Concrete nouns, even proper names, can become abstract when they occur in forms dissociated from space, in "the universe of discourse," for example, or in absolute historical time, the lyric soul, iambic pentameter, or the periodic sentence. Conversely, words like "truth" and "beauty," arrayed in space, are as concrete as the most specific noun.

In the *Maximus* the poet presides over his work not by virtue of a sensibility but by a stance. "I, Maximus of Gloucester, to You" is the third early poem, with "The Kingfishers" and "The Praises," in which Olson establishes the grounds for his practice. It is the poem of

[12]*Ibid.*, p. 12.

stance, and it will be discussed at length in Chapter III. For the present, it will suffice to say that the poet takes up his stance in a place of extreme tension. Try as he might to make himself a transparent medium in which space passes to fact, try as he might to eliminate any resistance he might occasion, he is shaken by the intensities that occur. It is not possible—at least not given the present condition of language and society—to avoid a fringe of abstraction. So the stance involves struggle. For all of the complexities which surround it, the central drama in the *Maximus* is relatively simple: the *agon* is between love and death.

These texts offer some measure of the consistency and meaning of "love" in Olson's poetry:

> what love alone is key to, form
> that feature nature wore
> before man turned her, woman, whore;
>
> (*Archaeologist*, 3)

> love is form, and cannot be without
> important substance (the weight
> say, 58 carats each one of us, perforce
> our goldsmith's scale;
>
> (*Maximus* I, 1)

. . . Okeanos the one which all things are and by which nothing is anything but itself, measured so

screwing earth, in whom love lies which unnerves the limbs and by its heat floods the mind and all gods and men into further nature;

> (*Maximus* II, 2)

> To have the bright body of sex and love
> back in the world—the moon
> has her legs up,
> in the sky of Egypt.
>
> (*Maximus* II, 52).

Love is the key to form; love is form; love is the driving force in the realization of form; form is secular. It is love that keeps free-floating facts *in* space and prevents them from remaining merely abstract, merely inert and deadly.

The process, however, is dynamic. It can develop only by verging on abstraction, by discovering facts which have not been placed in the concrete order of life (or in a poem, which is to say the same thing). These human loci in space, the creative sources, are also destructive and even self-destructive. This seems to be the basis for Olson's fascination with cannibalism:

> In *Moby-Dick* the sea, its creature, and man are all savage. The Whale is "athirst for human blood." Ahab has "that that's bloody on his mind." The sea will "forever and forever, to the crack of doom, insult and murder man."
>
> It is cannibalism. Even Ishmael, the orphan who survives the destruction, cries out: "I myself am a savage, owing no allegiance but to the King of Cannibals; and ready at any moment to rebel against him."
>
> It is the facts, to a first people. (*Ishmael*, 81)

The kind of participation in space which Olson demands of himself is a kind of self-cannibalism: "one loves only form, . . . of yourself, torn" (*Maximus* I, 3). And again: "We drink / or break open / our veins solely / to know" (*Maximus* II, 5). Otherwise our stake in the processes of space is naturalistic rather than participatory, and, of course, one dies abstractly as one lived.

Olson intends to establish a situation for the poet in which it is possible to engage speech *before* it has been formed to taste or even to thought. Speech must become a living thing, an instance of living rather than a reflection on, or a description of, life. It cannot allow the lyric withdrawal, the paradox of which Eliot states with painful precision:

> Trying to learn to use words, and every attempt
> Is a wholly new start, and a different kind of failure
> Because one has only learnt to get the better of words
> for the thing one no longer has to say, or the way in which
> one is no longer disposed to say it.

Olson proposes a language in which the use of words and what one has to say are aspects of a single engagement. Until speech is again returned to the condition of act, language will continue, as it has for the past three millennia, to separate men from the space in which they have their proper being and to replace the dependable actuality with a transcendence which, though perfect, can be drawn down into intercourse with men and women only through destructive acts of Ahabian will.

By allowing the energy of the poem to arise directly from its sources, Olson loses the opportunity to achieve perfected, static form, but he gains an immediacy of mythic and historical material which is missing in modernist poetry. The modernists were uncertain how to use the staggering amount of information which archaeology began to make available in the last part of the nineteenth century, whether arbitrarily, like Joyce, or as an extension of an orthodoxy, like Eliot, or nostalgically and as a source of authority, like Pound. Although Olson did not fully establish the theoretical basis for his practice until he assimilated Whitehead's cosmology in 1956, he was aware that the use of mythology and history depended upon "This biz of, getting rid of, nomination, so that historical material is free for forms now" (*Writings*, 81). That is, names (substantives, substances) must be redeemed from past contexts so they can enter the work as freely as contemporary things.

The modernists use mythology in their writings to give their images of life coherence. The *Odyssey* for Joyce and Pound and the grail legend for Eliot are forms to shape or ironically deny history. In *Paterson* even Williams expects recurrent narrative to appear and break the on-going flow of historical time. Like those other representatives of modernism, the psychoanalysts, they understand myth and history to exist in discrete dimensions. Primitives, the assumption is, live in some proximity with the soul. They move along the timeless idealities and, in their simplicity, project the innermost structure of consciousness onto the physical world. When men assume residence in time and space, however, as they did in Greece during the fifth or sixth Century B.C., the magic circle is broken and their acts become "mere" history or psychopathology.

Olson sees his opportunity as an engagement with stories which are the revelation of man's shape, whether the fact is "that / first season, 1623 / the fishing, Gloucester / was good" (*Maximus* I, 103), or "Zeus sent Hermes / to draw Agenor's cattle / down to the seashore / at Tyre, date / 1540 B.C." (*Maximus* II, 102). As we will see, in the Whiteheadian cosmology the *present* is the beginning, the point of genesis, and all that we call "past" is, in fact, a potentiality: "The tenses . . . of the mythological," Olson says, "are never past but present and future, a thing I have elsewhere called attention to, about

history as it has now re-presented itself" (*History*, 22). He admits
that, given our present language, it is difficult to understand how this
might be so, and he suggests that the language of the Hopi provides a
model for what English must become if it is to be most useful.

Benjamin L. Whorf, on whom Olson depends for his knowledge
of Hopi, points out that, as Indo-European languages divide all experience into past, present, and future, the Hopi divide experience
into what he calls the "manifest" and the "manifesting." The manifest
world comprises everything available to public scrutiny: the earth,
history, whatever can be documented. For obvious reasons it is identified with extended space, the horizontal axes which determine the
landscape. The transition from the manifest to the manifesting world
is at the point in time at which future projects begin in the present, the
point of inception. The manifesting world comprises not only some
indeterminate course of future events but also all of those phenomena
which are normally called "merely subjective": dreams, thoughts, de-
sires, hopes, fears, faiths, etc. In the *Maximus*, as in Hopi grammar,
the manifesting world is identified with the vertical axis:

> As far as space is concerned, the subjective is a mental realm of
> no space in the objective sense, but it seems to be symbolically
> related to the vertical dimension and its poles, the zenith and the
> underground, as well as to the 'heart' of things, which corre-
> sponds to our word 'inner' in the metaphoric sense. Correspond-
> ing to each point in the objective world is such a vertical and
> vitally INNER axis which is what we call the wellspring of the
> future.[13]

Olson associates this vertical axis with "the growth principle of the
Earth" (*Myth*, 12). It is this dimension, so long excluded from western
thought, that rejoins myth and history and allows man as physical to
re-enter the world as familiar place. The vertical is the dimension of
stance.

[13] "An American Indian Model of the Universe," in *Language, Thought,
and Reality* (Cambridge, 1956), pp. 57–64.

---

1   The Possibility of Measure

In an African folktale to which Olson refers, the personified Way, the ritual leader, dies. He writes: "Value is perishing from the earth because no one cares to fight down to it beneath the glowing surface so attractive to all. Der Weg Stribt" (*Human*, 8). The Way attends all ceremonies in which consciousness is transformed, in which passage is made, in which new coherence is found. To follow the Way is to explore consciousness uncritically, perhaps, from the point of view of ego, even stupidly, to its extremities. It provides a key to the labyrinth and the formulae by which the symbolic manifestations of the Earth as devouring mother, whether she is "represented as grave or underworld, as hell or Maya, as *heimarmene* or fate, as monster or witch,"[1] is overcome. Poetics for Olson is a study of the Way, methodology, "meta hodos, the way after."

Olson's methodology for the recovery of value is summarized in a piece he wrote shortly before he died. He juxtaposes these three terms: initiatic cosmos, world of nature, celestial world. The initiatic cosmos is where the work is done, the landscape across which the Way is followed: " . . . *initia* means to begin to find out" (*History*, 21). The world of nature and the celestial world, as increasingly large concentric circles, contain the initiatic cosmos and are discovered through it. They differ only in quantity, not quality, so they are partially revealed in any legitimate act of finding out. The piece concludes: "The spiritual is all in Whitehead's simplest of all statements: Measure is most possible throughout the system. That is what I mean.

---

[1]Erich Neumann, *The Great Mother: An Analysis of the Archetype*, trans. Ralph Manheim (New York, 1955), p. 175.

That is what I feel all inside. That is what is love."[2] Olson's career as
a poet was devoted to discovering the precise demands that vision
made on him. He is a primitive and a literalist. In a letter to John
Clarke he insists that he should be "read—as I were—as in fact etc—
Paleolithic" (*Pleistocene*, 9). The aim is to reveal the prosody and
syntax of what D. H. Lawrence calls the vertebrate intelligence in its
relation to that other primal condition which Olson discovers most
clearly in *Moby Dick*: " . . . things, and present ones, are the absolute
conditions; but they are so because the structures of the real are flexible, quanta do dissolve into vibrations, all does flow, and yet is there,
to be made permanent, if the means are equal" (*Human*, 122).

Judged by conventional standards—Matthew Arnold's touch-
stones, for example, which probably still define the music of poetry
for most readers—Olson does not have a good ear. The necessities to
which he is party seldom allow the resonance and regularity of
rhythm which we are accustomed to associate with "a high truth and
a higher seriousness."[3] The rhetorical stance which Arnold recognizes
as the movement of high seriousness, Olson would argue, is an illegitimate attempt to enlarge a man's proper truth by associating it with
some form outside himself, *outside* the active organism which establishes the only rhythm which can be taken as finally serious. Arnold
writes: " . . . the idea is everything; the rest of the world is of illusion,
divine illusion. Poetry attaches its emotion to the idea; the idea *is* the
fact."[4] In a critique of Cid Corman's "The Soldiers," Olson suggests
that the poem fails precisely because it does attach "its emotion to the
idea." The poem attempts, he says, "by a certain largeness of tone to
reinforce Man" in the abstract, while failing to recognize that "any
largeness is not extendable beyond your own size—which again, is a
matter of YR RHYTHYM" (*Origin*, 84). The revolution for which Olson
claims responsibility does not allow a poet to appropriate a public
ideal to shape his own private musings. Rather, he says, "I am proposing a rearising of the Olympic Game: the public is the body"
(*Prose*, 51). The prosodic beauty of the *Maximus* is like the beauty of
a hammer thrower; the rhythm is a product of the body's involvement
with its task. The assumption of Olson's poetic is that the voice, if its

[2]"Conditio," *Io*, 8 (1971), 274.
[3]"The Study of Poetry," in *The Portable Matthew Arnold*, ed. Lionel
Trilling (New York, 1949), p. 311.
[4]*Ibid.*, p. 299.

full potential can be recovered, is as insistent as any of the vital functions and as sustaining as traditional metrical conventions. The poet whose ear can tap that energy and find means to register it can establish a force which is purely his own.

In his essay "Lexis and Melos," Northrop Frye makes a distinction which can help us avoid some confusion in the discussion of Olson's poetic. He argues that the adjective "musical" is generally applied to the most unmusical poetry. When, for example, Tennyson is called a "musical poet," as he often is, it means that he "has produced a pleasant variety of vowel sounds and has managed to avoid the more unpronounceable clusters of consonants that abound in modern English."[5] A more appropriate adjective for Tennyson is "euphonious." As Frye goes on to observe: "Music is concerned not with beauty of sound but with organization of sound, and beauty has to do with the form of organization. A musical discord is not an unpleasant sound: it is a sound which throws the ear forward to the next beat: it is a sign of musical energy."[6] Olson uses "music" in Frye's precise sense when he praises a line from Shakespeare's *Henry VIII* in these terms: it "shows forth the weave of accent, quantity, breath which makes prosody the music it is: and here is a very close music, sharp, long and stopped, all in a small space of time" (*Human*, 85). He also uses "harmony" in the analogical sense which is implicit in Frye's distinction. Harmony is the function of verse which "throws the ear forward to the next beat." "It would do no harm," he says, "to both prose and verse as now written, if both rime and meter, and, in the quantity words, both sound and sense, were less in the forefront of the mind than the syllable, if the syllable, that fine creature, were more allowed to lead the *harmony* on" (*Human*, 53–54, my italics). That is to say, Olson would establish harmony as the *dynamic* component of the line and allow rhythm to take on its primary character as simple measure. The measure of the line establishes how much of the energy is used.

Olson's poetic, while in no sense an attempt to recover classical meter, is quantitative. It gives its attention to the line as temporal duration and to the management of durations in form. In his analysis of Shakespeare's prosody he says, "One should not have to be bugged

[5]In *Sound and Poetry*, ed. Northrop Frye (New York, 1957), p. xi.
[6]*Ibid.*, p. xiii.

because Shakespeare so often does knot up his speech in the last plays, does come up with rough polysyllables, 'stops' his line so much" (*Human*, 86). This roughness results directly from Shakespeare's rediscovery of speech as intensive. The syllable, in addition to being a mere potential accent, reasserts its power as duration or quantity. There is a new understanding of the syllable's command of a measured place in the line. Olson speaks of traditional end-stopped or enjambed iambic pentameter lines as demonstrating "the running power of verse" (*Human*, 84). He applies the same word to the blank verse of the early Shakespeare and of Milton as he applies to the character of space as it was understood until the mid-nineteenth century and the discovery of non-Euclidean geometry: it is merely extensive and so can be measured by a rigid foot or a rigid footrule. By contrast, he speaks of the "standing" power of quantitative verse or verse with a strong quantitative base, which Shakespeare anticipated. When he says that quantitative lines "come quietly to a stop as they take off, vertically" (*Human*, 82), he is trying to find a language to specify the measure of that other dimension which we identify as intensive or *inner*, the dimension which appears when space is understood, as it is by contemporary physics, to be flexible, capable of being expanded, concentrated, or deformed.

In his concern for quantitative measure, Olson is attempting to purify the language of the abstract pollutants which have been allowed to creep into it. Before poetry can be written, language must be returned to itself. In quantitative measure the duration of a syllable is an inherent factor. Olson objects, for example, that Milton's disregard for syllabic quantity results in what might be called rhythmic sentimentality. The "humanistic" elements in Milton's verse (those which are chosen, willfully, rather than given—the stress patterns, as opposed to the syllables) are allowed a weight in the determination of the verse which they can maintain only if they draw authority from some abstract source (attaching the "emotion to the idea," whether the idea be Christian dogma, Latinate syntax, or iambic pentameter) outside the proper concerns of the verse itself. In a letter to Cid Corman, Olson quotes a passage from Pierre Boulez which he takes as evidence that music, like the kind of poetry he is proposing, "is now capable of being absolute." Music and poetry were inextricably related in the preliterate poetry which provides him with his most persistent model for his art, and he is understandably excited by the fact that the mechanisms which had separated them are breaking down. The twelve-tone scale, Boulez says, results in composition which "amounts to arranging sound phenomena along 2 coordinates: duration and pitch. We are thus freed from all melody, all harmony and all counterpoint since serial structure has caused all these (essentially modal and tonal) notions to disappear" (*Origin*, 103). The prosodic interest is not drawn to the beauty of an individual passage, the thrill of hearing a complex harmonic relationship resolved, for example, but to the articulation of a complete serial structure.

After pointing out that Shakespeare has returned language in the last plays to the rhythms which are natural to it, Olson goes on to say: "The limit on new in the verse is syntax. Shakespeare did not particularly disturb the working sentence as it has served him and others in blank verse" (*Human*, 84). As Olson had found in his own work and in the work of Pound, Williams, and Crane, the periodic sentence is an abstraction which intervenes between the poet and his material as absolutely as iambic pentameter. The sentence, he suggests, imposes a logic on speech which is entirely foreign to it: "So long as a sentence stayed a 'completed thought'—and I'd guess it got that way when the Greeks did impose idea (to see) on act (dran, drama, to act) . . . the sentence ceased to be the capable animal it now is" (*Human*, 65). In a periodic sentence the words and the syllables as loci of meanings are subordinated to an abstract structure which reduces its burden, the noun and their actions, to mere weightless pointers which have no inherent force; objects move not by their own force but by the abstract drama of the sentence.

The epigraph which Olson takes for his lecture *Causal Mythology* consistently applies to his work: " . . . that which exists through itself is called meaning" (*Myth*, 2). Words in the *Maximus* cannot be taken as referring to objects which *give* them meaning. Olson attempts to recover a sense of the noun which he discovers in Mayan hieroglyphs: " . . . the signs were so clearly and densely chosen that, cut in stone, they retain the power of the objects of which they are images" (*Human*, 7). That an object is a "power" which can be named by another power of the same magnitude and shape is a possibility almost beyond contemporary comprehension. For us, the obvious association of language and magic is disconcerting. We have been convinced by our use of language, and the conviction has been bought and sold by Madison Avenue, that objects have "images" which can be changed at will. Like Pound, Olson returns to glyphic writing in an attempt to recover the language from the abstract shape which has been imposed upon it, but he recognizes that Pound's attempt to adapt the ideogram directly into English is foredoomed to failure. The noun must be treated as the symbol of a complex internal structure, not a mere surface, and by virtue of its inner structure it exhibits its own integrity. In the *Maximus* the inner structure of language recapitulates the inner structure of the world: " . . . every element in an open poem (the syllable, the line, as well as the image, the sound, the sense) must be taken up as participants in the kinetics of the poem just as solidly as we are accustomed to take what we call the objects of reality; and that these elements are to be seen as creating the tensions of a poem just as totally as do those other objects create what we know as the world" (*Human*, 56). The noun exhibits *all* of the complexities, as an articulated sound, that its "twin," as Olson calls it (not "referent"), exhibits as a sensuous thing. The energy for the poem comes inward from the external world, not outward from the lyric soul.

Like the noun, the verb too must be revalued. Given the weight and solidity of Olson's nouns, its burden is increased, and, as it has been invested with what Olson considers perhaps the most pernicious abstraction which has been introjected into the language, it is unequal to its task. If nouns (objects) are to be made genuinely usable, they must be freed from the abstract temporal continuum in which verb tenses involve them.

In "Projective Verse" Olson asks, "Do not tenses, must they not also be kicked around anew, in order that time, that other governing absolute may be kept, as must the space-tensions of a poem, immediate, contemporary to the acting-on-you of the poem?" (*Human*, 56). The problem is to prevent the past from remaining abstract, where it is separated from the act of the creation of the poem by the temporal gulf implicit in a verb tense. Maximus finds several approaches to the problem:

> I am seized
> —not so many nights ago—
> by the sight of the river
> exactly there at the bridge.

(*Maximus* I, 85)

In "Letter 14" Maximus comments parenthetically on a passage from one of Sir Richard Hawkins's letters to Queen Elizabeth. Hawkins's theme, his preparation for the exploitation of the New World, is timeless, and so Maximus treats it as both a contemporary and a historical document. The solution, however, is not so simple when Olson deals with more complex historical developments:

> (the LIE of history is that a man can find or take any relevance out of the infinite times of other man except as he pegs the whole thing on *his* time: and i don't means times, that sociological lie, I mean *your* TEMPI—mine, in short, all that TIME IS, is RHYTHYM (and there is no way of knowing any rhythm OTHER THAN YOUR OWN than BY your own. (*Origin*, 83)

Olson's spelling of "rhythym" (rhyt-him) is, of course, to underscore the personal, immediate sense of measure as the only useful understanding of time. In the *Maximus* the tenseless verb and the active noun are both aspects of the same energy. Verbs occur as manifestations not of abstract time but of the contemporary interaction of noun-objects, so historical material is free for present use, free from the rigid chronologies of absolute pastness. Maximus's own rhythm, the rhythm of his discovery, emerges so powerfully that all of the evidence, past and present, bends to the contemporary. Rather than submitting the process of the poem to simple historical sequence, Maximus draws on material when it is useful to the development of his *own* processes. The language is made to register the poet's own grammar. Olson quotes the linguist Edward Sapir: "All of the actual content of speech, its clusters of vocalic and consonantal sounds, is in origin limited to the concrete; relations were merely implied and articulated with the help of order and rhythm" (*Prose*, 30). In this light, measure takes on new significance. All of those elements which can safely be considered "sound effects" in traditional verse intrude into questions of *meaning* on the most elementary level.

When the noun is reconceived as an active power and the verb as a manifestation of one of its potentialities, the nature of syntax changes radically. In a review of Eric Havelock's *Preface to Plato*, Olson draws attention to Havelock's use of the word "parataxis" to describe the syntax of Hesiod and Homer. In paratactic order, Olson says, "the words and actions reported are set down side by side in the order of their occurrence in nature, instead of by an order of discourse, or 'grammar,' as we have called it, the prior an actual resting on vulgar experience and event" (*Prose*, 52). That is, in periodic organization, the order of conventional literate language, the concern is with the *whole* and the ways in which individual perceptions combine to form the whole. In parataxis the attention is given to the relationship among the individual perceptions themselves without reference to an abstract form. Robert Creeley speaks of the anecdotes in the *Maximus* as providing a "vocabulary of activities,"[7] the value of which is precisely that it is plural and the parts are individually active. The anecdotes which occur paratactically in the *Maximus* have their effect on the reader who, in turn, should not expect to find a hierarchy of subordinated actions. Rather than integrating categorically or according to chains of cause and effect, one discovers on-going associations, subject-puns, images answering to images, one moving to the next in terms which are purely local to them. Unlike stream of consciousness, however, which is passive, parataxis is active, attempting to bring the poem to an immediate coherence by developing concrete associations on multiple planes. In other words, when the abstract noun, which gathers the multiple faces of experience into a static concept, is repluralized by conjecture and explored through anecdotes, a new sense of order arises. Olson speaks of "a syntax of apposition" (*Prose*, 53), which can be opposed to a snytax of subordination. The order which emerges is analogous to the order of a map rather than the order of a scientific law or a periodic sentence, both of which tear objects from their contexts, rearrange them, and subordinate them to a controlling principle or, as Olson would says, *logos*.

Olson proposes an oral poetry as a reopening of possibilities which have been closed by literacy: "What we have suffered from is manuscript, press, the removal of verse from its producer and its reproducer, the voice, a removal by one, by two removes from its place of origin *and* its destination" (*Human*, 57). He has no interest in enforcing some previous orthodoxy or any illusion that his analogy to preliterate conditions is literal. When he says that "the only advantage of speech rhythms is illiteracy" (*Human*, 95), he is not proposing a return, as if it were possible, to mnemonic verse. He means that verbal possibilities which preliterate poets exploited can be freed from the context in which they originated and brought to bear on the technical

[7]"Some Notes on Olson's *Maximus*," in *A Quick Graph: Collected Notes and Reviews*, ed. Donald M. Allen (San Francisco, 1970), p. 172.

problems which verse must face in the twentieth century. The advantage of literacy to an oral poet is that his speech can be recorded with a reasonable degree of accuracy. He is freed from the limitations of a hearing. His speech can be spoken and respoken by his readers; time is allowed to stop the speech to think or to refer to collateral sources of information; but, as oral poetry, the poem is not to be apprehended without ultimate reference to the act of speech.

The language of the pre-Socratic Greeks made no distinction between *logos* and *muthos*. They both meant "what is said," which is, of course, necessarily the absolute arbiter in a preliterate culture. During the fifth century B.C., however, *muthos* came to mean "fictitious narrative," as opposed to *logos*, which meant, to translate it into literary jargon, "a story with thematic development," or, more generally, "the controlling principle, the Word," as it is used in the Gospel of John. In "Letter 23," one of the number of poems in which Olson breaks through to a new understanding of the general movement of the *Maximus*, Olson notes Pindar's "crack/at Homer's sweet versing." Then he adds:

> Plato
>
> allowed this divisive
> thought to stand, agreeing
>
> that *muthos*
> is false. Logos
> isn't—was facts. Thus
> Thucydides.

(Maximus I, 100)

The issue involved in the distinction is not merely the truth or falsity of what is said. *Logos* and *muthos* are structurally distinct, and Maximus, who says, "I would be an historian as Herodotus was," casts his lot with the muthologists.

In his *Preface to Plato*, Eric Havelock addresses himself to the crux of the matter in his explanation of Plato's attack on poetry. Havelock argues that *The Republic* should not be read as an essay in utopian politics, as has been assumed, but as a document in the power struggle between the oral poets and the literate philosophers for the control of Greek education. Havelock points to Plato's argument that "everything said by a *mythologos* or poet . . . is a 'going through of what has or is or will be.'"[8] Because of the nature of the poet's practice, the mnemonic dependence on *story*, the information in the poetic record of the past is necessarily referred to some specific event. Even the aphorisms which are common in Homer draw their authority from and "come to mind" because of their narrative context. As the story in turn comes to mind from the complex rhythmic organization of the poetic performance, the dynamic combination of meter, music, and dance which the poet brings to the service of memory, the authority for the *muthos* derives absolutely from the poet alone. Havelock writes: "The early role of the Muse has often been misunderstood. She was the symbol of the bard's command of professional secrets, not of his dependence on divine guidance. When the Greek poets voice their claim to fame or immortality they prefer to base it not as in the Hellenistic age upon inspiration but upon their skill."[9] The poet's authority derived from his ability to coordinate all of his faculties to the demands of the song. To the extent that the poet was "possessed," it was not a divine possession of the soul but a song's possession of the poet's total organism. The Greek word *mousike* means not only "music" but also "the state of self organization and intensity of attention which the bard must attain."[10]

The philosopher, on the other hand, or the philosophic historian, who is able to withdraw from specific incidences and compare them in the light of an ideal pattern or *logos*, is able to deal in principles which are apparently true for all times and places. For this reason, Thucydides' relevance to our own age is more immediately apparent. J. A. K. Thomson, on whose *The Art of the Logos* Olson was depending when he wrote "Letter 23," says, "The aim of Herodotus was to put the Persian Wars in their setting; the aim of Thucydides was to take the Peloponnesian War out of its setting."[11]

The *Maximus* is Olson's attempt to put the abstract world he confronts back into its setting. For the oral poet, however, "setting" is an inadequate metaphor if it leads one to think of a theatrical backdrop. The setting for everything that is said is *first* the poet's own

[8]*Preface to Plato* (Cambridge, Mass., 1963), p. 236.
[9]*Ibid.*, pp. 150–51.
[10]*Ibid.*
[11]*The Art of the Logos* (London, 1935), p. 43.

memory and the rhythm which allows it to be made manifest; second-arily, the setting is a geography, a culture, a milieu, which is to say, an *image*. Olson reports that he was given this formula in a dream:

> of rhythm is image
> of image is knowing
> of knowing there is
> a construct.

(Archaeologist, 51)

So fact (i.e. "construct") can never have greater authority than what it gains by testimony of the individual speaker's *mousike*. Everything rests on that foundation.

Plato characterizes *muthos* as *doxa* or opinion. It does not pri-marily mean, as the English translation suggests, "a judgment lacking positive confirmation." It rather describes a syntax and the relation-ship to experience which that syntax assumes. In an initial attempt to define the word Havelock writes: "It is a knowledge of 'happenings' (*gignomena*) which are sharply experienced in separate units and so are pluralized (*polla*) rather than being integrated into systems of cause and effect. And these units of experiences are visually concrete; they are 'visibles' (horata)." [12] *Doxa*, in other words, is knowledge not of being but of becoming, a following of a Way, which Olson would see as its great advantage. As we have seen, *muthos* is inevitably time-conditioned. It must refer to its "visibles" in terms of verb tenses. Consequently, oral intelligence cannot deal with timeless essences or static beings. Odysseus, for example, can never be separated from his specific deeds. He is never the Hero but always a man in the process of becoming a hero. If he is to provide a valuable model for behavior, he must be re-proven again and again by the person who is educated in Homer. *Doxa* is knowledge of a world which, seeming to betray some unifying wholeness, reveals itself only partially. The wholeness can only be suggested by repeating incident after incident in a series of incidents which is endless. The Way is of necessity open-ended and dynamic.

As the word is applicable to the *Maximus*, poetics is the study of how a man must behave when his words are out of control. The poem, as an instrument of self-integration, transcends ego (that part of self *under* control) and develops a force which is experienced by

[12]Havelock, *Preface to Plato*, p. 180.

the poet as other than his own: "You wave the first word and the whole thing follows. But—You follow it. With a dog at your heels, a crocodile about to eat you at the end, and you with your pack on your back trying to catch a butterfly" (*Human*, 79). At these extremities, beyond the limit of the controlled, and *only* there, men attain vision. This shadowy region of consciousness is the province of the alchemist, the astrologer, the shaman, and the poet. When there is no measure, it is also the landscape for the visions of madmen. Robert Duncan defines the risk as "the conquest of babble by the ear."[13] It can also be defined as the conquest of the abstract by the image.

Olson sees the poem as a field and composition as an activity which takes place in it: "the large area of the whole poem, . . . the FIELD . . . , where all the syllables and all the lines must be managed in their relations to each other" (*Human*, 55). The analogy of the field has begun to appear as suggestive for twentieth-century poets as the analogy of the organism was for the Romantics. As early as 1913, Pound writes, "We might come to believe that the thing that matters in art is a sort of energy, a force transfusing, welding, and unifying."[14] In his essay on Cavalcanti he says, "We appear to have lost the radiant world where one thought cuts through another with a clean edge, a world of moving energies . . . magnetisms that take form, that are seen, or that border the visible."[15] And William Carlos Williams speaks of "the poem as a field of action"[16] in a lecture which draws almost as frequently on Einstein as on literary masters. As a branch of physics, field theory deals with with the characteristics of a region which is under the influence of an electromagnetic force such as gravity or electricity. Applied to poetry, of course, the assumption is that consciousness defines a field under the influence of the imagination or the force of emerging selfhood. "At the root (or stump) what *is*," Olson writes, taking field theory in its broadest sense, "is no longer THINGS but what happens BETWEEN things, these are the terms of the

[13] "Notes on Poetics Regarding Olson's *Maximus*," in *The Poetics of the New American Poetry*, ed. Donald M. Allen and Warren Tallman (New York, 1973), p. 190.

[14] "The Serious Artist," in *Literary Essays of Ezra Pound*, ed. T. S. Eliot (Norfolk, Conn., 1954), p. 49.

[15] "Cavalcanti: Medievalism," in *ibid*., p. 154.

[16] "The Poem as a Field of Action," in *Selected Essays* (New York, 1969), pp. 280–91.

reality contemporary to us—and the terms of what we are" (*Human*, 123).

When a set of words is understood to generate a field, simple juxtaposition can establish a matrix of relations so complex as to defy linear syntax, as, for example, in this found poem:

The Account Book of B Ellery

vessels
goods
voyages
persons
salaries
conveyances

(*Maximus* II, 34)

What is happening between things in this field, needless to say, throws considerable force on the fourth item of account. The dynamics of the field are such that both B Ellery and the economic system in which he operates are indicated. This phenomenon provides a place for value in a world which, considered as a mere assemblage of inert things, allows only facts. "Judgement arises," Olson writes, "from a more accurate paratax, or is made more possible as an experience of experience" (*Prose*, 53). In the larger context of the *Maximus* this poem generates a field which intersects with the field of the Algonquin legend of the man-with-his-house-on-his-head (three poems earlier). This evidence of disregard for individual integrity is balanced against the evidence for the possibility of genuine integration. Through "The Account Book," "Maximus Letter # whatever" is also related to "The Song and Dance of," "Letter 16," and "Capt Christopher Levett." In the other direction it leads directly to "Maximus Song," which celebrates Phyrne, the Greek courtesan whose integrity could not be purchased. From this point too, as from any point in the *Maximus*, relationships proliferate: Phyrne is obviously associated with Aphrodite (as whom she modeled for several artists), and so "Maximus Song" looks back to "I faced the calm grey waters" and forward to "Maximus, at Harbor." The disturbance in the field which "The Account Book" creates has effects throughout the poem. The method of the *Maximus* might easily be misunderstood. It appears at first that Olson, as is sometimes said of Pound, states the evidence and allows the reader to draw the generalization. This reading of the poem, however, assumes that Olson *knows* the generalization and, perversely, for reasons of effect, will not share the secret with his reader. In fact, all judgment in the *Maximus* is strictly in terms of the specific required- ness of the matrix. The field renders generalization unnecessary. The gain which results from treating the poem as a field of action is that *value* is placed in a concrete geography.

In *The Special View of History*, Olson speaks of "the metrical" as a spatio-temporal involvement: "History is the practice of space in time" (*History*, 27). This is precisely the opposite of the usual under- standing of history as the practice of time in space. "Letter 23," as we have seen, is a summation of the first twenty-two poems and, at the same time, the declaration of a new beginning. The following poem, "A Plantation a beginning," responds directly to what is "required" by the field at that point:

> I sit here on a Sunday
> with grey water, the winter
> staring me in the face
>
> "the Snow lyes indeed
> about a foot thick
> for ten weeks" John White
>
> warns any prospective
> planter
>
> Fourteen spare men the first
> year who huddled
> above Half Moon Beach.
>
> (*Maximus* I, 102)

Faced with a new beginning himself, the grey water, the indeterminant range of his possibilities, Maximus's thought returns to the first two attempts to shape a city out of the possibilities which Cape Ann offers. With rimes on the short "i" and short "a" leading the harmony on, the mind playing among the syllables, Maximus's history moves from the scene before his eyes to John White's description of winter on Cape Ann (1640s), and to a conjecture about the conditions of Gloucester's first settlers in 1623. These casual facts, which are liter- ally abstract as they inhabit the records of the city's history, are actualized in the geography of the poem and begin to develop requirements of their own. The distinction between the actual, whether it manifests itself as history, as the natural, or as value, and the abstract is made on the basis of geography. " . . . the actual entity," Alfred North Whitehead writes, "in virtue of being *what* it is, is also *where* it is. It is somewhere because it is some actual thing with its correlated actual world." [17]

Since the fifth century B.C. the location of vision, the literal landscape of the poem, has grown persistently more obscure. Kant's stratagem saved a sense of the world at the expense of destroying the intimate connection between the place where men live among facts, locatable facts, and that *other* place where they experience value, beauty, where the possibility of morality resides. Both the body and its contents, the reach of the feel of will, and God, Being, whatever, the ultimate exterior, were rendered mysterious. As a result, intelligible experience under that dispensation usually called romanticism or, in its later form, symbolism, takes place at the margins, only where the internal and the external meet. It is littoral: Whitman on the beaches of Paumanok, mediating between the uncreated inlands, which are treated as a matter of conjecture, and the formless uncertainty of the sea. "The soul / Forever and forever—longer than soil is brown and solid—longer than water ebbs and flows" appears as the *place* of vision, rather like Mars in a sci-fi fantasy; we do not know where it is.

Olson's achievement is to discover a poetic which is so completely spatial that he can say simply, "metric is mapping." Maximus is not only local to the actual geography of Gloucester but also to history. He turns inland: "The Sea—turn yr back on / the Sea, go inland, to / Dogtown" (*Maximus* II, 9). He moves from the quotation of John Smith, "History is the memory of time" (*Maximus* I, 112), to the assertion "*my* memory is / the history of time" (*Maximus* II, 86, my italics). As always the movement is in both directions on a nonreversible axis: he grows more "subjective," inward, while at the same time he involves himself more thoroughly with the outwardness of history and space. In the latter books Maximus is two synchronous events. He remains a perfectly integrated organism, the form of which cannot be separated from his own content, shaping space to his form. At the same time, however, he is also the form which he gives to space-time or history. Maximus is not engaged in some romantic effusion of ego, which confuses simple inclusiveness with shape. The re-enactment of

[17] *Process and Reality: An Essay in Cosmology* (New York, 1969), p. 75.

history, with all of the outwardness it implies, in Maximus's own in-ternal processes allows ego to dematerialize as irrelevant. If experi-ence is grasped with the heat of attention Maximus demands, both ego and sequential time, like rational form, appear as mere apparent clarities which dissolve in space, and the self, the fully individuated potential of the human being, emerges as a location in spatio-tem-poral reality.

2   The Open Form of the *Maximus*

In "A Later Note on Letter # 15" Maximus says:

> In English the poetics became meubles—furniture—
> thereafter (after 1630)
>
> & Descartes was the value
>
> until Whitehead, who cleared out the gunk
> by getting the universe in (as against man alone
> (Maximus II, 79)

The mind, as Descartes argues, is unextended, immaterial, and im-mortal; the body is extended, material, and, in one of his favorite examples, prone to dropsy. He seems always to have the deepest un-certainties about his condition as an occupant of space. The spatial world, as its structure is totally foreign to the mental, can only be known indirectly, as a postulate derived from the consistent and self-evident axioms of analytic geometry. The difficulty of explaining the interaction between an immaterial mind and a material body ap-peared immediately and continued to plague the school of philosophy which Descartes founded throughout its important history. He had so successfully divorced the agoraphobic self from space that he had dif-ficulty explaining how the mind informed the body of a decision, for example, to walk or speak. One of Descartes's followers maintained that mind and body were related to one another like perfectly syn-chronized clocks which had been set into motion at the creation. An-other, seeing the inherent lack of free will in the two-clock theory, went so far in his attempt to solve the problem as to provide divine collaboration in every human movement. If the cleavage between mind and body is so great as to require divine mediation, the mind-body organization of oral verse is obviously not equal to the task. Measure, losing its status as an essential element in thought, is reduced to, as Maximus says, "furniture," an accidental rather than the absolute feature of form. Olson's reassertion of the syllable and line (the ear and lungs) as the determinants of form consequently calls the larger structures or organization into question.

In Chapter Two of *Discourse on Method*, Descartes is preparing the grounds for the process of doubt by which he arrives at the paradox which proves his existence. He draws an analogy to illustrate the advantages of a philosophy articulated from that isolated point of view:

> ... those ancient cities which from being at first only villages, have become, in course of time, large towns, are usually but ill laid out compared with the regularly constructed towns which a professional architect has freely planned on an open plain; so that although the several buildings of the former may often equal or surpass in beauty those of the latter, yet when one observes their indiscriminate juxtaposition, there a large one and here a small, and the consequent crookedness and irregularity of the streets, one is disposed to allege that chance rather than any human will guided by reason must have led to such an arrangement.[18]

Four points about Descartes's analogy, as an illustration of a sense of form which has persisted despite numerous attempts to break down its rigidity, need to be made. 1) The only order which Descartes comprehends is extension in three-dimensional space, form which can be represented on geometric coordinate systems. It is an order which he would have an architect *impose* on the face of his experience, not an order which he discovers to be his own. 2) Descartes can account for order but not for novelty. The rational city on the plain can grow only by repetition of the basic units of order. The form, which precludes discovery, has only a monotonous future, closed by the teleological principle which created it. 3) Although Descartes creates the form of the city, he cannot *participate* in it. Like the Demiurge's appreciation of his own creation, Descartes's appreciation of the city can only come at a distance, say, from a mountain above the plain where, isolated from the life of the city, he can bring the whole under a single view. He finds for metaphysics the point Archimedes coveted for physics. 4) Descartes's geometry and the metaphysics which support it make

[18]*Discourse on Method*, trans. John Veitch (New York, 1934), p. 10.

it possible to identify the rational structure of the ego with space itself. Erich Neumann writes: "Man's will to dominate nature is but an extension and projection of that fundamental experience of the ego's potential power over the body, discovered in the voluntariness of muscular movement."[19] Descartes projects the rational order of the ego on space. At the expense of the faculty which allows men to discover the fresh possibilities of space, Cartesian geometry, by dealing with all extension in terms of symmetrical graphs, allows honest expectations of familiar experience and extends the comfortable security of the ego to the limits of the universe.

Descartes's presence in Olson's *Maximus* conditions the birth of Massachusetts. His work is synchronous with the founding of the colony: "Descartes, age 34, date Boston's / settling" (*Maximus* I, 128). So Descartes is not only relevant, he is unavoidable, because, according to the law Olson offers in "Against Wisdom as Such," "whatever is born or done this moment of time, has the qualities of this moment" (*Human*, 70). Descartes becomes the prime representative of, in D. H. Lawrence's words, "the old white psyche" which "has to be gradually broken down before anything else can come to pass."[20]

The crisis of which Boston was born—the religious wars, the collapse of scholasticism in the face of science, the loss of distinction between private and public, the opening of space which the New World represented—was the product of a sudden expansion of ego on the part of seventeenth-century Europe:

> the things
> of this world (new
> world, Renaissance
> mind named
> what Moses men tried
>
> to twist back to Covenantal
> truth) Continental
> loci inside of which they'd
> dry, sweet souls to whom
> outward was inward

[19] *The Origins and History of Consciousness*, trans. R. F. C. Hull (New York, 1953), p. 110.
[20] *Studies in Classic American Literature* (New York, 1966), p. 65.

act when inward-outward
was, by being here, being

turned, in Corinth
cooling into mettle.

(*Maximus* I, 130–31)

Olson understands the problem as a denial of the proper *place* of phenomenon, a hopeless confusion of man's limits and so a loss of opportunity to expand in legitimate directions. To interiorize "outward" phenomena, to consume them in ego as a continuous extension of rational processes, is to lose the relationship between things in terms of which all meaningful action takes place. The balance of the factors which determine the American experience, however, like the sudden coalescence of accidents in Corinth which produced bronze, was possessed of a power which would allow phenomena to assert their true complexity as both inward and outward, their potential to be involved in man's doings without the loss of their own integrity.

The sense of form from which the *Maximus* grows is not antirational but postrational. The *field* of the poem includes not only the data which can be comprehended by humanistic rationalism but also all that humanistic rationalism excludes as irrational, random, or subjective. Descartes divides all experience into rational and nonrational elements. Consequently, he will find phenomena which are closely related to one another in space-time to have essentially different ontological statuses. One phenomenon will be seen as a vehicle of rational order, another as the encroachment of chaos. Olson, with his obedience to all phenomena, recognizes a possibility for order which derives simply from the contiguity of phenomena. "One wants phenomenology in place," Olson writes, "in order that event may re-arise" (*Prose*, 51). The freshness of space must be allowed to assert itself so it can reveal its *own* form. Perception in the *Maximus* is an interchange between outward space and the inward self which takes place at the surfaces of the body, before it is confronted with the abstract systems which form in the centers of consciousness: "There are no hierarchies, no infinite, no such many as mass, there are only / eyes in all heads, / to be looked out of" (*Maximus* I, 29). By confronting a reader with phenomena as he sees them, "over the waters / from this place where I am, where I hear" (*Maximus* I, 4), Maximus throws his reader on the mercy of his *own* phenomena, his breath, his hearing, the contents of his own consciousness; thereby the process engages those who begin as a mere audience as a third term in the event. Upon examination of the sort which Maximus demands, the conditions of consciousness appear as the exact contrary to what they have been assumed for the past three hundred years to be. The contents of consciousness, far from being most significantly rational, comprise fragmentary perceptions of the external world, shards of dreams, projections of wishes, fears, random memories, and lines of thought which turn on the most arbitrary relationships. The rationalistic sense of perfection, which demands radiance of poetry and rigor of thought, can be recognized as a confusion of form with clarity of vision. As Alfred North Whitehead writes: "Consciousness flickers; and even at the brightest, there is a small focal region of experience which tells of intense experience in dim apprehension. The simplicity of clear consciousness is no measure of the complexity of complete experience."[21] To maintain continuity of experience, despite the waywardness of attention, rational interpretation hews to the illuminated regions, to the most obvious and elemental components of consciousness, to the skeletons of experience which have been called forms. In the *Maximus* the possibility of form which measures the *complexity* of complete experience presents itself.

Olson demands repossession of his own organism, determining, as he goes, how far he extends as a thing "which exists through itself" and so, according to the criterion of meaning he develops in *Causal Mythology* (*Myth*, 2), the extent to which it is meaningful to speak of himself. Western man has been so long the victim of what Whitehead calls "the fallacy of misplaced concreteness," abstraction has so totally fragmented his perception of himself, that it is only with some difficulty that he realizes the concrete self must be created. As an initiation into an order of perceptions, the *Maximus* frequently finds a language in the established mysteries (Orphism, Gnosticism, alchemy, astrology, etc.), which have their own ideal structures, but the ceremony of the poem is a declaration of a unique personal order. Charles Olson, the casual man, is initiated into Maximus, the fully created man.

With his initiation into the body, however, Maximus discovers his participation in an energy which is his own only in a limited sense.

[21]*Process and Reality*, p. 312.

In "Letter 14," apparently quoting from an alchemy text, Maximus contemplates the necessities:

> "to unite in one lustre,
> of stars," it says
>
> And as it might,
> "dreams" (?)
>
> (*Maximus* I, 59)

In "Maximus Letter # whatever," the man united as a star, the fully individuated man, the astral man of alchemy,[22] appears as "The-man-with-his-house-on-his-head" (*Maximus* II, 31). It is obvious in the context of the *Maximus* that "house" is intended in the metaphoric sense which is common in Olson's work: "It is his body . . . , the house he is, the houe that moves, breathes, acts, this house where his life is, where he dwells against the enemy, against the beast" (*Human*, 47). Although "Maximus Letter # whatever" is taken whole cloth, as a found poem, from Charles G. Leland's *Algonquin Legends of New England*, it concretizes possibilities which have been latent in the *Maximus* almost from the beginning. The freshness of objects, when they are freed from the illegitimate uses that have been imposed on them, has been associated with the coming of spring since "Letter 9," in which "house" is used in both the metaphoric and the literal sense:

> the flowering plum
> out the front door window
> sends whiteness
> inside my house.
>
> (*Maximus* I, 41)

In "Maximus Letter # whatever" the identification is explicit. It is a legend on the vernal archetype: the re-entry to the body is the coming of spring:

> Hanging from the beams were deer-
> meat, hams, duck, baskets of berries and maple sugar
> and as he reached out for them the rug itself melted
> and it was white snow, and his arms turned into wings
> and he flew up to the food and it was birch-boughs on
> which it hung, and he was a partridge and it was spring.
>
> (*Maximus* II, 31)

---

[22]Butterick points out that this passage is, in fact, quoted from *Webster's Third International Dictionary*. The dictionary is, for Olson, an occult text.

To re-enter the body is to escape the apparent limitations of bodily life, to enter the natural world and, consequently, take up all of the advantages of the natural. The man with his house on his head locates his own time and space and, there, finds the possibility for being larger than himself which was denied when he began by directing his ego against his own physical limitations.

This energy is manifest in two modes, or *locations*, which have been traditionally called "objective" and "subjective." When Olson says, for example, that Shakespeare's tragicomedies "move without any internal combustion" (*Human*, 82), he is trying to distinguish a dynamic possibility which cannot be confused with willful overextension of the ego. There is a dynamic which Shakespeare shares and shapes but does not generate or, despite his shaping, does not ultimately control. Olson points out that English grammar makes a distinction in the infinitive between the obeying and the asserting functions of the self. It is a linguistic feature which has somehow survived the leveling will of humanistic rationalism. In most cases the infinitive appears in its full form: I want *to go*, I plan *to be*, etc. The implicit metaphysical structure of these sentences sees a finite noun participating in an infinite action. As Olson describes the situation, "the actionable is larger than the individual and so can be obeyed to" (*History*, 45). After auxiliary verbs indicating moods or powers, however, the infinitive is truncated: I *dare* say, I *will* do, I *can* make. The structure is reversed: the infinite noun limits the actions to its own design. "They are the act of the will of the self," Olson says, "and assert the unconditional, thus the self-contained and self-determining powers of the same" (*History*, 45). From Melville, Olson had learned that action as an expression of personal necessity, indignation, or whatever motive one might find for asserting private order against experience must be finally destructive rather than creative. He suggests that will may be a matter of obedience as well as assertion: "Will is the innate voluntarism of to live. Will is the infinitive of being" (*History*, 44).

Olson finds confirmation for this argument in Alfred North Whitehead's *Process and Reality*. The world, Whitehead maintains, is initially experienced as *merely real*, a locus of abstract potentialities or, in his terms, "eternal events." In his experience of the merely real the individual is overwhelmed by a perceptual chaos which is felt to be public and threatening. As Olson says, "the multiples, *crowd in* on the individual" (*History*, 50, my italics). The images immediately before the eye, the larger possibilities for argument, and the memory, as it is not initially distinguished as purely private, all vie for immediate attention and use. The first stage, then, in the development of form, or what Whitehead calls "feeling," is conflict.

The second stage, according to Olson, has been the limit for the development of poetry since the time of Pindar. It is "that most individual stage when he or she seeks to impose his or her order of order on the multiples" (*History*, 50). Here, the direct perception of outward chaos is subordinated to the comfortable clarities. The merely real is transformed into what Whitehead calls an actual occasion or an actuality. The "eternal events" which appear in the condition of pure receptivity are placed in a landscape which consciousness defines with itself as center: "An actual occasion arises as the bringing together into one real context diverse perceptions, diverse feelings, diverse purposes, and other diverse activities arising out of those primary perceptions. . . . In this way we assign to the percipient an activity in the production of its own experience."[23] In actual occasions of the second stage, however, the vector quality of experience, that force by which images come in, is contained in the equilibrium of rational order or aesthetic form. "The trouble has been," Olson says, "that a man stays so astonished he can triumph over his own incoherence, he settles for that, crows over it, and goes at a day again happy he at least made a little sense" (*Human*, 3).

In order to overcome the stasis, it is necessary to mount sufficient intensity of consciousness to become aware of the data which the private order of the second stage excludes. The energy by which one rises to the third stage develops from those causes of discomfort which are systematically excluded from experience as a personal and unified order. One enters the third stage with the understanding that the order of the second stage may be coherent but never complete. " . . . to be 'something,'" Whitehead writes, "is 'to have the potentiality for acquiring real unity with other entities.'" The form cannot close. In order to maintain its stake in reality, the private, rational, or aesthetic form of the second stage must perpetually open itself to the satisfaction of the third: " . . . the notion of 'passing on' is more fundamental than that of a private individual fact. In the abstract language here adopted for metaphysical statement 'passing on' becomes 'creativity,'

[23]*Symbolism* (New York, 1927), p. 9.

in the dictionary sense of the verb *creare*, 'to bring forth, beget, produce.'"[24] The tension between the uncontrolled energy of the first
stage and the resistance of the second is relaxed in the third as "the
innate voluntarism of to live," which can now be recognized as spring-
ing directly from space. It is in the endless uncertainty of the third
stage that the private forms tend again toward becoming public fact,
for, as we shall see, in the third stage the rational processes of the ego
begin to merge fully with the organic processes of the body. As the
known processes open themselves to the unknown, new possibilities
for form make themselves manifest.

Olson identifies the process by which consciousness moves beyond rational form as "autoclytic multiplication," the evolutionary
principle which explains life as "the chance success of a play of creative accidents" (*History*, 48). Irwin Schrödinger speaks of an organism's "astonishing gift of concentrating a 'stream of order' on itself
and thus escaping the decay into atomic chaos—of 'drinking orderli-
ness' from a suitable environment."[25] The poem, then, is not a metaphor to vegetable growth but to the literal organic processes of the
poet himself, a realization at the tips of consciousness of all that he is
genetically. By insisting that the poem is an open-ended field of action,
where the poet is free to take advantage of creative accidents when
they appear, he provides a context in which the genetic processes can
be made permanent in consciousness.

In this connection the following passage from Whitehead is
worth quoting at length:

> Order is not sufficient. What is required is something much
> more complex. It is order entering upon novelty; so that the mas-
> siveness of order does not degenerate into mere repetition; and
> so that novelty is always reflected upon a back ground of system.
> But the two elements must not really be disjoined. . . . The old
> dominance should be transformed into the firm foundations,
> upon which new feelings arise, drawing their intensities from
> delicacies of contrast between system and freshness. . . . It is by
> reason of the body, with its miracle of order, that the treasures of
> the past environment are poured into the living occasion. The
> final percipient route of occasions is perhaps some thread of hap-

[24]*Process and Reality*, p. 245.
[25]*What Is Life? The Physical Aspects of the Living and Mind and Matter*
(Cambridge, 1967), p. 82.

penings wandering in the 'empty' space amid the interstices of the brain. It toils not, neither does it spin. It receives from the past; it lives in the present. It is shaken by the intensities of private feeling, adversion or aversion. In its turn, this culmination of bodily life transmits itself as an element of novelty throughout the avenues of the body.[26]

This passage is largely free of Whitehead's ponderous vocabulary. It is only necessary to know that he uses the word "occasion" in a special sense to mean "object or event or both," as an object in Whitehead's cosmos is an event. The body, for example, is both an object with a more or less determined order and an evolving process, continually bringing the past into the creation of immediate experience . The ways in which the event of the body can develop are limited by what it is already as an object with a past. In the *Maximus* neither Maximus's own personal past nor the biocultural past is lost. Past occasions, whether established by natural selection, the universal unconscious, or repressed or active memories, arrange themselves in "the empty space amid the interstices of the brain" to provide a foundation for new immediacies. The body becomes the medium through which the "old dominance is transformed into the firm foundation, upon which new feelings arise." It is at this point in the process that the objective world is joined to the forms of bodily life which are otherwise known only in dreams and rare moments of vision. Olson speaks of the proprioceptive sense of the body: "the sense whose end organs lie in the muscles, tendons, joints, and are stimulated by bodily tensions (—or relaxation of same)" (Prose, 17). Through this connection the body lends its continuity to the fleeting flow of perception and modulates the contents of consciousness with in-*form*-ation from the suppressed self which would otherwise be lost. The dream life, which is rooted deeply in the processes of the estranged body, is gathered into the creation of a literal landscape.

The poem is a concrete continuum drawing the past into the present for the creation of a future which shares something of the shape of the man who created it. However an occasion is disposed of, it passes into the future as a determinant of possibilities. Every creative act is a self-creative act, every meaningful expense of energy, a rejuvenation. Similarly, if the occasion is squandered, merely drained of

[26]*Process and Reality*, p. 400.

its energy, reconciled or balanced in final form, it passes into the future as diminished possibilities, a seed bed of exhaustion. Whitehead's phrase "feelings . . . drawing their intensity from the delicacies of contrast between system and freshness" comes much closer to describing the spirit of the *Maximus* than Coleridge's "forms all into one graceful and intelligent whole."[27] The simple process of breathing, as the determinant of the poem's only measure, is recapitulated throughout the field. Breath is drawn from the circumference toward the center, turned in the lungs, joined to intelligence, and exhaled as speech, measured by the respiratory fact of the poet speaking. In Whitehead's analysis of feeling, percepta spring from the circumference of the circle of vision, are turned in the mind, joined to the biological mechanisms of speech, and returned as created form. Life, Olson writes, "is the equal to its cause only when it proceeds unbroken from the threshold of a man through him and back out again, without loss of quality, to the external world from which it came" (*Human*, 11).

In Whitehead, Olson finds a cosmology which is in keeping with his own processive sense of history. Although the past had been of importance to Olson since the very beginning of his career, he had chafed at the limits of history because of the gulf of abstract time by which, instant-on-instant, it separated itself from present usability. Writing to Creeley from the Yucatan, he refers to history as "the passage of time & time's dreary accumulations by repetition" (*Writings*, 84). He argues that the observations of the Mayans which are re-enacted in the hieroglyphs are as valid now as they were when they were made because "their workers had forms which unfolded directly from content." Through their involvement in space, they had lifted their work from the continuity of time and so were contemporaries with any other person who was not estranged from the external world. He concludes, "Therefore, there is no 'history.' (I still keep going back to the notion, this is (we are) merely, the second time" (*Writings*, 113).

The uselessness of history, as it has been practiced since Thucydides, is another product of the humanistic inversion of the world: "it has been turned about as everything else has" (*History*, 16). The historians have assumed that time is an absolute continuum in which men must find their way. It is Olson's burden in *The Special View of History* to demonstrate that time is obedient to the man who finds

[27] *Biographia Literaria* (Oxford, 1954), II, 13.

forms only in the extension of his own content: "History is the new localism, a polis to replace the one which was lost in various stages all over the world from 490 B.C. on" (*History*, 25). That is, history is a *place*, a city. As man himself is *in*, as well as *acting* in, a place, place itself is an activity. As Olson points out, Herodotus used the word "history" as a verb, "*istorin* finding out for oneself" (*History*, 20). The place which man inhabits is not a static space nor a static self but a process in which man himself is the active agent. The impact of this discovery revalues all of man's relationships to the external world. Historical order ceases to be chronology and becomes an order of discovery. The reality of history is not the narrative of events, which the historian offers as a final product, but the actual process of finding out for oneself. The order of history is that which is created as a man recognizes those instances of more and more inclusive design in the fragments among which he finds himself. Its continuity is the dynamic gathering in the emerging order. A piece of evidence is valuable to the extent that it contributes to the instensity of the on-going process which is, at once, historical and biological. Olson writes that "a life is the historical function of the individual. History is the intensity of the life process—its *life value*" (*History*, 18).

For over three millennia western culture had spread itself in space. Having broken away from the force of the old cosmic center in the eastern Mediterranean, the excitement and power, it appeared, was to be found on the circumference. The settlement of earth was impelled by a horror of the familiar. The old places, the cities which are always the first signs that the vertical dimension is vital, were images of an earth perpetually coming into being. The men and women who had begun to find some thing in themselves which seemed complete and perfect could not bear them. Their flight, their quest for some city in the world which mirrored their own perfection, ended in the nineteenth century, when the whole of the earth was finally known. The cities they had built were, for the most part, ruins, almost as soon as they were built. They were outposts, intended to last only until an opportunity to pass on presented itself. The ancient wisdom which had sustained them, almost despite themselves, was largely forgotten. The earth was explored, even in its remotest corners, and men were strangers on it. It is in this dark, uncreated space that Maximus begins.

Chapter III

The Maximus Poems

Among Olson's unpublished papers there is an essay, which appears to date from 1953, entitled "The Area & The Discipline, of Totality." It summarizes Olson's own understanding of his apprenticeship as leading specifically to an engagement with the *Maximus*. Recalling the writing of *Ishmael*, he says:

> I knew no more than what I did, than to put down *space* & *fact* & hope, by the act of sympathetic magic that words are apt to seem when one first uses them, that I would invoke for others those sensations of life I was small witness to, part doer of. But the act of writing the book added a third noun, equally abstract: *stance*. For after it was done, & other work in verse followed, I discovered that the fact of this space located a man differently in respect to any act, so much so & with such vexation that only in verse did I acquire any assurance that the stance was not in some way idiosyncratic & only sign of the limits of my own talent, only wretched evidence of the lack of my own engagement at the heart of life.
>
> But the mark of life is that what we do obey is who and what we are. And we have no other recourse than to see what we do as evidence of what we are, and use it, for good or worse, (1) to make more use of what we obeyed in the first place, & thereby (2), continue the pursuit of who we are. . . .
>
> With that introduction—those words *space, fact, stance*—you now know what I knew until now, if I add one more thing: the increasing, and at first most irritating, tendence on my part to see what I was getting at as a morality, specifically *a morality of motion*. This bothered me, at least until the sense of motion got added, just because I took it that if there was any virtue at all in

the vocabulary I was trying to engage that reality by (and, in my work, re-enact it, or at least throw what light on it) without reference to any known sanction systems. Not that I was seeking to be original. It was merely that all I knew—the moral, as well as metaphysical, as well as aesthetic formulations & their words for themselves—did not jibe with, actually prevented me from, what I felt and did. Yet there I suddenly was, adding such words as "obey," seeing some person as unredeemed (and unredeemable!), thinking of perfection (I, the proud relativist! even writing the line, "The idea is to be perfect," and putting it in Christ's mouth), and, finally, having the experience myself of knowing the need of God![1]

Maximus is the noun-magician. He is not simply the namer, he is "the man in the word," the flesh made Logos. The poem to which he refers in the closing lines of this passage is "In the Hills South of Capernaum, Port," a carefully expurgated version of the Sermon on the Mount. Olson's Christ says, "Take the natural for base / assume your nature as a bird his or the grass" (*Archaeologist*, 6). Christ, however, had been used so long and so relentlessly as a symbolic prop for a morality which was repugnant to Olson that His secular force could not be recovered. It is a daring poem, managing, as it does, to hew to the language of the original text, but ultimately it is a dry, lifeless thing. Maximus is the god Olson wanted, so like himself that the two seem sometimes to merge, in perfected secularity.

Although there are important secondary resonances, Maximus's name means, most simply, large. By implication, he is also the Neoplatonic philosopher and magician, Maximus of Tyre, as well as *homo maximus*, the redeemed man of alchemy, but above all, he is a big man, as large as his name, and, at the beginning of the poem, largely unknown. He is located in Gloucester, Massachusetts, a little fishing village on Cape Ann, which daily fills his eyes and ears, so it is his most common concern, but much passes there which has reference to other places and other times, frequently far away or long ago. Maximus is proposed as a figure who is equal to the immense spaces and stretches of history that comprise the outward facts of his existence. He is an image of possibilities inherent in that situation.

The association of Maximus and his Tyrian counterpart is erratic:

[1]Copyright by the University of Connecticut Library.

sometimes the two seem to merge totally; sometimes the Tyrian is almost forgotten. In *Ishmael*, Olson mentions the "occult art of the Neoplatonists in which, through self-purification and sacred rites, the aid of the divine was invoked" (*Ishmael*, 56), as an alternative to the black arts of Ahab. Like the alchemists of the seventeenth century, they seemed to Olson dark survivals, decadent and misguided as they often were, of an ancient, lost science. The "Foreword" to Lawrence's *Fantasia of the Unconscious* was a crucial text for Olson. Lawrence argues that the myths and rituals are, in fact, the remnants of a world-wide pleistocene science which was, in contrast to our own, a science of life: "And so it is that all the great symbols and myths which dominate the world when our history first begins, are very much the same in every country and every people, the great myths all relate to one another. And so it is that these myths now begin to hypnotize us again, our own impulse towards our own scientific way of understanding being almost spent."[2] Maximus of Tyre is one of the gates through which Maximus of Gloucester attempts to enter the lost mythic world. Olson is a literalist. If Lawrence's "science of life" is possible, he wants to find its laws.

Although one might find ways in which Olson's vision reflects the Tyrian's, it is not his philosophy which makes Maximus for Olson a conduit to the lost past. Tyre, like Gloucester, is "a town / placed on an island / close to the shore" (*Maximus* II, 103), and Tyre alone gave Alexander the Great and his destruction of the polis as a legitimate organization of life any serious resistance. Maximus was a civic gadfly—a role which Olson's Maximus reluctantly assumes—and, as a secular magician, still in touch with the ancient power, he offers a center on which to reconstruct a non-Christian history. "History was ritual and repetition" for Olson, as for Melville, when "his imagination was at its own proper heat" (*Ishmael*, 13). There is no implied mysticism or even mystery, no metaphoric use of exotic doctrine, like metempsychosis, to account for the Tyrian's reappearance. Like a number of other figures with whom Maximus becomes identified, Maximus of Tyre is relevant to the poem's process because he figures in several layers of the multiphasic form.

If Maximus of Tyre presides over the first volume of the *Maximus*, lending his example to Olson's hero, it is *homo maximus*,

---

[2]*Fantasia of the Unconscious* (New York, 1930), p. xi.

the alchemical man of the cosmos—in whose body the four cardinal directions, the four seasons, and the four elements, all of the oppositions, are united—who appears in the second volume as the embodiment of secular perfection. He represents the integrity of the cosmos, which the adept produces microcosmically in the philosopher's stone and in his own soul. "For heaven is a man," Paracelsus writes of the *homo maximus*, "and man is heaven, all men are one heaven and heaven is only one man."[3] Union with the *homo maximus* is the recovery of innocence, the integration in the world of the total self. The adept is freed from time and enters into unconstricted familiarity with space. Jung, on whom Olson depends for much of his alchemical lore, writes: "Union with the *homo maximus* produces a new life which Paraclesus calls 'vita cosmographica.' In this life, 'time appears as well as the body of Jesahach' [one of the innumerable names for the philosopher's stone]. . . . *Locus* can mean 'time' as well as 'space,' and since . . . Paracelsus is here concerned with a sort of Golden Age, I have translated it as 'time.'"[4] Olson would have translated "locus" in its more common sense. The Golden Age, as he understands it, comes with the assertion of space *against* time. The *vita cosmographica* is literally the life of cosmos-mapping which Maximus assumes in the second volume.

In these enlarged dimensions Maximus is a man of *stance*, the central figure in a geometry which involves space and fact in a "morality of motion." Olson will use a different vocabulary later, but these three, space, stance, and fact, are the first manifestations of Olson's secularized trinity. The terms are related to the three stages in Whitehead's analysis of the development of feeling, to the topos-typos-tropos paradigm in "Letter to Elaine Feinstein" (*Human*, 97), and to the world of nature, the initiatic cosmos, and the celestial world in "conditio."[5] They are at once simultaneous *and* stages in a ritual disclosure, which provide focuses for the first, second, and third volumes. The *Maximus* is an actualization of, a working through, these abstract nouns. If in the third volume both Maximus of Tyre and *homo maximus* disappear, to be replaced by Charles Olson himself, it is because the poem arrives at an image of man which must be lived.

[3]Quoted by C. G. Jung in *Alchemical Studies*, trans. R. F. C. Hull (Princeton, N.J., 1967), p. 131.
[4]*Ibid.*, p. 167.
[5]"Conditio," p. 274.

Although the terms are not precisely parallel, each set of them revealing the relationship in slightly different light, they all derive from an understanding of language which disappeared in the seventeenth century. In the Stoic analysis of language which had generally prevailed in the western world, the act of language had involved three terms: a significant, a signified, and a conjuncture (an active bringing together). Michel Foucault describes the nexus in which the linguistic act had occurred in these terms:

> . . . language exists first of all, in its raw and primitive being, in the simple, material form of writing, a stigma upon things, a mark imprinted across the world is a part of its most ineffaceable forms. In a sense, this layer of language is unique and absolute. But it also gives rise to two other forms of discourse which provide it with a frame: above it, there is commentary, which recasts the given signs to serve a new purpose, and below it, the text, whose primacy is presupposed by commentary to exist hidden beneath the marks visible to all. Hence there are three levels of language, all based upon the single being of the written word.[6]

In the seventeenth century, however, the linguistic situation became simply binary, a pure one-to-one representation of significant to signified. The mystery of language and the chief philosophic problem thenceforth became the link between the word and the object which it intends. As Foucault points out, language "in its raw and primitive being" has returned in the nineteenth and twentieth centuries, in Mallarmé and Artaud, for example, but criticism, as the modern form of commentary, has remained so utterly within the bounds of representational discourse, even for the poets themselves, that the occluded forms which rest *below* the written language have failed to emerge. Consequently, the various pure languages of poetry which have appeared are, despite the power we feel in them, essentially only counter-discourse, negations, rather than languages inside of which life can be conducted. Olson proposes to recombine the three terms of language in a single act of writing, commentary, and revelation.

Space, where both objects and words occur, is the first term and the most obvious: the topology, the beginning, the source. It is the place where the work is done, where the lines between significant and

---

[6]*The Order of Things: An Archaeology of the Human Sciences* (New York, 1971), p. 42.

signified are traced and retraced, where everyone and everything shares a common condition. Unrelieved space, however, is an infernal condition, the play of meaningless and destructive forces. In *Maximus* I, the hero deals in *surfaces*. He gathers the heroic tales of the Gloucester fishermen and steps off the property lines of the first settlers, in an attempt to bring the city to coherence. He pits his own will to cohere against the pejorocratic will to change and disperse, and he fails. Toward the end of the first volume he says: " . . . the present / is worse give nothing now your credence / start all over" (*Maximus* I, 150). "Melville," Olson writes, "saw his likeness in defeated and exiled heroes, not in successful sons who, by their triumph, became the fathers" (*Ishmael*, 82). *Maximus* I is the book of the unsuccessful son.

The stance which locates a man with respect to his own truth, however, is revealed as one works on these surfaces. It is the way a man is *typed*, how he is struck by the blows of experience (typos, from *typtein*, to strike, beat, carries these violent implications in its etymology). Space literally produces a condition in which something *has* to happen. Stance which cannot or does not act is solipsism; it takes from the world, but it gives nothing in return. In the first volume Maximus is able to define the active condition:

> That carpenter is much on my mind:
> I think he was the first Maximus
>
> Anyhow, he was the first to make things,
> not just live off nature.
>
> (Maximus I, 31)

It is not, however, just things which are demanded of Maximus but a coherent ordering of the world. The surfaces have been so degraded that Maximus must return to the interior, to the lost past. In the second volume he turns inland, literally, to Dogtown, the deserted village in the interior of Cape Ann, and to his own interiors: "I am making a mappemunde. It is to include my being" (*Maximus* II, 87). At this point, however, the map is called "Peloria," the monster. It is still isolated, and cannot be perfected until it is joined again to the external. *Maximus* II is the book of purgation and rebirth.

The event, the created thing—retaining all of the force of space, but in another form—is the fact, the trop, which is the issue of the moral stance, the revelation of the celestial, the unknown totality that provided a context for the original initiation. In the Beliot lectures

Olson identifies "trop" directly with image or vision. The third volume opens with this proposition:

> having descried the nation
> to write a Republic
> in gloom on watch-house point.
>
> (*Maximus* III, 9)

The passage seems to have been written shortly after the death of Olson's wife, and so the Republic is to be written in "gloom." Obviously the distinction between "to descry" and "to write" is at this point crucial to the turn which the poem takes as it moves into the third volume. It implies a change in both location and mode of action. "To descry" implies a distance: "to discover a view from afar," and, to this point in the poem, Maximus has been, as he is in the opening lines of the sequence, "Off-shore, by islands hidden in the blood" (*Maximus* I, 1). "To descry" also involves a certain passivity or receptivity: the space and the history are *given* facts of the nation, and they are revealed rather than made. In the third volume Maximus proposes to actively assume the role of the maker. The poem passes from sight to vision. The neat Freudian drama of the family, however, is never completely played out. Maximus does appear as the father (*Maximus* III, 69–70, 102, 120), but the mythos is no longer geneological and aristocratic. As we will see, the democratic dispensation is more interesting and complex than that. Like everything else in the written republic, fathers and sons are specific.

The expanse of the nation is mapped, by way of a non-Euclidean deformation, to a point. "It was even shown that in the infinitely small the older concepts of space ceased to be valid at all," Olson writes. "Quantity—the measurable and numerable—was suddenly as shafted into any thing, as it was also, as had been obvious, the striking character of the external world, that all things do extend out" (*Human*, 118). The opening passage of the third volume, then, can perhaps be paraphrased in these terms: Having descried the begetting and the birth of the nation, to take an active stance toward the Republic, which will shine from the trop of this point. That is in keeping with Olson's definition of "tropism" in *Poetry and Truth*:

> . . . that we *are* darkness. That our, like, condition inside is dark.
> In other words, if you stop to think of yourself as an impediment

of creation, I mean you. . . . I think you follow me, that the unknown is rather your self's insides. . . . I mean, literally, that to
light that dark is to have come to whatever it is I think any of us
seeks. And tropism to my mind—and actually here I do or again
express an experience of, say, twenty years ago, which was to me
dogmatic, when I knew there was a sun, I mean a helio inside
myself, so that every other human being, and every thing in creation, was something that I could see if I could keep that experience. (*Poetry*, 43–44)

Maximus III was to have been the book of paradise. Although it is
only nominally finished, and the published volume was compiled by
other hands, we are at least given some notion as to what Olson's
paradise might have been. There is much sadness and loneliness in the
third volume, and, if it does not manage to bring about the final secu-
larization of the mysteries, it does bring the poem to a point from
which its images can be lived.

I must underscore the fact that this triune form in in no sense
absolute. The *Maximus* develops through a series of self-corrections.
Both specific details, such as Maximus's assessment of John Winthrop,
for example, and the form of the poem as a whole are constantly
subject to revision. As long as the most insistent concern is the act of
knowing by the individual, the three loci which determine such acts
appear as formal conditions of the poem, where they inform the parts
as they inform the whole. In the third volume when the fact/trope of
the hero appears, it must be recognized as the space/topos of the redeemed city. Stance, the remaining vestige of the old ego, is absorbed
back into space and fact, and heroic action becomes the responsibility
of everyone. To use Olson's terms from *Causal Mythology*, space now
appears as The Earth and The History or City, fact as The Image of
the World and The Spirit of the World. Once this new shape makes its
appearance, it can be recognized that it has been emerging since early
in the second volume (see the four-part organization of "Later Tyrian
Business," *Maximus* II, 36, for example), and, of course, it has been
implicit since the beginning. The trinity, rather than being a limiting
device, can now be seen clearly as the vehicle for this new possibility,
which is no longer personal. It is a limit for Maximus. To go beyond
it, he can only impose his vision on others and so make the mistake
he condemns in Pound. The space of vision is open to all.

1

Taken from another point of view, however—and the challenge of open composition is to take all views at once into account—the whole of the *Maximus* is an exegesis of "I, Maximus of Gloucester, to You" and "Maximus, to Gloucester." Written in the spring and summer of 1950, they stake out a territory which Olson spent the next twenty years exploring.

If the *Maximus* is considered not as a completed form but as a process of revelation, it appears to arise from the play of two simultaneous relationships which "I, Maximus of Gloucester" (*Maximus* I, 1–4) embodies fully but articulates only in broad outline. These relationships are at once syntactical and spatial:

1) The relationship between nouns (or objects) which English registers circuitously as subject to indirect object: "I, Maximus of Gloucester, *to you*." We say, "I grab you by the collar," but "I speak this poem *to you*." Speech, as it is treated in English grammar, is profoundly involved with itself. Its *direct* reference is to the Apollonian sun, to the Platonic heaven, to the Logos which was in the beginning. Both speaker and audience climb their own *ad hoc* ladders to reach the height where they come into contact. The approaches to that place, perfect in itself, are so rickety and uncertain, so dangerous, that they have given the attempt to *say* anything a bad name. Whitman's efforts to come into touch with his audience ended in a merging of egos which violated everyone's integrity. When Olson began writing poetry in the 1940s, Eliot's prescription for indirection, the objective correlative, had been received as scripture. The condition described by F. H. Bradley, in a passage which Eliot quotes in a note to *The Waste Land*, was implicit, so perfectly was language conditioned by the Delphic assumption, in the grammatical situation: " . . . my experience falls within my own circle, a circle closed on the outside; and, with all its elements alike, every sphere is opaque to the others which surround it."[7]

The mode of the *Maximus*, however, is not speech but address: "Isolated person in Gloucester, Massachusetts, I, Maximus, address you / you islands / of men and girls" (*Maximus* I, 12). Olson proposes a projective verse: "projectile, percussive, prospective" (*Human*, 51), a direct contact between himself and what was formerly understood

[7] *The Waste Land and Other Poems* (New York, 1934), p. 53.

as indirect object, audience. "A poem is energy transferred from where the poet got it . . . , by way of the poem itself, to, all the way over to, the reader" (*Human*, 52). One process of the *Maximus*, then, is its own publication (making-public), an engagement with the literal biological mechanism of speech which happens also to supply the oxygen necessary to sustain life, a modulation of the column of air which runs up and down the core of both poet and reader. If the poem is to be of essential use, rather than mere decoration, it must break the veil of syntax which separates rhythm from its confirmation in speech as gesture.

Olson's solution to the problem which Whitman raises for American poets is to write letters. The address of the poem demands that specificity. Some of the poems are literally letters, and it is sometimes possible to determine to whom they are addressed, but there is another meaning here. The Alexandrian scholars divided the Homeric epics into twenty-four roughly equal parts and, to simplify citations, assigned letters of the Greek alphabet to each part. They would refer to a passage as beta, line such and such, or they would speak of the twenty-four letters of the *Iliad*.[8] The address of the *Maximus* is at once personal and epic.

2) The relationship between nouns which English registers as the genitive of place: "I, *Maximus of Gloucester*, to You." From Williams's *Paterson*, Olson had learned that the local referent, like the specific address, was a necessary condition of the poem. The particularity of Paterson or Gloucester is required because the grammar has weakened the relationship between the speaker and his place and opens distances between the poet and the ground he stands on which are recapitulations of the distances between the poet and his audience. It assumes that, if everyone is far enough away from earth, if they can, as the Delphic tradition demands, make the sun the center of reference, the difference in what is seen will be negligible.

The westward movement of culture away from ancient Sumer, which according to Olson's reading of history began about 1200 B.C., was both a socio-cultural imperialism and something that might be called "syntactical imperialism." The language was forced into ever more generalized forms which, having the advantage of universal

[8]Victor Berard, *Did Homer Live?* trans. Brian Rhys (London and Toronto, 1931), p. 19.

applicability, destroyed the integrity of every place. Olson's "Grammar—a 'book'" (*Prose*, 27–31) traces part of the process which has, in effect, emptied all relational words of any specific content. He quotes the linguist Edward Sapir on the fact that "of," like the Latin genitive suffix, was "originally an adverb of considerable concreteness of meaning, away, moving from . . . " (*Prose*, 30). It defined an *active* condition, and it derived its meaning from a relationship to a specific center. In the *Maximus*, being *of* some place provides the impetus for the narrative movement of the poem.

Olson recognizes that, in *Paterson*, Williams allows the local referent to become only another variety of provincialism. The language of the *Maximus* comes from a center which, by engaging itself with Gloucester's antecedents, with Dorchester, Tyre, and the lost capital of Gondwanaland, engages itself totally with Gloucester. Language in the *Maximus* becomes a map in which nothing has spatial reality except that it comes into relation with that center. Such mapping requires a retooling of language in order to return the personal genitive of place—as against the subject alone—to a position of linguistic control.

Gloucester is an arbitrary place, chosen perhaps for no other reason than the happy summers Olson spent there as a child. He had not been there, except for an occasional visit to his mother, since 1939. Washington, D.C., where he was living when he began the poem, would seem a more likely place. It was, in 1950, flushed with atomic arrogance and beginning to conceive of itself as policeman of the world. The point is, of course, precisely that Gloucester *is* arbitrary. The Center is not a place as such but an engagement of attentions which is necessarily *located*. Maximus himself is "off-shore by islands hidden in the blood." His most immediate involvement is not with the city but his own circulation, his own pulse, which provides him with his most immediate sense of measure. "A metal hot from boiling water," he lends nothing to the process but the heat of his own attentions. He does not act in any willful sense: "he obeys the figures of / the present dance."

The dance is an important and persistent concern, especially in Olson's early work, but it is not used simply as an image of the unity of body and soul, as it is so frequently in twentieth-century verse. He is interested in techniques which dance and poetry once shared and which have been lost to the literate poet. In a plan for Black Mountain

College which he drafted in 1956, he writes: "It is not the appreciation or the listening or the creation of music, but the work side of
music as of dance—the direct necessity of either, if you make, as we
do, work in writing and theater pivot on process."[9] He insists that the
poem is, like the dance, a coming into, and process of, the literal body.
"Apollonius of Tyana, A Dance, with Some Words, for Two Actors,"
which was written the year after "I, Maximus of Gloucester, to You,"
is Olson's investigation into the nature of the obedience which the
dance requires. Maximus's obedience to Gloucester is directly parallel
to Apollonius's obedience to Tyana. He is the dancer, the city is the
voice.

It should be noted perhaps that Apollonius is forty years old,
roughly Olson's age when he began the *Maximus*, when he becomes
"aware of the dimensions of his job" (*Human*, 37). By that time,
Apollonius has studied with the masters of the Aesculapian-Pythago-
rean school, for whom the disciplines of the mind and of the body are
inseparable, and he has understood, as Olson says, "the body as the
first part of the way" (*Human*, 30). He has traveled to Bagdad, where
he imposed a five-year silence on himself, and thence to Cadiz, the
western limit of the known world, in search, Olson says, of a methodology. The comparisons to Olson's own biography are too obvious
to avoid: the early involvement with Melville (Olson's master), the
five years of silence in Bagdad-Washington, the hitch-hiking trip to
San Francisco (1947) in search of materials and methods for his proposed history of the West. It would also be mistaken to overlook the
fact that Apollonius's task is precisely Olson's:

> . . . how to offer man a correction which will restore (1) point by
> point sharpness; and (2) what he knows makes such sharpness—
> the allaying of any doubt in a man he belongs, the restoration to
> him of the sense that every thing belongs to him to the degree
> that he makes himself responsible for it as well as for himself.
> And Tyana, as his given, as a first fact (no more than that, but no
> less) looms for him, at this juncture, as in some way intimately
> connected with the job. (*Human*, 37)

Olson had used the phrase "first fact" before, as the title of the prologue in *Call Me Ishmael*, which recounts the story of the whaleship

[9]"A Draft of a Plan for the College," in *Olson: The Journal of the
Charles Olson Archives*, 2 (Fall, 1974), 55.

Essex, the story which fired Melville's imagination for *Moby Dick*. Their cities are first facts for Apollonius and Maximus because they are, for their citizens, images of working coherence, the centers which tie the wanderers back to their sources and are in turn transformed by the abilities of certain men to confirm the sources in their knowledge of the world as a totality and a coherence. This doublet of energy flow Olson calls "verticality." It "is the proper way a human body can indicate penetration downward . . . : dignity, after all, is as much a sinking of the feet into the earth as it is containment of the round of the self" (*Human*, 38).

Unlike the conventional epic which begins with the statement of a theme, the *Maximus* opens with a complex relationship, a juxtaposition of the hero with his audience and his local space. The entire fabric of the poem will be woven in this nexus. Maximus is not a communal figure, nor is there any communal spirit in Maximus's concern for the city. Robert Creeley points to the relevance of the ancient Pythagorean tradition which defined the social classes at the Olympic Games: the lowest class comes to buy and sell; the next class comes to participate; the high class comes to *look on*.[10] Maximus seeks to join his passivity to the intense action which a city must bring to focus. In "Equal, That Is, to the Real Itself" Olson writes: "I pick up on calm, or passivity, Melville's words, and about which he knew something, having served as a boat-steerer himself, on at least his third voyage on a whaler in the Pacific. He says somewhere a harpoon can only be thrown accurately from such repose as he also likened the White Whale to, as it finally approached, a mighty mildness of repose in swiftness in his phrase" (*Human*, 122). "A mighty mildness of repose in swiftness" is the condition of perception and speech which Olson proposes in his hero. Maximus is "one of a company" which exhibits a will the opposite of Ahab's; Melville calls them men on "the hustings of the Divine Inert." His personal strength never extends beyond the "repose of swiftness" in which he participates by finding "the actual character and structure of the real" in himself (see *Human*, 122).

The chain of association which ends with Maximus's transformation into a partridge in "Maximus Letter # whatever" is implicit

---

[10]"Some Notes on Olson's *Maximus*," pp. 167–68.

in this opening poem of the sequence. In the first section of "I, Maximus of Gloucester," Maximus's off-shore vision is juxtaposed, literally, with a bird's-eye view of Gloucester: "the roofs, the old ones the gentle steep ones." The vowels leading the harmony on (island/I/lie/time, obey/may/slain, Maximus/land/lance/dance/after/mast), the persistent element through this radical change in viewpoint (from Maximus, to Maximus's projection of himself, as in any dream), is concern for the *quantity* of attention which experience receives. Olson incidentally provides a gloss for his passage in an explanation of his interest in the ancient Maya: "It was better to be a bird, as these seem to have been, they kept moving their heads so nervously to stay alive, to keep alerted to what they were surrounded by" (*Human*, 64). With his attentions absorbed in local reality, Maximus discovers the "vertical" dimension of space, so that he recognizes an *instant* is not a mechanical duration but a coincidence of consciousness and space which can be concentrated or expanded indefinitely by use: "second, time slain, the bird! the bird! / and there! (strong) thrust, the mast." After this initial act of will, this declaration of his own local situation as absolute, Maximus, in a position to take up the dynamics of his situation, is released from willfulness. When he erects the mast, he institutes the new geometry: time falls away, space is reordered, and he becomes like Apollonius, "geometric and annunciative man measurer and to be measured" (*Human*, 26).

The cosmos which Maximus will reveal is founded on this center which he erects. In the course of Maximus's voyage, the mast will become the *axis mundi* which joins the city to the heavens and to the underworld. So located, Maximus discovers the will which Apollonius finds manifest in Indian culture, "a will which asserted itself inward, a sort of will the West had lost the law of, and so only turned outward" (*Human*, 39). The first volume of the *Maximus* records the hero's attempt to turn *inward* and to take Gloucester with him. He reaches out to the world in an effort to join the city's diversity to a greater and more useful diversity. The invocation of the kylix and Anthony of Padua suggest a range of things and people that offer themselves as allies to anyone who would stand up straight. Although the specific local force of the kylix is not clear, it contributes, like Anthony, the patron saint of the Portuguese fishing community in Gloucester, to the coherence which any polis brings to bear in itself.

In the growing circle of coincidents, which constitute the discovered form of the *Maximus*, Anthony, like John Smith and John Hawkins, are rhymes for Maximus himself. In 1964 Olson writes, "I cldn't advise you than to study more the/13th century especially the 1st half," which was Anthony's period, "& particularly the contrast (4th century Athens!) of the 2nd Half" (*Archaeologist*, 206), when, of course, those more characteristic carriers of the Delphic tradition—Aquinas, Eckhart, and Bacon—were clearly in the ascendancy.

The second section of "I, Maximus of Gloucester" is a re-enactment of the process by which Maximus, as center, exercises his force. Form is *not* disciple, as it has been since the rise of the Greek lyric, and form is *not* the product of hatred and revenge, as it has been since the will in western culture began to confront its limits: "love is form." In light of our most venerable traditions, it is an outrageous statement. We believe that our form-making abilities reside in the most dispassionate and sublimated part of ourselves. Maximus, however, has nothing but his own desire and the belief that it is of such superior force that it can draw a world into shape around him. Metrical judgment is made strictly in terms of quantity, "feather to feather added," rather than discrete qualities, such as those which have dominated aesthetic, ethical, and metaphysical thought. The process by which the instant is possessed does not develop through judgments of taste, value, or arbitrary conventions. The necessity is to make a place to *be*. Feathers, bits of hair and string, the documents of other activities, which precede and contribute to the building of the nest, are carried in, from the ambience to the center, to build a new coherence from the signatures of other processes which have dispersed. The materials carried in "make bulk, these, in the end, are / the sum." Only by his insistence on quantity can Olson return measure, as against syntax or Idea, to a place of crucial significance in the poem. The syllables—and the images, as love "cannot be without / important substance"—are measured as they pull down, have *weight* in the line: "58 carats each one of us, perforce / our goldsmith's scales." Measure, in other words, is not across the linear expanse of the line; it is rather a quantity which occurs in the instant and gives a reading of how the instant is disposed of: "This is eternity. This now. This foreshortened span" (*Human*, 47). Maximus does not measure himself against some "never-time" which appears beyond the end of the poem. The design of the poem arises from the effort to inhabit the eternity which opens to one who, in the heat of attention, realizes the form of his eros in the present.

After Maximus asserts quantity as the measure of totality, the muse of the poem appears to him:

> (o my lady of good voyage
> in whose arm, whose left arm rests
> no boy but a carefully carved wood, a painted face, a schooner!
> a delicate mast, as bow-sprit for
>
> forwarding.

Our Lady is the first manifestation of the feminine archetype or, as the Jungian color of that term is not precise, Maximus's other. If the *Maximus* can be said to be an exercise in hero-worship, an attempt to resolve the dichotomy which Ahab and Ishmael represent, its success depends upon Maximus's restoration of the rites of the Mother behind whom stands, as at Delphi, the Earth itself. She is the object of Maximus's desire. More immediately, however, Our Lady, whose image overlooks Gloucester harbor from the tower of the church to which she lends her name, provides the counterbalance, the forward force to ensure that the inwardness of will which is being proposed does not become subjectivity and provinciality.

It should be pointed out, incidentally, that the movement from section to section of the poem does not develop in time, according to some narrative or logical scheme. Olson's revisions of the poem[11] amount largely to a rearrangement of chunks of lines, and, for the most part, the changes seem to be intended to draw Maximus and the process in which he is engaged into a position of prime importance. The potentiality of the poem is timeless, and it is called into linear sequence by the poet's discovery.

The early version of "I, Maximus of Gloucester, to You" opens by recalling one of Pound's dictums in the Imagist manifesto: "By ear, he sd." He appeals to the organ at which contact between the poet and the voice of the city is made and attempts to clear the channels in a burst of protest against the conditions which compromise the ear's hearing:

---

[11]For the original version of "I, Maximus of Gloucester, to You," see *The New American Poetry* (New York, 1960), pp. 8–11.

> But that which matters, that which insists, that which will last
> where shall you find it, my people, how, where shall you listen
> when all is become billboards. . . .

These are not the questions of a man whose *tastes* have been offended.
Something more profound is at stake. Advertising is only the most
obvious sign of a social order which attacks the inward coherence at
the gates of perception.

A more confident Olson, however, revises the poem to establish
more clearly the relation between the process which the poem proposes and the protest which the workings of the process unfortunately
involve. In the revised version the poem moves from the establishment
of the Center, to a consideration of measure, and, in section three, to
the *content* to be measured.

If form is the emergence of the body of Eros—or the embodiment
of eros—as the second section suggests, rather than a state which is
qualitatively distinct from what would then be called "chaos," the
attention must be directed to the point where the casual world is
transformed into local unity. Maximus is in the position of selecting
details from the mass of indeterminant possibilities to "fill out" a
form which is visible to him only in the vaguest sense:

> the underpart is, though stemmed, uncertain
> is, as sex is, as moneys are, facts!
> facts, to be dealt with, as the sea is, the demand
> that they be played by, that they only can be, that they must
> be played by, said he, coldly, the
> ear!

The poet's most immediate erotic involvement is with the music of his
own verse. The poem is a sensual experience which gives voice to both
the occuluded interior and the occluded exterior; it is the audible sign
of those two "out-riders" of space which are usually called "the unconscious" and "the noumena." Maximus's gain, from the beginning
of the poem, is that he has located these crucial and elusive dimensions of the real in the *same* space that he inhabits physically.

Olson stands at the end of a tradition of poets who have courted
the unconscious for well over a century, have allowed it to fill their
songs with an energy which is sometimes beautiful and sometimes
perverse. Although the poets of the nineteenth century applied to it

indirectly, letting their speech arouse it through symbolic equivalencies, its revelation was attended in a remarkable number of instances by despair, madness, and destruction. The demonic genius, who presides over the work of Byron, Goethe, Poe, and Melville, accepts damnation as the cost of knowledge. Olson recognizes, however, that the Romantic poets had attempted to contain knowledge which was transpersonal and worldly in the limited vessel of personality. It is their evidence which leads Freud to imagine the unconscious as a psychic carbuncle which must be lanced. The surrealists, on the other hand, who are the twentieth-century representatives of the tradition, submit themselves and their personalities so totally to the unconscious that they lose any personal relationship with their created forms. Although the lines of influence are not direct, of course, it was an impulse similar to the surrealists' which directed Jung in his hypostasization of the unconscious as a transcendent reality.

Olson might be said to secularize Jung's universal unconscious. What is unknown, what must be known, if men are to be whole and "healthy," is the world itself. As he will say in "Proprioception," " . . . the unconscious is the universe flowing-in inside" (*Prose*, 19). The Socratic injunction to self-knowledge and psychoanalysis are both expressionistic; they insist that the required task is to "push out" the lost contents of the self. In the *Maximus*, Morpheus, the shaper of dreams, is neither some forgotten drama of childhood nor a godlike repository of archetypes; he is the world from which modern man is estranged.

Identifying the process of form-creation with self-creation, the fourth section returns to a current of energy which was left undeveloped in the second section:

> one loves only form
> and form only comes
> into existence when
> the thing is born.

Things have been so abused and degraded that even the word "thing" is weak, almost empty. Maximus, however, casts his poem in a space where things and selves are so intimate, so dependent upon one another, that either is vague, even nonexistent, without the other. The thing—the concrete formal thing of the poem—is "born of yourself" and the free-floating, abstract percepta, the "hay and cotton struts, / street-pickings, wharves, weeds" the bird carries in. The act of *doing* history draws the personal and the past together in the recognition that these documentary fragments are the terms of the present. The past, comprehending only itself, is never more than the context for the indeterminant possibilities of the present: "the thing is born / . . . of yourself, torn." The self, unable to comprehend the new act until it is complete, must perpetually rediscover its own shape.

The fifth section brings together the largely unrealized concerns of section three with the more or less complete analysis of form which section four provides in a "clot" of images and references which will not be fully sorted out for some time. He discovers the reign of abstraction, which, borrowing a term from Pound's canto LXXIX, he calls "pejorocracy," interposes itself between him and the necessary objects of his love. The evidence that he gives is an early example of what we have since come to know not as "mu-sick" but as "mu-zack," which was piped into the streetcars in Washington, D.C., when Olson was living there in the late 1940s. In the second song of Maximus he returns to the same incident:

> all
> wrong
> And I am asked—ask myself (I, too, covered
> with the gurry of it) where
> shall we go from here, what can we do
> when even the public conveyances
> sing?

(*Maximus* I, 13)

And in the following song the "mu-sick" of the street car is identified with the "musickracket / of all ownership" (*Maximus* I, 14). As it can be documented that Olson did not learn that the Greek words for "myth" and "mouth" derive from the common root "mu" until 1956,[12] his use of "mu-sick, mu-sick, mu-sick" (a line probably taken from a popular song: "Put another nickel in, in the nickelodeon, all I want is loving you, and mu-sick, mu-sick, musick") is a clear case of the kind of discovery which Olson describes as doing "what one knows before one knows what one does."[13] It is this kind of "tear" in

[12]See Olson's lecture at the Institute of the New Science of Man, in Ann Charters, *Olson/Melville: A Study in Affinity* (Berkeley, Calif., 1968), p. 86.
[13]*Ibid.*

the self (i.e. the self exceeding the self) which Olson recognizes as the sign of genuine creation, for it is precisely oral myth-making which Maximus demands. Things, wherever they have their casual existence, must be extricated from their abstract context and reworked by the *voice* of the poem:

> American
> braid
> with others like you, such
> extricable surface
> as faun and oral
> satyr lesbos vase.

The section ends with Maximus raging against the pejorocrats:

> O kill kill kill kill kill
> those
> who advertise you
> out.

In the final section the *outwardness* of the pejorocracy, the perfected will which inevitably turns itself toward the circumference rather than the Center, is opposed to Maximus's own struggle to bring the multiplicity of outward experience to an inward coherence: "in! in! the bow-sprit, bird, the beak / in the bend is, in goes in." This contention between the will which directs itself outward and the will which bears inward is the prevailing condition in horizontal space in the *Maximus*. In fact, it is a central feature of any *open* structure, because existence in an open structure is nonsimultaneous: it contains elements which cannot be explained in terms of a single conception. In explaining why "outward" is a meaningless concept in Einsteinian (open) physics, Buckminster Fuller writes: "'In' is unique to individual bodies but 'out' is common to all and 'out' has no shape. Inside-outing of non-simultaneous event relationships from heterogeneous time viewpoints of universe is inherently shapeless, ergo non-conceptual."[14] The *agon* of the first volume of the *Maximus* pits the hero's efforts to bring Gloucester to a dynamic coherence which moves inward in horizontal space and downward in vertical space. It would misrepresent the nature of the process which produced the *Maximus* to imply that Olson was aware in 1950, when "I, Maximus of Gloucester" was written, how completely this pattern would per-

[14]*Utopia or Oblivion* (New York, 1969), p. 72.

vade the completed poem. As it turns out, however, the two nonreversible axes which are defined by the statements *the way in is the way out* and *the way down is the way up* characterize the nature of the space in which Maximus maps his being.

"Letter 2" (*Maximus* I, 5–8) picks up directly from the suggestions in "I, Maximus of Gloucester, to You" and explores them in another context, while at the same time it opens another sight, another archaeological dig. The discovered artifacts, the first from the shrine of the local hero, the second from the shrine of the mother-goddess, to press the metaphor which is essential to one aspect of Olson's method, becomes evidence in the continuing conjecture about the unrevealed city which is Gloucester, Massachusetts.

In Ernest Fenollosa's "The Chinese Written Character as a Medium for Poetry," Olson had read: "A true noun, an isolated thing, does not exist in nature. Things are only the terminal points, or rather the meeting points, of actions, cross-sections cut through actions, snap-shots. Neither can a pure verb, an abstract motion, be possible in nature. The eye sees noun and verb as one: things in motion, motion in things, and so the Chinese conception tends to represent them."[15] Olson recognized that Pound's attempts to form English on a Chinese model had resulted in the substitution of one kind of discontinuity for another, but it seemed to him that glyphic language did retain a density of involvement in the dynamics of the world to which it referred that his own language desperately lacked. In 1951 he spent six months in the Yucatan, studying Mayan glyphs. "Human Universe" and the lovely sequence of letters to Creeley, published as *The Mayan Letters*, are at once meditations on the lost language and, indirectly, on the relationship between the first two poems of the *Maximus*. The underlying question is, "Can one restate man in any way to repossess him of his dynamic" (*Human*, 8). Olson's answer—to the extent that he is able to give it at this date—is that man can become a participant in the dynamics of the world to the extent that he can recover the sense that *things* are potentialities which manifest themselves and their endless kinetic energies as *both* object and nouns:

> There is only one thing you can do about kinetic, re-enact it. Which is why the man said, he who possesses rhythm possesses the universe. And why art is the only twin life has—its only valid

[15] In Ezra Pound, *Instigations of Ezra Pound with an Essay on the Chinese Written Character by Ernest Fenollosa* (New York, 1920), p. 364.

metaphysic. Art does not seek to describe but to enact. And if man is once more to possess intent in his life, he has to comprehend his own process as intact, from outside, by way of his skin, in, and by his own powers of conversion, out again. (*Human*, 10).

The focus in "I, Maximus of Gloucester, to You" is largely interior, tracing out the lines of force involved in the hero's "powers of conversion." In "Letter 2" (*Maximus* I, 9–12), Olson seeks to engage his hero with larger, more resistant chunks of reality, which are exterior to him.

The prologue to "Letter 2" consists of two glosses on the previous poem. Maximus is now able to see himself established in the poem as hero, and so life's preoccupation with itself becomes an *explication de texte*. He points out, rather flippantly, that he is not required to offer himself as a ritual substitute. He is no scapegoat; he can justify only himself. The recognition of this fact allows him tentatively to restate the terms of the poem's process in a single apothegm:

> he was right: people
>
> don't change. They only stand more
> revealed. I,
> likewise.

In the first section he discovers that the *city* does not change but, likewise, stands more revealed:

> coming from the sea, up Middle, it is more white, very white
> as it passes the grey of the Unitarian church. But at Pleasant
> Street,
> it is abruptly black
> (hidden
> city.

Maximus alternately absorbs and is absorbed by the external world. The subjective and the objective, the masculine and the feminine, the conscious and the unconscious, are ultimately no more than spatial forms which Maximus discovers to be aspects of himself.

Under the excitement of this discovery, "Letter 2" becomes a celebration of Maximus's muse. Although she is imaged at first as the Virgin, she appears, as *Maximus* continues, as the Great Mother in all of her manifestations. Catharine R. Stimpson has objected that Olson's "most sweeping tributes to women are conventional, to their procreative powers and their sexuality. Olson dislikes American cheerleaders and girls in cute Capri pants, but he apparently fails to imagine women who act other than as mothers or lovers, be it in a conjugal or cosmic setting."[16] Without doubt, there is a measure of blustering *machismo* in Olson, but men and women alike are alienated from the eternal feminine as they are alienated from the heroic principle. The roles of women, like the roles of men, are *all* strictly proscribed by the failure of both to live in a physical world: " . . . the bodies," Maximus will say in one of the songs, "all buried / in shallow graves" (*Maximus* I, 13). In the *Maximus* "male" and "female" do not define social roles. The formal principles are masculine, the energy which fills the forms is feminine, and everyone, both men and women, must realize both in themselves, if there is to be a *polis*.

In the non-Maximus poems from this period Olson conjectures on a number of different occasions about the nature of femininity. In "Adamo Me" he writes:

> The riddle is (beside femininity, that is)
> that of which beauty is only the most interesting expression, why
> we persist, why we remain, even in the face of, curious
> even before the example of. . . .
>
> (*Archaeologist*, 23)

In "Letter 2," however, the riddle of femininity and the riddle of the persistence of the Gloucester fishermen are a single riddle. Our Lady's precise vision is proven in the heroics of the fisheries:

> She looks
> as the best of my people look
> in one direction, her direction, they know
>
> it is elements men stand in the midst of,
> not these names supported by the false future she,
> precisely she,
> has her foot upon.

The anecdotes reported in section two, which can be confirmed in Connolly's *Book of the Gloucester Fishermen* and the Gloucester

---

[16]"Charles Olson: Preliminary Images," *Boundary 2*, 2, nos. 1 & 2 (Fall, 1973, Winter, 1974), 152.

Times as literal fact, are Maximus's dreams, or at least they carry the personal force of dreams. The inversion has already taken place: "the unconscious is the universe flowing-in."

In section three, however, as Maximus walks down along the wharves, he and a fellow citizen of Gloucester eye "(with a like eye) a curious ship." They are sharing the privilege of citizens, joined in common perception. When "the lad from the Fort" turns to one of the handsomest of the docked ships, however, and says, "I'll own her one day," the false future intrudes, and Maximus is thrown back into the pejorocratic isolation. The poem ends with Maximus assuring himself, perhaps trying to convince himself, that "the demand / will arouse / some of these men and women."

These two poems define the limits of the polar geometry inside of which the *Maximus* is articulated. The objective landscape and history of Gloucester are the dreams which Olson will attempt to restore to his isolated hero. The work of art and the process of art begin to merge. Each act of speech becomes a revision of the poem as a whole and a realization of the possibilities which have been opened by previous revisions.

Although a number of Olson's finest individual poems—"The Praises," "In Cold Hell," "For Sappho," "An Ode on Nativity," and "To Gerhardt"—were written in 1950, 1951, and 1952, the *Maximus* was slow in declaring itself. The first two letters were written in 1950; the third was not added until 1952; and the poem did not get genuinely underway until 1953. During this period, however, the poems and the prose pieces were moving toward solutions to the problem of writing a poem of epic scale which finds its impulse in sources so remote from the pervasive cultural tradition that they require archaeological recovery. The difficulties were not simply the distances in time and space which separated Maximus of Gloucester from Maximus of Tyre and, behind him, the seed-time of pleistocene civilization, nor was it those equally immense distances which separated Maximus from his own inner vitality. Olson was most troubled by those conventions which are used to hold experience, which *might* be immediate, at arm's length: aesthetic distance, historical perspective, and scientific objectivity. The painting is framed, the play and the dance exist only behind the proscenium arch, the poet is the embodiment of a genius which removes him from the immediacy of experience to an isolated place of vision. History, geography, archaeology, economics,

and political science are all, no less than the aesthetic, disciplines of
distance. In "In Cold Hell" (1951) Olson asks:

> How shall he who is not happy, who has been made so unclear
> who is no longer privileged to be at ease, who, in this brush, stands
> reluctant, imageless, unpleasured, caught in a sort of hell, how
> shall he convert this underbrush, how turn this unbidden place
> how trace and arch again
> the necessary goddess?
>
> (*Archaeologist*, 66)

In the first two letters of the *Maximus*, Olson establishes a form
which is inherently unstable, demanding confirmation and reconfir-
mation in the poem's process. As one would expect of a poem which
allows the recognition of creative accident to declare its necessary direction, it is necessary first to create a context in which "the unac-
counted for" can be allowed, and then a range of evidence must be
brought to bear before the larger parts of the world can begin to make
their relationships manifest. Roughly speaking, these two projects are
the burdens of letters 3 through 9 and letters 11 through 22, respectively. To schematize in this way, however, oversimplifies the process
of the poem almost to the point of falsification. In the dynamic emergence of Maximus's world, which finds its true vein in "Letter 23," it
becomes apparent that the first twenty-two poems are not merely cast-
ings in the dark but the determinants of a form which is not articulated fully enough to be recognized.

The juxtaposition of Maximus and Gloucester has two immediate issues: the first sustained attack on pejorocracy, in "Letter 3"
(*Maximus* I, 9–12), and song, in "The Songs of Maximus" (*Maximus*
I, 13–16). These are both acts of Maximus, the private man, the man
limited to complaint and lyric. "Letter 3" is specifically a response to
a bad review of Vincent Ferrini's magazine *Four Winds* (which is again
an issue in "Letter 5") in the *Gloucester Times*. It becomes the occasion for a speculation about the relationship between the modern city,
in which language is used to intimidate, and Tyre, the ancient polis,
where a word is "meant to mean not a single thing the least more
than / what it does mean" (*Maximus* I, 11). The language has been
brutalized, caught up in a self-contained discourse which can be used
for commercial purposes, *without* involving the complexities of total

revelation. It has become a tool for sundering the public and the private, rather than for revealing the inner forms, the inner strengths, in public forms. In "The Songs" Maximus invokes Yeats at his most escapist, echoing a line from "The Lake Isle of Innisfree"—"I know a house made of mud & wattles" (*Maximus* I, 15)—to underscore the isolation of his situation.

Inside the space which the coincidence of Maximus and Gloucester defines, however, other relationships appear, immediately modifying one another and establishing new loci of energy, fields within the larger field. The first of these, which becomes sufficiently important to carry through a group of poems, has to do with matters arising from Vincent Ferrini's magazine. Olson's desire to avoid that stance which he characterizes as "the private soul at any public wall" leads, in letters 5 through 9, to a concern with making public, publication in the larger sense. The field of composition attracts images of self-manifestation: "The mind, Ferrini / is as much of a labor / as to lift an arm flawlessly" (*Maximus* I, 23); "what *sticks out* in this issue" (*Maximus* I, 24, my italics); "as Olsen, two days out, would appear / in a new white shirt and new fedora" (*Maximus* I, 27); "They are but extensions of their own careers" (*Maximus* I, 28); "as he used to wear a turquoise / in one ear, London / to let them know, here / was an American savage" (*Maximus* I, 32); "how to dance / sitting down" (*Maximus* I, 35); "The flowering plum / out the front door window / sends whiteness / inside my house" (*Maximus* I, 41). Taken up in Maximus's self-revelation, things emerge from their privacy, their one-dimensionality; the world profusely makes its inner being known.

A poetry magazine is, of course, in itself of no particular consequence. It seems a lightweight theme to hold a commanding place in a poem which proposes to extend itself to epic size. What is at stake, however, is large: the poet must, if he is to be a force in the city, exist, as his work must exist, in a space which the city shares. The diminution of the poet as a figure of power stems directly from the fact that, after the fifth or sixth century B.C., the poem came to have a tenuous relationship to the place in which daily life is conducted. A few months after "Letter 5" was written, Olson writes to Corman: " . . . certain New Englanders . . . have exposed the local by demonstrating that the particular is a syntax which is universal, and that it can not be discovered except locally, in the sense that any humanism *is* as well place as it is the person, that another of Socrates' crimes (who was improperly punished) was, that he did give polis its death blow when he cried, Be, a Citoyen, du monde . . ." (*Origin*, 127). The counter-thrust, opposing and frustrating the kind of "publication" Maximus values, is the deathly energy of abstraction which opens gaps in space and creates discrete orders of being. In "Letter 5" (*Maximus* I, 17–25) Maximus considers the places where he and Ferrini might meet, and he maps the city with the kind of specific knowledge any citizen might have: "I'll meet you anywhere you say (the beer's best—the pipes are kept cleaner— / at the Anchor Inn," and so forth. But the city which Maximus traces in his mind, as he will literally walk the streets in "Letter, May 2," is not Ferrini's Gloucester, which is, like "the wharves, absentee-owned" (*Maximus* I, 10).

The underlying issue in "Letter 5," as in the two following poems, is the poet's relationship in his audience, an issue provoked by Ferrini's characteristic Whitmanizing. He had published a book enti-tled *The Infinite People* (1950), and the implications of that phrase are much on Maximus's mind:

> And there is nothing less applicable
> than the complaints of the culture mongers
> about what the people don't know but oh!
> how beautiful they are, how infinite!

Olson began publishing his poetry in popular magazines, *Harper's*, *Atlantic*, *Harper's Bazaar*—the most in the way of a mass audience any American poet can hope for. In "The Praises," however, which was written at about the same time as "I, Maximus of Gloucester, to You," he says:

> What has been lost
> is the secret of secrecy, is
> the value, viz., that the work get done, and quickly,
> without the loss of due and profound respect for
> the materials
>
> which is not so easy as it sounds, nor
> can it permit the dispersion which follows from
> too many having too little
> knowledge.
>
> (*Archaeologist*, 63)

In these lines he gives up: 1) Whitmanism, 2) liberal politics, and 3) popularity. It is a rare time when the great spokesmen are given a form which the mass audience can share. Shakespeare's was such a time; Milton's was not. Olson must have realized that he did not have the energy both to do his work and to educate the masses to it. Our best understanding of the physical world has been, at least since the time of Copernicus, available only to the specially educated, and Olson proposes a discipline of attentions as rigorous and demanding as cosmology or physics.

In an attempt to restore himself to a useful placement in space, Maximus proposes, in "Letter 6" (I, 26–28), a radical phenomenology: "polis is / eyes." The fishermen provide a model of perceptual precision and care for both the city, which mistakenly promotes "young Douglas, who never went to sea," and the poet. While humanism deals in terms of qualities which inherently separate one discrete condition from another, Maximus insists upon the absolute primacy of the visual:

> There are no hierarchies, no infinite, no such many as mass,
> there are only
> eyes in all heads,
> to be looked out of.

The perceptual field is nowhere broken by the disjunctions which are implied by such abstractions as "hierarchy" or "the infinite people."

The audience to which Maximus address himself is small, but it does not constitute an elite. It is only necessary that the city make room for legitimate work to be done:

> So few
> have the polis
> in their eye
>
> . . .
>
> So few need to
> to make the many
> share (to have it,
> too).

Maximus is, as it becomes apparent in "Letter 7" (*Maximus* I, 30–34), a *worker* in precisely the same sense as the carpenter and shipbuilder, who will emerge as one of the heroes of the *Maximus*, William Stevens ("he was the first to make things, / not just live off nature"), and Olson's father, "who'd," as Maximus says, "never have turned the Whale Jaw back / to such humanness neither he nor I, as workers / are infatuated with." The poet makes a world in which it is possible to live, precisely in the way Stevens makes ships in which it is possible to sail, and they both claim their right by the same law of precise attention to quantitative reality:

> Only: no latitude, any more than any, elite. The exactness
> caulking, or "play," calls for, those
> millimeters

> No where in man is there room for carelessness.

In "Tyrian Businesses" (*Maximus* I, 35–40) Maximus becomes a teacher to replace the humanist teachers who have dominated western education at least since the seventeenth century. The tone is literally pedagogical: "This is the exercise for this morning." Olson was, of course, teaching at Black Mountain College, where he had taken a position upon his return from the Yucatan in 1951, and that experience, creating a radical alternative to the structuring of knowledge implied in the traditional college curriculum, meshed precisely with the restructuring of knowledge which is the most fundamental concern of the *Maximus*.

Tyrian business, whether in this poem, "Maximus, at Tyre and at Boston," and Phoenician business, as in "Maximus, to himself, as of 'Phoenicians,'" has to do with a clot of images which are involved directly with Tyre as the *omphalos*: the nasturtium, the alchemical symbols of transformation, and the swastika or "flyfot" which is identified variously as a glyphic flower or sun or as Lady Luck who is herself an avatar of Our Lady of Good Voyages and the external, feminine earth. Tyrian things, in other words, are the jetsam of the ancient Indo-European culture and the coherence it embodied before the occident and orient were sundered toward the end of the second millennium B.C. Compared to Gloucester things—the landscape, the history recorded in the town records, and so forth—they are remote and difficult to define with precision. They tend to have bearing on "matters of the soul," which are, given the prevailing condition of language, inevitably vague and uncertain. For Maximus, however, they are distinct only because post-Socratic culture has lost the methodology by which they are revealed. Inherently, Tyrian business is as immediate and as important as what goes on in City Hall—or what *should be* going on in City Hall, if it were not devoted to the kinds of waste and destruction of possibilities that results from the alienation.

As a practical matter, Tyrian business is for Olson an involvement with what he called, during this period, the problem of nominalization: how does one name something so the word is the equivalent of the thing it names. Of the Mayan hieroglyphs he says, "the signs were as clearly and densely chosen that, cut in stone, they retain the *power* of the objects of which they are the images" (*Human*, 7, my italics). Even the suggestion that objects, other than human objects, have "power," smacking as it does of animism and magic, is somewhat disconcerting to the modern western mind. In phonetic languages, of course, those powers must be transformed into rhythm and sound, but, if poetry is to be of any *essential* use, it must find a language which does more than manipulate a set of arbitrary signs in their relationship to the surface facts. Melville is sometimes able to manifest the sense of the world which Olson feels in the Mayan glyphs, especially, it seems to Olson, in the chapter in *Moby Dick* on the whale's tail: "'The Tail' is as lovely an evidence as any other of Melville's ability to go *inside* a thing, and from its motion and his to show and to know, not its essence alone (this was mostly the gift of ideality—of Gautama's, Socrates', or Christ's), but its *dimensions*, that part of a thing which ideality—by its Ideal, it World Forms or Perfections—tended to diminish . . ." (*Human*, 113). Naming, if it is not mere representation, brings namer and named into an intensely active relationship which is endlessly transformed by the way both behave. The space which opens, when one goes inside a thing, to try it on for size, is powerfully alive, continually shifting, modifying itself and everything that appears in it, but at the same time nothing is violated. The action which occurs is the action of the thing being itself, existing through itself, as a thing in space. The inertial energy which any thing has in its simple spatial being is almost dizzying. "Tyrian Businesses" is an approach to that sense of naming action: "how to dance / sitting down."

The germ of the poem is to be found in a series of letters which Olson wrote to the Indian dancer Natarja Vashi. They are, in effect, meditations on a text from the Vedas which Olson transposes as " . . . man is a thing which thinks and dances," and he adds, "I should imagine the meaning is a thing which simultaneously thinks and dances."[17] The problem with dance in the West, as with thought, according to Olson, is that movement lacks a base in *things*. In languages which have been biased by the humanistic assumptions, it is possible to account for the immediate and particular only in terms of an abstract or general case. All act becomes deathly or shapeless because the only alternatives are rigidity of mind or the euphoria of chaos—those modes of consciousness of which Apollo and Dionysius are the types:

> Or there are those sing ditties, that dead reason
> of personality, the will of, like a seal
> of a mealy justice: the body a shell, the mind also
> an apparatus
>   There are so many, children
> who want to go back, who want to lie down
> in Tiamat. They sing:
> euphoria.

India seems to Olson, as it did to Apollonius of Tyana, to have stayed closer to the ancient sources of culture than the ever-restless West. " . . . your Vedas," he writes to Vashi, "because they got moved from a homeland to India at a time and to a people who were then fresh, did not suffer the thinning out that the same doctrines did, not being displaced, but merely worn down by the stay-at-homes, the near Easterners, who begot the West."[18] The Indians have retained the mark of true culture: the ability to join intense action with passivity. They know "how to dance / sitting down," and, although he appeals to Vashi to "teach us what you know about sitting," he realizes that the West cannot recover itself directly from the Orient, as Ginsberg, Snyder, and the afficionados of eastern culture have tried to do. Maximus must trace the lines of force from his own, immediate, vertical situation—"the land-spout's / put all the diapers / up in trees"—back through physiology and etymology, to the true nouns which have been lost.

The first four sections under Roman two in "Tyrian Businesses" move with such density of reference that they do not make much linear sense. It's a gathering of images, puns and definitions—several

[17] "A Syllabary for a Dancer," *Maps*, 4 (1971), 9.
[18] *Ibid.*, p. 12.

of them quoted directly from *Webster's New International*—which will be sorted out as the *Maximus* continues. It is the dance of naming, a dance with the dictionary.

The nearest and most perfect instance of an organ which joins intense action and passivity is the heart: "a hollow muscular organ which by contracting vigorously, keeps up the. . . ." But it is also, for Maximus, the body as a whole which contracts, as he shows in "I, Maximus of Gloucester, to You" ("in, the bend is, in, goes in"), and keeps up ("around the head, call it / the next second"). He imagines the heart or the body growing as a flower, "a whorl of green bracts at the base." He may be recalling a Mayan figurine which he describes to Creeley as having a "calyx of clay with little humans sitting where the pistil might be" (*Writings*, 117). Whatever the specific reference, however, there have been few poets who have identified with plants and vegetable growth as consistently and as closely as Olson does. "Letter 9," in addition to being a conjecture about poetic process, is a kind of ode to vegetation. In "Maximus, at Tyre and at Boston" Maximus says, "the history of weeds / is a history man" (*Maximus* I, 94), and in the third volume he becomes so much an embodiment of the annual circulation of the sun that he seems almost to merge with Osiris or one of the vegetation gods.

"Ling" is a variety of cod, and the "she" in "ling / she is known as" seems to be Lady Luck herself. She presides over the ill-fated voyage of the *Hawes* (in section II, 5), at any rate, and provides cod to save its crew from starvation. The syntax of the passage, however, is open. She might also be the weather, which for fisherman is also a matter of luck. Maximus is, after the metaphrastic exercise of the first five sections, taking a passage of pure dance. From time to time Olson's language becomes so elliptical that one can only follow the passage as it moves toward a fuller revelation of itself.

The passage ends with a definition of "metacenter," the critical point in the distribution of weight which determines the orientation of a floating body. Of course, it is relevant to a ship, in which the metacenter must be kept above the center of gravity or "there's upset," and, by implication, to the dancer who drags herself across the ground, her metacenter and center of gravity coinciding, and to western culture as a whole which has spread itself horizontally.

The definition of "nasturtium" in II, 2, leads directly back to those prime nouns—the noun-things of Olson's secular trinity—in which the language of the poem is confirmed: "Peltate / is my nose-twist, my beloved, my trophy." "Peltate," which means, "shield-like," is the botanical designation for leaves which join the stem on the back surface, rather than at the base. The nasturtium is known as a nose-twist, for its pungent odor, and it is of the genus *Trapaeolum*—a family of smooth, peltate herbs. *Trapaeolum* is the Greek for trophy, and goes etymologically to *trepein*, to turn, and is related directly to *tropos*, way, manner, style, trope. Olson's "Topos/typos/tropos" is obviously hovering about in these radicals, and it will be Maximus's success in finding a coherent order in such suggestions which will allow him to carry the poem on, despite his initial failure to make Gloucester itself cohere.

Olson's use of etymology, as a way to restore language to its primitive usefulness, is, of course, hardly original. In a passage which no American poet can escape knowing, Emerson writes: "Every word, which is used to express a moral or intellectual fact, if traced to its *root*, is found to be borrowed from some material appearance." [19] To Emerson, however, this fact seems a confirmation of a transcendent morality or intellectuality. His use of language is limited to those functions which extend the personality, the ego, and, consequently, the image can be taken up only as a public correlative of private emotion, and the public world is reduced to a simple mirror of the private, a possibility which the Mayan farmer in "Tyrian Businesses" (section II, 2) knows must be resisted at all cost:

>   (The farmer whose nephew we knew
> was so expasperated
> he used to heave anything at the bird, swearing
> if his face got reflected in that burnished tail
> he'd die
> right then & there.

Olson first tells this story in *Mayan Letters*, where he introduces it with the comment that the Mayan "nouns, undone, are my nouns" (*Writings*, 121). Although Butterick cites a number of sources for the lines in the following section (II, 3), the passage obviously has to do

[19] *The Complete Essays and Other Writings*, ed. Brooks Atkinson (New York, 1940), p. 14.

with "undoing," distinguishing the fresh and useful from the dead, focusing on centers of energy which can carry the poem forward.

In section II, 5, Maximus defines "eudaemonia," Aristotle's term in the *Ethics* for "felicity resulting from life in accordance with" reason. But here the *noun* is missing: "Which is the question: in accordance to what?" The immediate answer is, in accordance with the metacenter: "The vertical / through the center of buoyancy," etc. Issuing this pronouncement, Maximus erects the mast which draws physical space to a center in "I, Maximus of Gloucester" in linguistic space—almost literally in the center of the dictionary. Interior space, where questions of ethics occur and where language is used, is suddenly in no way distinct from exterior, physical space.

The prose narrative which follows recounts Olson's one experience as a fisherman. Definition inevitably comes to "story." Maximus has no other vocabulary, because names as they occur in dictionaries are isolated but they are not particular and they are not active. The story bears directly on the fact that the problem of naming is deeply rooted in Gloucester's history: "Come aboard CeCe—come aboard and get some cod! it sounding, over the water, like the barrel of God." "Letter 10" (*Maximus* I, 45–47) will pick up directly from this point: "on founding: was it puritanism / or was it fish?" And the question, "in accordance to what?" is given a statement which has specific and local reference: "And how, now, to found, with the sacred & profane—both of them— / wore out."

"Tyrian Businesses" calls attention to language as a resistant, physical material. Maximus presents us with words as such, for the most part without any significant reference to any thing outside the poem. If the reader is to look for a confirmation of his use of "metacenter" or "nasturtium," he can only look to their further use. The poem is not a sign directing the reader's attention to objects in his experience; it is a place with exists only in the precarious, thin lines of ink across the pages. What happens at any juncture in the language involves a large measure of randomness or casual indeterminancy. "The crooked timbers" are "scarfed together to form the lower part of the compound rib": "futtocks / we call 'em." It is a definitive specification, but these lines gather their force because of their multiphasic relationships to the other definitions and images in the poem. The technical vocabulary of the shipbuilders plays against those who "sing: euphoria." A metaphoric relationship between these ribs and the heart suggest itself; the point at which the futtocks are scarfed together is on the line of a ship's metacenter; and so forth. Looking up "futtock" in *Webster's Third International*, Olson apparently noticed the strange word "flyfot" in the joining column:

> But a flyfot,
> she look like,
> who calls herself
>
> (luck.

In *The Special View of History* Olson will point out that it is she who confirms the creative process in both life and the poem: " . . . life is the chance success of a play of creative accidents. It is the principle of randomness seen in its essential application, not in any serial order imposed at random on either chance or accident (the new tautologies of the old chaos) but in the factual observation of how creation does occur: by the success of its own accidents" (*History*, 48). "Letter 9" is a further inquiry into the process by which the poet becomes the center at which creative accidents are recognized and become factors in the growth of consciousness.

In "Letter 9" (*Maximus* I, 41–44) there is obviously no necessary connection between the facts that Olson has just written a vicious attack on his friend Vincent Ferrini, that the plum outside Maximus's "window sends whiteness inside" his house, and that he has just received a copy of his new book, *In Cold Hell, In Thicket*. These events, however, lend themselves to the occasion of the poem, and Maximus discovers that these accidents, more or less imposed on him, come together in a conjecture about the nature of the poetic process. Maximus's immediate past, the four previous poems, his less immediate biography ("as in another spring"), and historical fact (Alfred at Ashdown) assimilate the immediate conditions in a new and unexpected coherence.

In a passage from *The Prehistorical Foundations of Europe*, to which Olson calls attention more than once (see, for example, *Origin*, 102), Charles F. D. Hawkes writes: " . . . the collective experience of the human groups become an inheritance handed down by means of that human peculiarity, a spoken language. So the capacity to create and transmit the elements of culture is the direct outcome of man's organic evolution, and thereby that evolution in humanity has been exchanged for culture."[20] Men ceased being mere expressions of the cosmic creative impulses and made their entrance as conscious participants in the creation of their own experience. The period which began with man's capacity to transmit order to his offspring by means of an oral tradition as well as genetic structure and ended, as it will become apparent in the second volume of *Maximus*, with the paternalistic assertion of human transcendence of the natural order, presents the possibility of a relationship with Earth which is again perfectly consistent with the necessities of the contemporary situation. Space and history, which in the post-Einsteinian cosmos of the poem are only different manifestations of the same order, form the body of the feminine to which Maximus must submit his ego. Only inside such a submission does one realize that "there is no other issue than / the moment of / the pleasure of / this plum." The song, the sources of the song, the self, and the forces which impel the self are all specifically congruent, as Maximus recognizes toward the end of "Letter 9," and if "things" are allowed to "carry their end any further than / their reality in / themselves," the circuit is broken, the culture is divorced from its only reliable source of energy, and man is thrown back into dependence upon his own willful strength. With this knowledge and some understanding of what it demands of him as a poet, Maximus is prepared to turn to the more fundamental and persistent concern of the poem, the founding of Gloucester itself.

2

It would be simple, and true, to say that letters 11 through 17 ("On first Looking out through Juan de la Cosa's Eyes") deal with the range of responses to the opportunities which the New World offered to "the last first people." The schematic possibilities are obvious. John Smith, who is taken as a model, has an eye for usefulness and the care to prevent use from turning to exploitation. Olson speaks of Smith as "the psyche that split off and went to America at exactly that moment of Shakespeare, Daniel, and Campion,"[21] and, consequently, he has

---

[20]Charles F. D. Hawkes, *The Prehistoric Foundations of Europe* (London, 1940), p. 4.

[21]Quoted in George F. Butterick, "Notes from Class," *Magazine of Further Studies*, 2 (1965), n.p.

the freshness of vision which that instant offered, just as Renaissance humanism was running its course and before it reformed itself as Puritanism and capitalism. "Why I sing this John Smith," Olson writes, "is this, that the *geographic*, the sudden *land* of the place, is in there, not described, not local, not represented" (*Human*, 132). Smith's precision of attention, of which Maximus gives direct evidence in letters 11 and 15, is juxtaposed with Columbus's description of the New World in section II of "The Song and Dance of." Columbus's expectations are literary rather than geographic, and he sees only some conventional Mediterranean paradise. He is *not* the discover but the romantic prototype of the conquistador and the commercial exploiter. In retrospect, the advertising which Maximus denounces in the earlier poems, and again in "Letter 15," bespeaks the horror of a space which has been reduced to mere expanse. The geography was, almost from the beginning, recast in a calculus of profit and loss, national wealth, and abstract ownership, which denies the articulation of the will which seeks a coherence to include man as precisely the *equivalent* of the world. Nathaniel Bowditch, Miles Standish, John Hawkins, and Stephen Higginson ("the son of a bitch," *Maximus* I, 75) are avatars of Columbus, all men who stay inside of some previously determined and closed concept of reality. Maximus demands a "knowledge of man in his place and culture" and joins his own will to similar wills, John Smith's, Richard Hawkins's, and Juan de la Cosa's, in an attempt, as Olson says, to return "to what I took it to be the heart of his totality, the centrality he cannot, for the life of him, go away from: his 'mythological present,' I found myself calling the familiar I took it, as Heraclitus had, that he was estranged from."[22] To reassert that will is the "undone business" Maximus speaks of in "Maximus, to himself" (*Maximus* I, 53).

In "Letter 15" Maximus reports this exchange:

> He sd, "You go all around the subject." And I sd, "I didn't
> > know it was a subj-
> ect." He sd, "You twist" and I sd, "I do." He said other things.
> > And I didn't
> say anything.
> I sd, "Rhapsodia."
>
> > > (*Maximus* I, 68)

[22]Copyright by the University of Connecticut Library.

Olson is fully aware that the Homeric poets were "rhapsodists," and that the word derives from *rhaptein*, to sew, to stitch together, and *aidein*, to sing. The poet is a stitcher of songs. Through these poems, which are in one sense a continuation of the attack on pejorocracy, two other structures (or perhaps one very complex structure) are simultaneously stitched into the emerging pattern. They will become, if not the spine of the *Maximus*, at least two important spinal nerves which carry much of the information.

One has to do with the migration of the center of culture away from the eastern Mediterranean, toward western Europe, and northward, into "the sludge," which Pytheas "took the water and the air and the sky / all to be one of / ultima Thule" (*Maximus*, I, 62). The north was for Pytheas, the fourth-century B.C. explorer and geographer, the place where the created world gives way to the primal unity. It becomes in the *Maximus* that distant point at which "objective" and "subjective" meet and are transformed into one another. As Olson understands it, Thule was for Pytheas, who was still of the old dispensation and so a man who came from and returned to a Center, the *unknown* which modern men, in their expansive egotism, call "the unconscious," and locate at their own lost cores rather than at the limit of the world. Pytheas's description of Thule—"there is no longer either land proper so-called, or sea, or air, but a kind of substance concreted from all these elements"[23]—parallels the alchemist's description of the *prima materia* in which Jung finds a profound image of the unconscious.

The other motif which opens in these poems also has to do, one might say, with a migration route, but through interior space, by way of history, personal biography, and dreams, to the Center of the physical body, where things of consciousness join with things of space. In a letter to Cid Corman in June, 1953, when Olson was in the midst of this first sustained engagement with the *Maximus*, he says, " . . . you will know, of course, how much I take dream to be such a sign of that confusion out of which all but the highest art emerges: I put it that way—so condition it—because I am led to think that there is a stage where man is free of dream" (*Origin*, 104). The dream itself, in other words, is a route, a way from the totalitarian reality of objective space

[23]*Geography of Strabo*, trans. Horace Leonard Jones (New York and London, 1923), I, 399.

and time to an inner coherence in which one sees that the totality of which he dreams is really the world itself, or, more exactly, himself as a commonplace part of the world.

In the world which Maximus confronts, however, dream experience is private and isolated. His own attempt, in "Letter 14" (*Maximus* I, 55–56), to bring his dreams and documentary history into a common space is strained. The specificity of which dream is the first sign has been excluded:

> It was the hat-makers of La Rochelle, the fish-eaters of Bristol who were the conquistadors of my country, the dreamless present.
>
> (*Maximus* I, 58)

Beginning with "The Twist" and through "Letter 22," Maximus attempts to situate dream in a context from which he can emerge into the highest kind of art. The poems in this group are not as mystifying as they may at first appear. Juan de la Cosa's map has brought Maximus to a vision of the earth as a reliable image of unity. As Olson will say much later, as an indirect reflection on this point in the poem, "The Earth . . . is conceivably a knowable, a seizable, a single, and *your* thing" (*Myth*, 5). If the *Maximus* can be said to embody an epistemology, the world itself, as a whole, knowable thing, *including* man, comes to replace the Cartesian ego and the Socratic polis as the source of authority. The land itself appears, like a dream, from the unknown:

> The New Land was,
> from the start, even by name was
> Bacalhaos
> there
> swimming, Norte, out of the mists
>
> (out of Pytheus' sludge
> out of mermaids & Monsters.
>
> (*Maximus* I, 78)

This revelation, however, still stands at a distance from Maximus's own immediacy. Beginning in "The Twist," dreams and personal memory are juxtaposed to the largely historical and geographic concerns of the previous eight poems. He is, as it were, working from both ends of the objective / subjective axis toward the Center, which will become, literally, the new *omphalos*.

Juan de la Cosa's map represents an immense gain: " . . . before La Cosa, nobody / could have a mappemunde." Along with John Smith's prose, it represents the New World as pure potentiality, unspoiled, open space. It is, however, also objective: while it presents a geographic image of a possible unity, it is also a reminder of the immense distance between the hero and the *embodiment* of that image.

The poem which follows, "The Twist," is one of the most personal of the first volume: Maximus counters the objectivity of La Cosa's map with his early life in Worchester, his first summer in Gloucester (see the first lines of section II), and his beginnings as a poet. In the second volume he will say, "I am making a mappemunde. It is to include my being" (*Maximus* II, 87). But here the mappemunde and Maximus's being can only be juxtaposed. The title, "The Twist," functions simultaneously in several different structures which are active through this dangerous part of the voyage, which Maximus images as sailing past Skylla. Most immediately it signals "the twist" inward, toward the more "subjective" material with which the next several poems deal. It is more precise than that, however: the literal space in which the poem exists is being twisted back on itself. What has been considered "subjective" and "objective" suddenly appears as locations on a moebius strip. In an early poem entitled "The Moebius Strip" Olson imagines a man so twisted back on himself that he wears "himself as amulet" (*Archaeologist*, 10), and that figure seems to be recalled in "Tyrian Businesses": " . . . a man is a necklace / strung of his own teeth" (*Maximus* I, 37). Now, however, it is not the hero who is "inside-outed"—*he* is standing upright, "arms out, legs out, leaping" (*Maximus* I, 61)—but the *form* of the poem. " . . . the structures of the real are flexible," Olson says, "quanta do dissolve into vibrations, all does flow, and yet is there, to be made permanent, if the means are equal" (*Human*, 122). The twist is figured forth as the tidal flow of the Annisquam: "the river / exactly there at the Bridge / where it goes out & in." In the poems of Maximus's conception and birth in the second volume, the twisting of the Annisquam becomes explicitly sexual. As in perhaps no other poem, the reader of the *Maximus* is witness to the process by which metaphors come into being. Okeanos, the massive figure of space-as-active-force, who almost replaces Maximus as the center of the poem in volume two, is still an unrealized potentiality, but in retrospect he is obviously present here in inchoate form.

The "twist" is also the nasturtium, "the nose-twist," from "Tyrian Businesses," and that complex etymological cell is reintroduced as a factor of the process. The poem is cast in the space where dream, memory, and external reality meet, and if Maximus is to attain that clarity which is inclusive, mythic, this "pin-point" on which everything "turns" must respond so agilely that it can incorporate the entire world. The nasturtium is the unwritten poem, the still largely unknown self, and so it becomes a shield, a defense certainly, but also the point of engagement. Olson frequently sees the poetic situation as a contest or battle. In "The Escaped Cock" he says, "I take it that contest is what puts drama (what they call story, plot) into the thing, the writer's contesting with reality, to see it, to SEE" (*Human*, 123). And in "Letter 22" (as well as, again, in "Letter 27 [withheld]"), he refers to the ancient Irish custom of allowing the poetic commemoration of a battle, as it was established by the poets of the opposing armies, to determine victory and defeat:

> And what I write
> is stopping the battle,
>
> to get down, right in the midst of
> the deeds, to tell
>
> what this one did, how,
> in the fray, he made his play, did grapple
> with that one, how
> his eye flashed
>
> to celebrate
>
> (beauty will not wait).
>
> (*Maximus* I, 97–98)

Maximus takes this custom both as evidence of the poet's absolute authority, as the one who sees what happens, and as an image of the immediacy of grasp which the poet must exercise.

Although the precise source of Olson's information on heraldry in "Letter 20" and "Maximus, at Tyre and at Boston" has not been located, it seems, despite Olson's wide range of interests, an unlikely terminology to attract his attention. As it looks forward to the equally unlikely concern with traditional fortification in the second volume (see, for example, *Maximus* II, 186–87), however, it deserves some speculation. Olson was possibly thinking of a passage in Jane Ellen Harrison's *Themis*. In her discussion of the Delphic rituals she asks,

" . . . what did the *omphalos* really stand for, really mean?" The information on the etymology of the word which she provides may have seemed more useful to Olson than it did to Harrison herself: "The name *omphalos* is little or no help. Like its correlative *umbilicus* it came to mean *navel*, but originally it only meant any sort of boss or thing that bulged, the boss of a shield or a phiale, an island that stands up on the 'nombril' of the sea." [24] Gloucester/Tyre is, of course, an island city, standing on the "nombril" of the sea, and its status as *omphalos* is directly related to Maximus's "contesting" with reality.

These poems, "Letter 19" through "Letter 22," are conjectural approaches to an impasse which will not be crossed until "Letter 23." "The Twist" defines Maximus's relationship to an immediate space, which involves history, but it leaves the specific demands of that involvement unstated. One of the great attractions of the *Maximus* and, at the same time, one of the chief causes of difficulty is that the process is continually unstable. Any given passage presents a blend of precisely defined reality and unrealized or inchoate possibilities. It moves forward sometimes by great leaps and sometimes by intensification. Olson never coerces his material. Maximus dances sitting down, and when he goes to battle, he fights sitting down. The faith to which the *Maximus* bears witness is that the world *coheres*. If the relationships on which the developing coherence of the poem depends are not immediately apparent, he assumes that he still lacks innocence and clarity. The poet can only bring his own god-like, child-like perfection against "the clouds of all confusion, / of all confusers / who wear false faces" (*Maximus* I, 88). The world is specific in its presentation of itself and shows itself forth only to those who find an equal specificity in their language. That, in itself, is sufficient. In "Letter 22" Maximus says:

> The real
> is always worth the act of
> lifting it, treading it
>
> to be clear, to make it
> clear (to clothe honor
> anew.

> (*Maximus* I, 92)

[24]*Themis*, p. 396.

Beyond that, the process depends upon forces which are utterly out of his control, and he must appeal to the random combinations which constitute the only reliable, creative force:

> that just at the moment that the heat's on,
> when it's your dice or mine, all
> or nothing, that she be there
>
> in all her splendor.

> (*Maximus* I, 92)

The engagement requires precision and consciousness rather than force.

In both "The Area, and Discipline of, Totality" and "Maximus, at Tyre and at Boston," the model for the kind of attention required is found in the work of the botanist-historian Edgar Anderson. He and the geographer-historian Carl O. Sauer, who had exercised an important influence on Olson since 1947, propose a variety of history, which, for the first time since Herodotus, understands man and his culture as *continuous* parts of what had formerly been distinguished as "Nature." Maximus quotes Anderson's *Plants, Man and Life* in "Maximus, at Tyre and at Boston": "The history of weeds / is the history of man" (*Maximus* I, 94). The city becomes an extension of the landscape, as Tyre was, rather than the expression of a supposed universal order, like Boston's theocracy—a dichotomy which Maximus states succinctly: "our / perfection. Not / His."

Between the summer of 1953 and the winter of 1957–58, Olson wrote a sizable number of Maximus poems which he subsequently rejected. In September, 1953, he writes to Corman: " . . . the real thing is that I have been lost in a quandary about the Maximus poem since I wrote you that letter abt such problems of a long poem in June, was it? And it has been a heady thing, to try to lick it—to see where (as I felt I had) I had got off its proper track (with #24 and through #33). And it has meant the hardest sort of both wandering away and cutting it" (*Origin*, 128). Either the letter to which he refers is not extant, as there is no such letter in Glover's edition of the letters to Corman in June or any time during the spring or summer of 1953, or he was thinking of one of the many letters which bear directly or indirectly on the problem of the long poem. The difficulty, nevertheless, is clear. The dream material which dominates the movement of the poem from "The Twist" through "Letter 22" opens a gap in the objective space-time of Gloucester, and Olson was uncertain how to fill it.

Although Olson never showed any interest in surrealism as a movement and seems not to have read the surrealists with any enthusiasm, he shared many of their sources, and the program for poetry outlined in "Projective Verse" fails to satisy André Breton's definition of surrealism in only one substantial detail. Breton writes: "SURREALISM, N. Pure psychic automatism, by which it is intended to express, verbally, in writing, or by other means, the real process of thought. Thought's dictation, in the absence of all control exercised by the reason and outside all aesthetic or moral preoccupations."[25] Olson never intends to *express* any thing; he insists that the poem must *enact* the reality which is its content. He is, however, never closer to the spirit of surrealism than he is in "Lester 22." Maximus proposes that senseless particulars as they occur in dream are themselves sufficient:

> "Satie, enough"
>
> was what it said
>
> > Satie,
>
> enough
>
> And I wear it,
>
> as my blazon
>
> > moving
>
> among my particulars, among
>
> my foes.
>
> > > (*Maximus* I, 97)

In the *Maximus* dream objects occur not with symbolic reference to waking life but, rather, as fortunate incursions of the common world from which man as personality is alienated. The immediate landscape, history, and the contents of the unconscious all have precisely the same status. They are separated from one another and from man himself by the intrusion of man as rational, aesthetic, or moral principle. Before the *Maximus* could continue, Olson was required to find ways by which to articulate the *dynamics* as well as the sufficiency of the dreamworld. He had to find the jointure of that sufficiency with the

[25]*Manifestoes of Surrealism*, trans. Richard Seaver and Helen R. Lane (Ann Arbor, Mich., 1969), p. 26.

sufficiency of the world—the so-called "objective" world—to which
Pound and Williams addressed themselves.

3

If the poem is to be more than an artifice by which the poet says
what he thinks or feels, it must reveal a structure larger than the poet,
the city, or the age, by participating directly in the movement and self-
revelation of what Olson was calling during this period man's *archai*
(i.e. the root of archaeology, from the Greek *archē*, beginning). In an
unpublished essay on mythology which apparently arose from his
reading of Douglas Fox's articles on Frobenius in the *New English
Weekly*, Olson writes that man is infinite by virtue not of his apoca-
lyptic possibilities but of his beginnings: " . . . one is infinite to begin
with—not afterwards. Genetically, one is infinite: by possession of *archai*." In Olson's growing understanding of the nature of the demands
the *Maximus* makes on him, the poem itself begins to appear as a
most profound ritual, the practice of the self which is also an enact-
ment of the real. The history, the dream, the biography as told and as
it is being told "IS THE RE-ARISING OF PRIMORDIAL REALITY IN NARRA-
TIVE FORM." Structurally, "myth" and "primordial reality" corre-
spond to the earlier terms, "fact" and "space." The third term,
"stance," becomes, simply, the making of the poem, literally the realization of one's own archaic, genetic structure as the informant of
speech. Olson writes:

> . . . any myth explains itself: Malinowski—a tale told and a
> reality lived . . . a living reality believe(d) to have occurred in
> primordial times *and* likewise occurring now . . . the tales are
> neither invented nor true, they are, and assert an original, larger
> and more important reality (Keats' each man's life is an allegory)
> which the present life fate work of a man are capable of, are, in
> fact governed toward, and the knowledge of the mythological
> provides men with (1) motives for ritual and practice and (2) with
> directions for their permanence.[26]

Myth—and history, as the two merge in Olson's narration of primordial reality—comprises all of man's particulars, all he thinks and says,

[26]Copyright by the University of Connecticut Library.

all he does. Fundamentally, myth is *speech*, and its structure is also the structure of space.

"Letter 23" is a crucial poem for Olson, because in it he finds his hero as historian involved in a process which draws his private acts and the public telling of the *archai* into a seamless whole. The poem begins by re-engaging the question which is posed in "Letter 10" and considers the early history of Gloucester. These groups of poems, "Letter 10" through "Letter 22" and "Letter 23" through "April To-day Main Street," are in effect parallel rather than sequential. The reader of the *Maximus* must continually remind himself that, while language is by its nature linear (in the simple sense that one word follows another), everything in the *Maximus* happens simultaneously. Charles Boer reports Olson as saying, "Anywhere is everywhere."[27] The corollary for a poet whose perception is thoroughly conditioned to Einsteinian space is "Anytime is everytime." It is useful, of course, to follow out certain patterns which occur in the poem, as our attentions tend also to be linear, but the whole of the poem is implicit from the beginning, and the progress, if it can be called such, is toward a fuller revelation of the form which inevitably occurs where a purely physical geography, a human history, of, say, five or six millennia, and an absolutely specific human organism impinge upon one another: "we are only / as we find out we are" (*Maximus* I, 95).

In letters 10 through 22, the history of Gloucester occurs inside the relatively broad context which is established by John Smith and Columbus. The issues are Gloucester in the New World, real use of the unspoiled land versus exploitation, the man of specific perception versus the humanist.

Beginning with "Maximus, at Tyre and at Boston," however, the opposition between Gloucester, as the island city, and the mainland begins to emerge, and "Letter 23" (*Maximus* I, 99–101) receives the burden of that conflict: the concerns of Maximus of Gloucester must be Gloucester. "The facts are . . . ," the poem begins, and the facts are clearly of a different order than the information which has thus far sustained the poem. Although John Smith and Columbus are treated specifically, some times literally in their own words, they are *still* treated as representative cases. They are types, almost allegorical fig-

[27]*Charles Olson in Connecticut* (Chicago, 1975), p. 110.

ures, representing two modes of perception. John Tilly and Thomas Gardener represent nothing but themselves. In fact, little is known about them beyond what the poem relates: "John Tilly to oversee the fishing, / Thomas Gardener the planting. . . ." They are relevant to the poem only because they are specific to the place: "the two of them / 'bosses,' for a year. . . ."

The gain in "Letter 23" is significant. In 1951 Olson had written to Creeley, "The trouble is, it is difficult, to be both a poet and, an historian" (*Writings*, 130). Although he knew he was required to break the almost irreversible tendency of history to declare itself chronologically, so the poet's time (his rhythm and his breath) could emerge as the factor of control in the poem, the only possibility which he had conceived at the time was Pound's. In the bibliography included in the letter to Creeley, he mentions Pound's *Guide to Kulchur* and annotates it, saying, ". . . just because it razzledazzles History. And any learning." And he adds, "But its loss is exactly that." He was painfully aware that razzledazzling history was not enough. While it freed Pound from the relentless flow of linear time, it did not give him a meaningful order.

Herodotus, as J. A. K. Thomson explains him in *The Art of the Logos*, provides Olson with a sense of order which is immediate and local to the *discovery* of the past:

> I would be an historian as Herodotus was, looking
> for oneself for the evidence of
> what is said.

Research has a formality of its own. It develops by hints and hunches, but, as the researcher stumbles through the endless false leads and irrelevancies, dynamics appear. Olson, who had done some significant scholarly detective work in his research on Melville, knew this fact well. In fact, he has allowed the inevitable dynamics of his finding out to carry parts of the poem already. In "Letter 16," for example, he draws much of his material from *Letters of Stephen Higginson*, and the poem includes a note of the kind anyone doing research might make to himself: "cf. Forces' American Archives, / Fourth Series, I, 1645–1648—*get*" (*Maximus* I, 74). As far as we learn from the poem, he never does. Maximus not uncommonly opens possibilities which he does not follow out, but the note remains in the poem as a specific, formal directive. In Thucydidean history, of course, this kind of material would be revised out, because the form which it commands is a static logos rather than a dynamic process. Maximus's discovery in "Letter 23" is that to practice history strictly as a process of finding out for one's self places the historian as dreamer and knower in the center of process. It is his own body, in the act of his work, by which he joins dream-space and "real-space."

The final poems of the first volume were written after Olson's return to Gloucester in 1957, and he was able to look in the city itself "for the evidence of / what is said." In Whitehead, Olson had read: "There is nothing in the real world which is merely inert fact. Every reality is there for feeling: it promotes feeling; and it is felt."[28] With that assurance, Maximus begins to gather the facts.

"A Plantation a beginning" and "Maximus, to Gloucester" are investigations into the continuities which allow the history of Gloucester to be engaged as directly relevant to Maximus's on-going life. These are the poems of Maximus's homecoming. It can be said without grossly exaggerating that Olson's single impulse in the *Maximus* is to experience the landscape—where "fourteen spare men . . . huddled above Half Moon Beach"—which he could see from the windows of his "rented house / on Fort Point," with the same freshness as its first inhabitants:

> He left him naked,
> the man said, and
> nakedness
> is what one means
>
> that all start up
> to the eye and soul
> as though it had never
> happened before.

(Maximus I, 107)

Maximus has proposed a form which, inhabited, overcomes the alienation "from that which is most familiar." In these poems he inhabits the form.

Gloucester was settled in one of those rare resurgences of primordiality when unmediated, historical space asserts itself. In the reading of history which the *Maximus* provides, the seventeenth century, especially the period from 1610 to 1630, is the seed-time from

[28]*Process and Reality*, p. 364.

which the present must grow. In "the hinges of civilization to be put back on the door," Olson calls the seventeenth century a "brilliant secular" age (*Prose*, 26). Its advantage over the intervening two centuries is that it is secular without the loss of the sense of the divine. The factors which contribute to the auspicious time of Gloucester's founding include the exhaustion of Renaissance humanism, the living tradition of alchemy as a science of archaic archetypes, and the appearance of the kind of language which is common to the writings of John Smith and Shakespeare's last plays. It is a time in which it is possible to feel that "we are in the presence of the only truth which the real can have, its own undisclosed because not apparent character. Get that out with no exterior means or materials, no mechanics except those hidden in the thing itself, and we are in the hands of the mystery" (*Human*, 94). "Some Good News" celebrates that mystery.

"Some Good News" and "Letter, May 2, 1959" provide much of the impetus for the second volume. They bridge the gap between the largely historical matter with which Maximus has been concerned and the mythical impact of that matter as it begins to emerge. Whitehead speaks of a kind of "perception which merely, by means of sensum, rescues from vagueness a contemporary spatial region, in respect to its spatial shape and its spatial perspective from the percipient," which he calls "perception in the mode of presentational immediacy."[29] The *Maximus*, in its earlier parts, is the product of such perception: Maximus finds his evidence in documentary history, geography, and sight, in the commonplace sense. It is still very close in spirit to Pound's pronouncements in the Imagist manifesto and Williams's "no ideas but in thing." The dream material in the poems leading up to "Letter 23," however, suggests to Olson that there are other sources of information. The dreams themselves are isolated occurrences and problematic in their apparent lack of continuity with waking consciousness, but Olson is never convinced that they are genuinely distinct. Whitehead's analysis of "perception in the mode of causal efficacy" provides him with a middle ground where the precision of image—"an intellectual and emotional complex in an instant of time," as Pound defines it—joins the vaguer but more dynamic sense, which seems to arise from some depth of the human organism. The instant only completes

[29]*Ibid.*, p. 143.

itself and fulfills itself as it moves toward another instant. Whitehead writes:

> [The mode of causal efficacy] produces percepta which are vague, not to be controlled, heavy with emotion: it produces the sense of derivation from an immediate past, and of passage to an immediate future; a sense of emotional feeling, and passing from oneself in the present toward oneself in the future; a sense of influx of influence from other vaguer presences in the past, localized and yet evading local definition, such influence modifying, enhancing, inhibiting, and diverting, the stream of feeling which we are receiving, unifying, enjoying, and transmitting. This is our general sense of existence, as one item among others, in an efficacious actual world.[30]

In "Some Good News" Maximus begins an investigation of causal efficacy. It is in this perceptual stratum that the *archai* moves, where it is to be experienced directly as the narrative movement of one's own speech. Later Olson will speak directly of "causal mythology." The Good News of the poem is that the archetypes are real, efficacious factors of history.

The first and most general of the archetypes is what, following Melville, Maximus calls "the Divine Inert":

> shifty new
> land, sucks
> down, into the terrible
>
> inert of
> nature (the Divine
> Inert, the literary man
> of these men
> of the West,
>
> who knew private
> passivity as these
> quartermasters knew
> supplies, said
> it has to be
>
> if princes
> of the husting

[30]*Ibid.*, p. 207.

> are to issue from
> the collapse
> of the previous
>
> soul.
>
> (*Maximus* I, 122)

The specific reference is to Ishmael's discussion of the "external arts and entrenchments" by which men like Ahab keep "God's true princes of the Empire from the World's hustings." They are "men who become famous more through their infinite inferiority to the choice hidden handful of the Divine Inert, than through their undoubted superiority over the dead level of the mass." The most useful commentary on "Some Good News" and the complex series of modulations which lead into the theogonic second volume is Olson's essay on Melville, "Equal, That Is, to the Real Itself." Olson finds in Keats, in Melville, and in the non-Euclidean geometers a synchronous set of events which profoundly altered the conception of measure. Still, of course, we have made little progress in reifying the change, as "measure" in poetry is generally understood as grossly beating out the endless subtle variations of stress as either hard or soft, but, for Olson, art *is* measure—nothing but measure. It is as measurer that men come to participate in their experience at all, unless they are to be the grasping, willful, destructive beings they have been.

John Smith appears in "Some Good News," paired with Melville, as a sign of the fact that "a permanent change had come / by 14 men setting down / on Cape Ann." For the first time since Dante, it is possible to figure forth a hero who need not act "solely in terms of man's capacity to overthrow or dominate external reality" (*Human*, 20). Smith is capable of revealing the heroic dimension by no device other than his statement of "quantity and precision." His presence in the *Maximus* is now subtly unlike it was in earlier poems. The metaphor from his poem "The Sea Marke"—quoted in "Letter 15"—returns here carrying the full burden of Maximus's sense of the world. The sea as an image of chaos has been one of the most persistent in western poetry, but in "The Sea Marke" Maximus finds an awareness of the "undisclosed because not apparent" forms of the sea. If one is to fish the shoals off Sable Island, the surface chaos of the sea is superficial. It is necessary to adjust the course to subaquatic conditions: "Shoals, worse / than rock because / they do blow shift lie, / are

changing as you sound." Smith stands as a jointure between, in Whitehead's terms, presentational immediacy and causal efficacy. As such,
he appears as "the Androgyne"—a prefiguration of both the androgynous product of the alchemical marriage and Maximus himself as
"Whelping mother, giving birth, with a crunch of his own pelvis"
(*Maximus* II, 87). In "Letter 11" Maximus speaks of Smith's "femi-
ninities" and quotes him as saying "for all their discoveries I can yet
heare of are but pigs of my owne sowe" (*Maximus* I, 50). In his review
of Philip L. Barbour's *The Three Worlds of Captain John Smith*, Olson
writes: "He is still some waif, presiding over Atlantic migration like
a 5 foot 4 lead figure, Mercury or an Hermaphroditus of the whole
matter" (*Prose*, 57). He had already realized the possibility which we
inherit from the nineteenth century: like the post-Melvillean man Olson describes in "Equal, That Is, to the Real Itself," "he was suddenly
possessed or repossessed of a character of being, a thing among
things, which I shall call his physicality. It made a re-entry of or to the
universe. Reality was without interruption" (*Human*, 118–19).

The most inclusive shape to be known—and John Smith was the
first to reveal it in the New World, as Melville was the second—is the
inertial structure of the world itself. These men, who were, when they
were at their best, without sense of themselves but as physical beings
in a physical world, are the prototypes of Maximus. The restless,
striving soul of western man—"the previous soul," Maximus calls it
in "Some Good News"—is replaced not by some *other* soul but by
the physical, both men and gods as physical. In a footnote to "John
Burke" Maximus speaks of a language "adjusted to the topological as
a prime and libidinal character of man" (*Maximus* I, 144). Space, that
is to say, is both the location and the content of man's desire. It is, as
it appears in Norse mythology, the primordial hunger which creates
the cosmos. This is the profounder meaning of Maximus's dictum,
"love is form." Eros is an inertial vector of precisely the same kind as
keeps the earth spinning in its orbit. The forms of the world are not
invented or conventional; they are real facts, to be discovered, if man's
actions are equal to them.

Maximus must, however, play out fully his engagement with
Gloucester as literal space and history. If the city is to be reborn as a
trope of Maximus's energies, the whole of it must be engaged as literal. The evidence which begins to accrue in "So Sassafrass," "History
is the Memory of Time," "The Picture," and "The Record" is complex

and conflicting. Even the earliest evidence establishes a future for Gloucester which is all too familiar: "each generation / living 33 years / of shoddy & / safety—not at all / living" (*Maximus* I, 113). Maximus's original assessment of Gloucester as a place "where polis / still thrives" turns out to be too optimistic. He can find only one man, John Burke, who has his "attention / on what was happening / to the city" (*Maximus* I, 143). The gain which John Smith makes is "futile / until the place / and time burned / with the same heat as / the man" (*Maximus* I, 123).

Although John Winthrop will be resurrected in the second volume as a heroic figure, he stands in "Stiffening, in the Master Founders' Wills" (*Maximus* I, 128–32) as a sign of the confusion of the social and the political which renders the very basis of life problematical:

> American space
>
> was 1630 still sailors'
> apprehension not Boston's
> leader's: "A family," he says
> "is a little
> common wealth, and a common wealth
>
> is a great family" Stop
> right there, said time, Descartes
> 's holding up
> another hand and your own people
> in this wilderness
>
> not savages but thought
> has invaded
> the proposition.

His is the characteristic modern misunderstanding of the state as housekeeper and leads to the various neatly tautological formulae which partition the city from the only reality which might lend it legitimate forms. Public facts can only be credited, as Maximus says toward the end of the poem, if their "dimensions stay personal." Otherwise, any public act becomes intolerable and even as gregarious a character as Maximus himself is driven into isolation:

> We'll turn
>
> to keep our house, turn to
> our house where our kind,
> and hungry after them,

> not willing to bear one short walk
> more out into even what they've done
> to earth itself, find
> company.
>
> (Maximus I, 134)

The poem which follows, "1st Letter on Georges," documents the most tragic storm in the history of the Gloucester fisheries: "There was hardly a home which didn't have a loss" (*Maximus* I, 138). Following immediately upon Maximus's withdrawal into his own privacy, the storm is a signature of Gloucester's—and perhaps Maximus's—failure.

In "Letter, May 2, 1959" (*Maximus* I, 145–51), Maximus faces the consequences of his recognition in "Capt Christopher Levett" that

> the newness
>
> the first men knew was almost
> from the start dirtied
> by second comers. About seven years
> and you can carry cinders
> in your hand for what
>
> America was worth.

Maximus returns to the only prime that he knows: the body moving in space. As the poem opens, he is walking northwest along Washington Street toward the sight of the original Meeting House, counting his steps. He is immediately involved in all of the primitive sources of meaning in the poem: the landscape and the history as it is measured by his stride. Maximus begins as an outsider—"off-shore, by islands hidden in the blood" (*Maximus* I, 1)—and in "Letter, May 2" he is still "in the mud / off Five Pound Island," but the passivity and the distance from which Maximus observes are now joined to an activity which is not theoretical. Maximus moves in space and history as fluently as any man, taking its measure by his form, which is also strictly spatio-temporal.

As he begins to speculate about Obadiah Bruen—"What did Bruen want?"—Maximus realizes that the evidence demonstrates clearly that Bruen was one of those restless, unsettled souls who are responsible for the destruction which the city has suffered: "N.G. the point not here I am not here to / have to do with Englishmen." The significant history is that which is specifically local to the landscape. He must, for example, deal with the way in which the settlers adapted the Indians' canoes to their purposes or the Venetian gondolas to farm work on the tidal rivers. Only when the landscape and the people who live in it are measurers of one another does history reveal the archaic reality.

The process of "mapping" history toward which the sequence has been building, however, is rendered impossible by the fact that, in Gloucester, Maximus's footsteps (his measure) betray him to a space which has been made abstract. The landscape has taken a form shaped by projects guided by less than total intelligence. Space itself has been deformed by the humanizing will:

> Take the top off
> Meeting House Hill
> is 128 has cut it
> on two sides.

The location of the first Meeting House, which should be a place of power for the city, is a traffic circle. Maximus has overcome his own estrangement from that which is most familiar to find that "it's earth which now is strange." In the context of the city as a whole, Maximus's inward force is unable to contain the outward thrust of the pejorocracy. It is the moral low point of the *Maximus*.

Toward the end of the poem, however, Maximus imagines the glacial ice sheets returning to purify Gloucester:

> step off
> onto the nation   The sea
> will rush over   The ice
> will drag boulders   Commerce
> was changed the fathometer
> was invented here the present
> is worse give nothing now your credence
> start all over step off the
> Orontes onto land no Typhon
> no understanding of a cave
> a mystery Cashes?

The cell of images which is introduced here and in the prose passage which follows will carry much of the burden in the remainder of the

Maximus. In the temporal order of "the genetic world" in which Francis Rose-Troup places Gloucester, Maximus is identified with Typhon, the monster-child of Earth and Tartarus who does battle with Zeus at Mt. Casius (Maximus will play on the pun Casius / Cashes in later poems), near the mouth of the Orontes, in an effort to revenge the Giants. From this point, which is, as always in myth, the present, Maximus will go forth to a future, which is, in linear time, the even more distant past, and find

> that one suddenly is walking
>
> in Tartarian-Erojan, Geaan-Ouranian
> time and life love space.
>
> (*Maximus* III, 228)

In Hesiodic terms, Maximus restores to primacy the most primitive of the divine beings. The task of the two following volumes is to shed everything which does not bear on man and language as directly as hell, desire, earth, and sky. In one of the letters to John Clarke, Olson writes: "It's almost like poetry. In fact it is poetry, Pleistocene, in that simplest alphabetic sense, that you can learn the language of being alive" (*Pleistocene*, 9). If the city does not present itself as a living image of order, Maximus must find his way to the archaic conditions which make the city possible. He must alone become the center, standing between all that is known and space. At the end of "Letter, May 2" Maximus is literally a force, drawing together in his private vision the ancient cultural knowledge, which derives from the Orontes and environs, and the active center of space, the vicinity of the New Siberian Islands ("novo siberski slovo"), which in the Wegener-Wilson theory of continental drift is the fulcrum on which the earth's crust turns.

"Maximus, to Gloucester, Sunday, July 19" (*Maximus* I, 152–54) reworks the same structure as the previous poem in a more specific context: the failure of the citizens to understand the memorial services for the lost fishermen is the true signature of the city's condition. Quoting Heraclitus, Maximus says, "as if one were to talk to man's house, / knowing not what gods or heroes are." Again, however, in the face of the failure, both of the primary sources which Maximus locates in "Letter, May 2" reappear. The sea itself, in a prefiguration of Okeanos (see *Maximus* II, 2), appears an active and informing manifestation of space:

> in the Charybdises of the
> Cut waters the flowers tear off
> the wreathes.

And the earth appears as the philosopher's stone, the emblem of man's potential knowledge:

> When a man's coffin is the sea
> the whole of creation shall come to his funeral,
>
> it turns out; the globe
> is below, all lapis
>
> and its blue surface golded
> by what happened
>
> this afternoon; there are eyes
> in this water.

As "polis is / eyes" (*Maximus* I, 26), the implications of this image are obvious. The energy is still there but it is utterly dispersed in the forgotten history of the city.

"April Today Main Street" (*Maximus* I, 155–60) is Maximus's private celebration of Gloucester's coherence. The brooding of the previous poems gives way to Maximus's enjoyment of his own ability to go *with* the landscape, to hold the whole of the city's past in the context of the gossip he gathers as he strolls down Main Street:

> the street
> was rife
>
> of its hills
> and me going
>
> with its
> polyconic
>
> character.

Nothing in the *Maximus* begins at the beginning, or the poem is always beginning again, an extended investigation into beginning as the sole condition of existence. In retrospect, however, Maximus's tracing of the space and history of Gloucester has been moving toward a more specific mapping of interior space. The relationships between the human / natural landscape (topos), the lives of the hero and the citizens (typos), and the deep, inhering forms (tropos, the shoals of "Some Good News"), which might have been in a more favorable situation transparent, given a more careful use of both the human and natural resources, temptingly and temporarily surface. The first volume—the book of space—traces those relationships to the extent that they have been allowed to manifest themselves.

Chapter IV

Maximus IV, V, VI

The character of the *Maximus* changes in the second volume in some rather obvious respects. Olson is less hesitant to let the rough edges of the process show. Although *Maximus IV, V, VI* includes a number of beautifully articulated poems—"Maximus, from Dogtown-I," "Maximus, at the Harbor," and "at the boundary of the mighty world," to mention only a few—he insists on the unfinished quality. The pieces seem at times to be notes for poems rather than poetry as such. The minimum poetic utterance is a simple discovery, a synapse connection which establishes a necessary relationship in the on-going form:

> Gee, what I call the upper road was the way
> leading by Joshua Elwell's to the wood-lots
> 1727
>
> and Cherry or the lower road was, 1725, the way that
> leads from the town to Smallmans now Dwelling house
> (Maximus II, 47)

Maximus becomes only a factor of the process which he initiated. He is, at once, minutely local and cosmic. It is a dangerous passage; the poem is continually on the verge of cracking into two halves. The primary centers of action in the second volume, the mapping of Dogtown and the emergence of Earth as an archetypal form, are held in relationship to one another through the first two books only by the clarity of Maximus's voice. In "Projective Verse" Olson had written: "For a man is himself an object, whatever he may take to be his advantages, the more likely to recognize himself as such the greater his advantages, particularly at that moment that he achieves an humilitas sufficient to make him of use" (*Human*, 60). In the first volume the *assertion* of humility turns out to be inadequate. Maximus must consciously witness his own dissolution, gather himself from his dispersed particularity, re-father himself, and be reborn of Earth. That is, briefly, the narrative.

1

"Letter 41" (*Maximus* II, 1) opens with a counterthrust, the equal and opposite reaction to the thrusting up of the mast in "I, Maximus of Gloucester, to You": "With a leap (she said it was an arabesque / I made, off the porch." He returns to ground zero: Valentine's Day, 1940. During that winter Olson had written his first poems (see *Maximus* II, 129). When the great snow storm of that year appears in "The Twist" (*Maximus* I, 84), it is associated with Pytheus's sludge, the primal chaos. Maximus's leap into the snow signals the beginning of his dissolution, which is also a recapitulation of the break-up of the pleistocene cultures in Asia Minor ("Like, right off the Orontes") and the reversal of the continental drift ("The war of Africa against Eurasia / has just begun again"). The upward thrust—in both its destructive and creative aspects—is now purely telluric:

> Nobody else will grant
> like he said the volcano anyone of us does
> sit upon, in quite such a tangible fashion.
> Thus surprise, when Yellowstone kicks up
> a fuss.

Jung, the unidentified "he" of this passage, uses the image of the volcano metaphorically: "What is actually happening is due not merely to 'dim remnants of formerly conscious activity,' but to volcanic outbursts from the very bottom of things."[1] Information about Olson's sources, however, is frequently misleading. Olson takes Jung literally and identifies his volcano with the geysers of Yellowstone (cf. *Maximus* I, 153). In the *Maximus* the Earth is the universal unconscious.

Although the old animism had been more or less lost even by the time of Hesiod, it has re-emerged in this century in Whitehead's cos-

[1]*The Development of Personality*, trans. R. F. C. Hull (Princeton, N.J., 1964), p. 12.

mology, and it is now Maximus's task to articulate possibilities which
are submerged in the *Theogony*. At this point, however, "Letter 41"
can only break off. There is much unfinished business before Gondwanaland can reappear as the sign of the earth's primal coherence.

The *Theogony* is a central source in *Maximus IV, V, VI*, but Olson heavily reworks Hesiod's material. Okeanos, the *first* born of
Earth and Sky, rather than Cronus, is the crucial figure in Olson's
cosmology. In "Maximus, from Dogtown-I" (*Maximus* II, 2–6),
Maximus says:

> The sea was born of the earth without sweet union of love
> > Hesiod says
> But that then she lay for heaven and she bare the thing
> > which encloses
> everything, Okeanos the one which all things are and by
> > which nothing
> is anything but itself, measured so
> screwing earth, in whom love lies which unnerves the limbs
> > and by its
> heat floods the mind and all gods and men into further
> > nature.

The sea, the barren waters on which earth floats, is still closely associated with the primal chaos or void. Hesiod speaks of its "raging
surge," but, as it is born without sweet union of love, it is formless.
Only desire is formal, and the formed world appears strictly as the
issue of passionate encounter. Okeanos is the figure of space in the
sense Olson has used that word since the writing of *Call Me Ishmael*.
The implicit distinction is between the raging surge of the sea and
deep-swirling Okeanos. Okeanos's force is directional, formal, flowing in currents, rather than simply surging. He is the dynamic force of
space, the power of the volcano in "Letter 41," "flooding all gods and
men into further nature." "Nature" in this passage obviously carries
a double burden: it means both "essence" and "the physical world."
Okeanos is active in both of these realms which have been figured in
western culture not only as distinct but also as inimical. He is the
measurable vector of primal energy which "steers all things through
all things."

The syntax of the passage as it continues is unexpected. At first glance the lines which begin "screwing earth" appear to be a hand-book example of a dangling modifier, and it does carry on the thought of the previous four lines. The measure which Okeanos makes possible is in Hesiod's word *lusimeles*, the unnerving of the limbs, or, as Olson translates it elsewhere, "the loosening of the limbs of love" (*Berkeley*, 45). In a sense, however, all the modifiers in the *Maximus* dangle. The poem is perpetually modifying itself with terms which occur simultaneously in different processes of the larger structures. So these lines are also an address to the muse of the second volume: earth as lover comes to replace "my lady of good voyage."

The bullfight which enters the context of the Hesiodic genesis is a ritual celebration of the power of earth, "the ring of Okeanos," as she will be called in "Maximus, at the Harbor," the poem in which Maximus has his own sexual encounter with her. James Merry, a young sailor of Gloucester who was, Olson's source tells us, six feet seven inches tall—exactly the same as Olson himself—had shipped to the Mediterranean and, while visiting Spain, had seen several bull-fights. According to Erich Neumann, on whom Olson depends for much of the information and some of the language in the poem, the ritual bullfight corresponds to a period in the history of consciousness which marks the dawning of the ego's transcendence of its instinctual union with the natural world. The feminine archetype which presides overs Merry's struggle "to manifest his soul" is a relatively late form of the Great Mother whom Neumann identifies as "The Lady of the Beasts": "Man's experience of this goddess in human form is the first indication that he now knows the multiplicy of his own instinctual drives, which he had experience in projection upon animals, to be inferior to the human principle that is specific to him. He experiences the authority that conditions and orders the instinctual drive. The great Goddess is an embodiment of all those psychic structures that are superior to instinct."[2] Obviously the bullfight is an appropriate celebration of the Lady of the Beast, because she is the symbol of man's emerging domination over the natural world. In his failure, Merry, as a projection of Maximus himself, participates in an anti-ritual which makes it possible for the Great Mother in her more primitive forms to re-emerge.

[2]*The Great Mother*, p. 278.

Merry's death and the end of the age of Pisces (i.e. the astrological age of Christianity) are synchronous events. Merry is specifically identified with that other figure of Christian heroism, Billy Budd, who is described in Melville's novel as a "superb figure [i.e. his 'Handsome Sailor ism'] tossed up by the horns of Taurus against the thunderous sky."[3] Olson, however, finds Billy's humility and innocence insufferable, because they are essentially earth-denying (see "David Young, David Old," *Human*, 105–8). "Maximus, from Dogtown-I" is Olson's rewrite of Billy's story, or, more accurately, rewrite*s*, as it is told three times. Each version of the story celebrates one of the manifestations of Olson's trinity, which is, in *Maximus IV, V, VI*, closely identified with the feminine archetype.

The first telling, which begins "WATERED ROCK" and ends "life spills out," deals with Merry's encounter with objective space. The rock of Dogtown, according to N. S. Shaler, Olson's authority on the geology of Cape Ann, is highly permeable; it is literally *watered* rock. Okeanos is demonstrably present as an active force. In fact, the boulders themselves are, as much as the bull, the agents of Merry's death: "scattered / boulders little bull / who killed Merry." The manifestation of the Great Mother who presides over the first telling is the earth as topos, which is both immediately the source of energy and indifferent. She defines the space which Merry and Maximus share, and it is only here that Maximus appears in the poem, to see life spilling out, the inner vitality of things profusely presenting the signature of itself.

The second telling, which begins "soft soft rock" and ends "the night sky / looked down," focuses on Merry's decomposition, the necessary rending apart which allows Merry's transformation. The presiding goddess, Magauel, the Mexican goddess of four hundred breasts, presents herself to man's use. She is Okeanos's force as typos, the vector, and because Merry seeks to contain the energy, rather than to allow it to "twist" through him, it is destructive.

In the final telling of the story, beginning "Dogtown is soft," Merry confronts the great goddess in her absolute form, the pure archaic reality which is prior to all consciousness: "The *deadly* power of her / was there that night" (my italics). Only through the death of ego and its inherent insecurities, which must perpetually submit itself

[3] *Billy Budd and Other Prose Pieces*, ed. Raymond Weaver (New York, 1963), p. 6.

to the test, can men participate in the flood of energy which they share as celebrants of the world-creating Mother. Merry's death returns Maximus—as Merry, like all of the figures in the poem, is a projection or agent of Maximus—to a totemistic psyche. Man's emerging ego develops, Neumann tells us, as he successfully identifies his so-called "lower" human capacities with plants and animals—that is, with forms which can be objectified and dominated. Merry is born under the pulque-sign, a time when "The plants of heaven / the animals of the soul / were denied." He seeks "to manifest his soul," precisely "as the stars manifest their souls." Overstepping his proper bounds as a creature of Earth, however, he loses the source of energy for any kind of meaningful action. The ritual, which begins as a celebration of instinct successfully denied, ends with Merry's marriage to the Great Mother in the very form which he sought to deny:

> Then only
> after the grubs
> had done him
> did the earth
> let her robe
> uncover and her part
> take him in.

In "Proprioception," which was written about the time he was beginning "Maximus IV," Olson concludes: "The 'soul' the is equally [as the body] physical" (*Prose*, 19). It is not, like the soul of the stars, transcendent, unearthly. Although the argument of "Proprioception" is very condensed, it can be summarized quite simply. It is an attempt to *locate* the Jungian unconscious. Although Olson's use of Jung in *Maximus IV, V, VI* is extensive and obvious, he is also continually suspicious of Jung's "spiritualism." By this point in Maximus's elaboration of his own form, he is, at once, totally dependent on the external—space and history—*and* the absolute determinant of his form. In the *Maximus* "subjective" and "objective" describe locations which events assume in the process of becoming. In one of its realizations the event is perceived in objective space; in the other it is known in the same *way* as "the 'body' itself as, by movement of its own tissue, giving the data of depth" (*Prose*, 18). The identity gained, in the loss of the ego, is the unity of earth itself which, like the physical body, is an instance of archaic reality.

In 1946 Olson was thinking of doing a book which he described in these terms:

> . . . the book on the Human Body. A record in the perfectest language I can manage of the HEART, BRAIN, LIVER, KIDNEY, the organs, to body them forth, to give a full sense of the instrument of the organism, approached on the simplest of premises: viz., the BODY is the first and the simplest and most unthought of fact of a human life. . . . I want to give a simple, straight, dramatic sense of the animation. (*Pound*, 82)

It is perhaps true that no one ever has more than a single idea. The *Maximus*, at any rate, is Olson's physiological drama. Of course, it does not take exactly the shape which he first imagined, but the two isomorphic narratives which are the prime concern of *Maximus IV, V, VI*—one tracing the hero's progress from the ancient Near East to contemporary Gloucester, the other tracing the hero's less obviously epic journey from Gloucester harbor to Dogtown—are metabolic.

"All My Life I've Heard about Many" (*Maximus* II, 7) introduces the first of these narratives in outline form. The hero, who sometimes appears as a sea-serpent (see *Maximus* II, 94), leaves Mt. Casius on the northern coast of modern Syria, near the mouth of the Orontes, and sails to Gades, the ancient Tyrian outpost on the Atlantic, thence to Ireland, the home of Olson's maternal ancestors (John Hines, in "Maximus, from Dogtown-II," for example), where he dies and is reborn, before sailing to Gloucester, as John H. Hammond, builder of the gothic castle at Norman's Woe and inventor of the fathometer. Olson's source is L. A. Waddell, whom he mentions in a letter to Creeley as a scholar "for those who have the wit to tell the unconscious when they see one." Waddell, he says, "was sure that the Sumerians or the Hittites or the Trojans founded the British Hempire, and that Menes the Egyptian was Minos the Cretan and ended up dead, from the bite of a wasp, in Ireland, at Knock-Many" (*Writings*, 130). In the transtemporal world of the *Maximus*, Many is truly many. He is associated with the crew of the Rattler which vaults Cashes Shoal (*Maximus* II, 19), Zeus with Europa on his back (*Maximus* II, 102), and, as we learn in "A Note on the Above" (*Maximus* II, 8), with Odysseus, who appears in the *Maximus* as the emblem of the restless, questing spirit of western man. In *Ishmael*, Olson writes: "Homer was an end of the myth world from which the Mediterranean began. But in Ulysses he projected the archetype of the West to follow. . . .

Homer gave his hero the central quality of men to come: search, the individual responsible to himself" (*Ishmael*, 117–18). In *Maximus IV, V, VI* Olson not only reaches back to the origins of the myth which Homer was beginning to transform, but he also confronts all of the rootless, ego-driven heroes who literally discovered the unity of the earth. The whole thrust of cultural movement from Gondwanaland to Gloucester is a factor of Maximus's physiology which the poem proposes to contain in the divine inertia of the new coherence.

The second volume of *Maximus*, standing between the failed attempt to bring Gloucester to coherence in the first and the projected effort to bring it to coherence in the third, is profoundly dualistic. Maximus is an avatar of Odysseus, but he is, in the second volume, half-turned against himself: his song is the chthonic song of the sirens. Odysseus is a figure of energies which he *uses*, but the energy is brought to bear on Maximus's own local concerns. Olson juxtaposes Odysseus's frantic movement with Maximus's own precise observation of the turning of country roads. Maximus's journey in the second volume, from Gloucester to Dogtown, rimes with the larger cultural quest, but, as Maximus reveals the very large in the very small, he has the boundless time to map the road to Dogtown—a matter which absorbs his attention in an important group of poems in "Maximus IV."

In "Maximus, from Dogtown-II" (*Maximus* II, 9–11), Maximus again turns *in*, recapitulating the formal movement of the first volume in the literal geography:

> The Sea—turn yr back on
> the Sea, go in, to
> Dogtown.

Dogtown is now a deserted village, north and slightly east of Gloucester in the interior of Cape Ann. From about 1720 until the Revolution, it was a thriving farming village. As the fisheries along Gloucester harbor grew, however, Dogtown began to decline, and in 1830 its last resident was taken to the poor house. In no company but that which the past provides, Maximus establishes a new center in Dogtown. He does not abandon Gloucester; rather, he attempts to create his own polis in Dogtown which is, as Sumer was, of "such exact and superior force that all peoples around" are "sustained by it, nourished, increased, advanced" (*Human*, 19).

"Maximus, from Dogtown-II" gathers motifs which will carry through the remainder of the volume. The chronology which was summarized in "All my life I've Heard about Many" is further developed, the whole history is set in an astrological context, and the identity of the earth and the philosopher's stone becomes more explicit. The turn inland marks the beginning of an experience for Maximus which corresponds to Melville's experience of the Pacific. Olson writes that the Pacific was to Melville *"an experience of SPACE most Americans are only now entering on, 100 years after Melville. Of waters, as Russia of land, the Pacific gives the sense of immensity. She is* HEART SEA, *twin and rival of the* HEARTLAND." And he points to Melville's persistent metaphor of the Pacific as a prairie: "The Pacific is, for an American, the plains repeated, a 20th century Great West" (*Ishmael*, 114). Dogtown is, for Maximus, the Pacific, the Great Plains, and, by that metaphor that inevitably rests there, his own interior. "The Atlantic / Mediterranean / Black Sea time" was marked by skillful soundings of the subaquatic terrain, to discover the forms which lay hidden in the depths. Jack Hammond's invention of the fathometer (see *Maximus* I, 50, and II, 174), however, has in effect emptied the "bottomed" oceans. What is now to be known is, as it was in "Some Good News," the way in which the "shifty new / land, sucks / down, into the terrible/inert of/nature" (*Maximus* I, 122). Maximus's experience in Dogtown is directly comparable to Melville's in the Pacific: "The Pacific carried him, much as it did the little Negro Pip, when he drowned, to 'wondrous depths where strange shapes of the unwarped primal world glided to and fro before his passive eyes'" (*Ishmael*, 115). Maximus's turn inland is also, in the non-Euclidean space of the poem, a turn into the earth's interior, where the subterranean rock is discovered to be both living and the source of life. Beneath Dogtown Maximus finds "the watered / rock Carbon / flowers," deposits of coal from the Pennsylvanian age, which are identified later in the poem with "the Black Gold Flower" of Chinese alchemy.

Olson had Melville's gain to go by. ". . . Melville grasped the archaeological man," Olson writes, "and by doing so entered the mythological present. *Moby-Dick* is the evidence. The rest of his work is the defeat which is still our own" (*Human*, 115). Melville's attentions are Piscean. Though he is the sign of another possibility which emerges through his work, he cannot realize it; "Melville was agonized over paternity. He suffered as a son. He had lost the source. He demanded to know the father" (*Ishmael*, 82). But the *knowledge* is his limit: he cannot *be* the father. Melville—by way of his agent, Ahab—discloses paternity by declaring himself "the rival of earth, air, fire, and water." Maximus is not the rival of the earth, air, fire, and water." Maximus is not the rival but the lover of earth:

> there is One!
> One Mother
> One Son
>
> One Daughter
> and Each the Father
> of Him-Her-Self

The archaeological evidence which was available to Melville did not make apparent the primacy of the Great Mother. His tradition derived from the stern patriarchy of the Old Testament in which the eternal feminine and her chthonic accomplices are thoroughly discredited. As Erich Neumann writes: ". . . because the patriarchal world strives to deny its dark and 'lowly' lineage, its origin in the primordial world, it does everything in its power to conceal its own descent from the Dark Mother and—both rightly and wrongly at once—considers it necessary to forge a 'higher genealogy,' tracing its descent from heaven, the god of heaven, and the luminous aspect."[4] The failure of Melville's later work, which Olson feels so keenly, is that the significant portents that Melville *tries* to read have been misplaced by the patriarchal tradition. The protogonic reality in the *Maximus* does not descend from heaven but rises directly from the genetic power of earth, to the morphological fact of the hero. Maximus says:

> the weather
>
> on Dogtown
> is protogonic but the other side of heaven
> is Ocean.

The distinction which Maximus is implicity making in this passage derives from a discussion in Jane Ellen Harrison's *Themis*. She points out that *ta metarsia*, which can be translated "air" or "weather," is the protogonic (literally, first-formed, primal) reality which the Mother Goddess controls. It is earthy and responsive to earth: the ancients practiced thunder-rites and bird-magic. The sources of mean-

---

[4]*The Great Mother*, p. 212.

ing were near at hand. The patriarchal, Olympian religion, however, regarded *ta meteura*—the superlunary realm, the *aither*—as primary.[5] The Olympian dominance was asserted mythologically in the story of Apollo's slaying of Python; the radiant god of the upper heaven slays the earth-bound serpent.

In the *Maximus* the situation is inverted. The serpent is resurrected as a companion of the hero, and *ta meteura* is seen as a *consequence* of the weather:

> ta meteura
>
> meteor things
>
> after the weather the
> meteors.
>
> (*Maximus* II, 58)

"The Sodality of the Female Rule" is declared (*Maximus* II, 83), and Enyalion, carrying only the earth-formed image of his own being, goes forth to do battle with formless eternity (*Maximus* III, 38).

Many of the difficulties in "Maximus IV" are a result of the fact that the action takes place at precisely the intersection between the topos and the tropos. In the interior Maximus stands at the point which he could only describe in "The Twist":

> the whole of it
> coming,
> to this pin-point
> to turn
>
> in this day's sun,
>
> in this veracity
>
> there, the waters the several of them the roads
>
> here, a blackberry blossom.
>
> (*Maximus* I, 85–86)

In the second volume the twist is *enacted*. Maximus is simultaneously turning inward and confronting the outward thrust of the Diorite Stone, simultaneously decomposing, along with Merry, and reforming as the representative of the new age.

[5] *Themis*, pp. 391–92.

In the first volume the swastika, which seems a glyphic flower, appears as a sign of luck. It symbolizes the condition in which the receptive mind recognizes happy accidents as creative. In "Maximus IV," however, Maximus recognizes the possibility and necessity of taking total possession of himself. Olson points out that "*gignere*, to beget," is the root of "genius," which he defines as that stage a man can reach, "where he is utterly clear, limpid, in this sense that he has possessed his own 'form,' so he knows the structure of himself (in the face of all other forms) that he works from that alone" (*Origin*, 104). "Maximus, from Dogtown-II" is a gathering of images in terms of which Maximus intends to claim his own genius. In "Maximus, to himself" (*Maximus* II, 11–12) he says:

> the fylfot
> she look like
> who called herself
> luck: *svas-*
>
> *tika* BREAK HER up as the lumber
> was broken up in the screw.

Maximus is released to shape *ta meteura* as he will. Born in December, he is, of course, a Capricorn, but now he can assert: "NO LONGER / the dead of winter be / the birth time." When it becomes evident that the age of Capricorn is still at least two millennia away, Maximus gives himself over to

> the hand of Isis which
> unweavest even the inextricably tangled
> web of fate, assuages
> any of us ("buried in us to
> assuage") & puts the stars
> to rights.

The swastika is now seen as a glyphic sun, and Maximus puts out the light of *ta meteura* altogether: "All the heavens, a few mile up—and even with the sun out—is BLACK" (*Maximus* II, 11). It is, of course, a literal fact, and Maximus takes it as evidence that meaning—light—occurs in the proximity of the earth.

After Maximus has firmly re-established himself, the primary action of the second volume, Maximus's conception, gestation, and birth, begins to develop. In "The River-I" Maximus finds an unexplained outcropping of diorite in the Annisquam River, which separates Cape Ann from the mainland, and he associates it with the Diorite Stone in the Hittite epic "The Song of Ullikummi." Olson says:

> ... it's the story of how this aborted creature, whom the poem calls the Diorite Stone, started growing from the bottom of the sea, and grew until he appeared above the surface of the water and then, of course, attention was called to him and he continued to grow and he became so offensive to the gods, and dangerous, that they had to, themselves, do battle with him. . . . And the Diorite, for me, this Diorite figure is the vertical, the growth principles of the Earth. He's just an objectionable child of Earth who has got no condition except Earth, no condition but stone. (*Myth*, 12)

The phallic implications of the Diorite Stone become explicit in "The River-2." The formal movement, which was defined in "I, Maximus of Gloucester, to You," is re-envisioned in the second volume as Maximus making love to the earth.

In the note at the end of "The River-II," Maximus realizes that his turn away from the harbor is not a revulsion, as it might appear, but a necessity of his self-revelation. The poimanderes, which appears to him, is a gnostic figure, sometimes manifest as an angel of enlightenment and sometimes as a krater, the vessel, according to Jung, "which the demiurge sent down filled with nous, so that those who were striving for higher consciousness could baptize themselves in it."[6] The specific revelation is recorded in the poem which follows:

> Dogtown   the dog town
>
> of the mother city   the C-
>
> city : METRO-
>
> POLIS.

(*Maximus* II, 18)

The dog/god pun appears to be unavoidable in the literature of this century (see "Later Tyrian Business" for its further development), but it is clear that Dogtown is the masculine counterpart of the mother city—at least for the present, as gender is a slippery business in the

---

[6]*Alchemical Studies*, p. 73.

second volume, where androgyny is the dominant mode of sexuality. Maximus recognizes the implications of the mapping of Meeting House Green which he began in "Letter, May 2" (i.e. "chomping around those street, measuring off distances"). Meeting House Green is literally the meeting place between the city and Dogtown. Historically it was settled before there were permanent settlements either at the harbor or in Dogtown, and, geographically, it stands more or less between. The krater appears as a sudden concrescence of abstract possibilities which determine a course of action. The demand is that Maximus, as cartographer, extend his work into the interior.

With "Cashes" (*Maximus* II, 19), Maximus begins one of the periodic gatherings of narrative material which is relevant to the ongoing process of the poem. "Mr. Pester acknowledges his sinfulness" (*Maximus* II, 20) is a reminder of the confusion of public and private, further evidence of what happens when the dimensions of public fact fail to stay personal. "Of old times" (*Maximus* II, 21) is both a gloss on one of the enigmatic lines in "Maximus, from Dogtown-II" ("she-who-Lusted-After-the-snake-in-the Pond") and looks forward to Maximus's own encounter with the serpent in "I forced the calm grey waters" (*Maximus* II, 32). "A Maximus" (*Maximus* II, 23) is a glyph, apparently of a crouched figure of the hero, rising from his "primitive buttocks" to "Pound, a person of the poem." It might be seen as a fleshed-out version of the glyph which stands opposite the title page in the first volume.

In each book of the second volume there is a poem which deals with the fishing grounds off the coast of Maine: "December, 1960" (*Maximus* II, 24–30), "The Gulf of Maine" (*Maximus* II, 108–10), and "A Letter, on FISHING GROUNDS [of, THE GULF OF MAINE] by Walter H. Rich" (*Maximus* II, 175–76). They require special consideration as a group, in part because they all seem relatively disconnected from the specific poetic environments in which they occur. Of course, in the poem of Gloucester the fishing must hold a place; it is the concern of the city which cannot be forgotten, so pervasive is its influence and smell. The more important fact, however, is geographic. In "Letter, May 2," Maximus speaks of "NW shifting man," and one of the persistent forms which he finds in the historical evidence is traced out by those routes of migration, the gradual movement, north and west, of the cultural center: "it ends, as Stefansson couldn't / stomach the dead end of his own prop- / osition, in the ice" (*Maximus* I, 146).

Vilhjalmar Stefansson, the Arctic explorer, appears in the *Maximus* as a modern Pytheus; to be more specific, he is almost a modern Pytheus, because he finds a power in the North which he almost describes as the unformed sludge of the cosmos: "Stefansson's ice, what trade replaced Pytheus's sludge with" (*Maximus* I, 151). The three poems in this group deal with the continuing northwestern shift of man and the threats which that "frontier" poses to those who test themselves against it. As if to hold Gloucester's northern border against chaos, the fishermen stake out a territory on earth *and* in the poem. In this middle passage of the *Maximus*, which is so deeply concerned with interior matters, these agents of the hero open a route northward, holding open a space which will not be filled until the third volume. In retrospect, it will be clear that the fishermen stand as representatives of those rather enigmatic figures of the North, the Bulgar and his sons (see *Maximus* III, 35).

Similarly, "Maximus Letter # whatever" (*Maximus* II, 31) is a sign of unfinished business. It provides an image of the integration which Maximus himself has not yet achieved and will not for some time. Like "Of old-times," the poem is lifted almost word for word from another source, one of the pieces "of hay and cotton struts, / of street-pickings, wharves, weeds" (*Maximus* I, 3) that Maximus carries in. The emerging coherence is capable of assimilating these substantial chunks of material.

"Maximus, March, 1961—1&2" (*Maximus* II, 32–33) were written shortly after Olson's participation in Timothy Leary's research on psilocybin at Harvard. This fact is apparent in an earlier version of the poem in which Maximus speaks of his "mushroom eyes." In the drug experience, however, Olson found only confirmation for the visionary process in which he was already engaged. In "Experience and Measure" he writes:

> Now this of course is the startling & unbelievable first impression
> of going under the Sacred Mushroom—or in fact the general state
> once one is successfully into Pot itself (Marijuana): that just that
> everyone & everything is nothing but anything but itself so that
> all—everything—is therefore well, and there's no push, there's no
> fuss, there's nothing at all to worry about, or press at, no sweat
> of any sort called for, its all too real and way beyond any attitude
> or seeking some greater or bigger answer than what so plainly is

quite in front of everyone of us all the time anywhere whatever it is: that it *is*, and that it got there from somewhere and that in fact it—and we share this extraordinary condition.[7]

The drug-induced consciousness is only a shortcut to an experience of the world consonant with a passage from the Chinese alchemical text, *The Secret of the Golden Flower*, which impressed Olson so profoundly in 1958 (i.e. before the drug experience) that a version of it had occurred to him in a dream: "that which exists through itself is what is called meaning."

Direct apprehension of this primordial reality is associated in the *Maximus* with the figure of the serpent. Whether as Uroborus, Hepit Naga Atosis, Typhon, or the Gloucester serpent, it is, like Melville's whale, an image "of Chaos or Pre-form" (*Human*, 116), a sign of the great primal unity from which everything springs. In a letter to Cid Corman in 1951 Olson writes, ". . . one needs . . . to keep in mind the tremendous image that a snake was . . . that the snake and the phallus were, together, of immense resonance for Mediterranean man." As with so much else, however, modern man has inverted the situation and, consequently, has failed to find use in the ancient insight. In the same letter he says:

> It is difficult to reify this, now, because none of us, now, find it easy to take a phallus as an image (i have a hunch we reverse the ancients, and make metaphors out of bananas and such rather than, as they, make the phallus, in a sense, a metaphor. For my assumption is that they took the phallus—&sex—as simply man's most immediate way of knowing nature's powers—and the handiest image of that power. (*Origin*, 57)

In "Maximus, March 1961—1" Maximus faces the archaic reality directly. The necessity to which he responds is the embodiment of the primal coherence in *conscious* generation of the world. The evolution which "floods the mind and all gods and men into further nature" must become aware of its own workings.

In the second part of the poem Maximus begins to establish a methodology, specifically relevant to his local conditions, which will allow that necessity to be obeyed:

[7]"Experience and Measure," in *Olson: The Journal of the Charles Olson Archives*, 3 (Spring, 1975), 60.

                         by the way into the woods
 Indian   otter   orient
 "Lake:"   ponds

     show me   (exhibit
     myself

                                              (Maximus II, 33)

This poem, like a number of others in the *Maximus*, cannot be read
as a linear movement of language. Maximus is creating a spatial field
in which both direction and juxtaposition are significant elements. He
is depending on Henry Corbin, who speaks of "an occident and an
orient of the cosmos" in the philosophic drama of Avicenna, the elev-
enth-century Arabic philosopher. The complexity of the poem results
from the multiple pun on "orient." In the simplest sense, of course, it
means "east." The road into the woods, the Dogtown road, which
Maximus will follow again in "for Robt Duncan" (*Maximus* II,
37–39) goes eastward, past Indian Lake and the otter ponds. As "orient" (from prp. of the Latin *Oriri*) is etymologically related to the
verb "to rise"—a fact that Olson with his endless curiosity about the
radicals of words would have known—Maximus also suggests that
the move inward is also a growth along the vertical axis. In "Maximus, at the Harbor" he will speak of "the soul / in its progressive
rise" (*Maximus* II, 71), and this possibility is confirmed by the landscape itself. The Dogtown road turns eastward at the base of Gravelly
Hill, on top of which Maximus will "orient" himself, marking off the
boundaries of "the mighty world" (*Maximus* II, 160–62).

   Maximus's map of the road to Dogtown is engaged specifically as
a map of himself: "show me / myself." The implications of this line,
though perhaps not immediately apparent, run through the remainder
of "Maximus IV." Maximus's efforts to show himself to himself revolve on a series of insights which derive from an essay by Henry
Corbin, "Cyclical Time in Ismailism and Mazdaism." The reflexive
(middle voice) verb reflects a crucial stage in the process which the
Arabic gnostics call *ta'wil*. Corbin gives a quotable definition of the
term in his book on Avicenna:

   Ta'wil is etymologically . . . to *cause to return*, to lead back, to
   restore to one's origin and to the place where one comes home,
   consequently to return to the true and original meaning of a text.
   It is "to *bring* something *to* its origin. . . . Thus he who practices

the *ta'wil* is the one who *turns* his speech from the external (exoteric) form . . . towards the inner reality. . . ." This must never be forgotten when, in current usage, *ta'wil* is said, and rightly, to be a spiritual exegesis that is inner, symbolic, esoteric, etc. Beneath the idea of exegesis appears that of a Guide (the *exegete*), and beneath the idea of exegesis we glimpse that of an exodus, of a "departure from Egypt," which is an exodus from metaphor and the slavery of the letter, from *exile* and the Occident of exoteric appearance to the Orient of the original and hidden Idea.[8]

In the margins of his copy of "Cyclical Time," where an abbreviated version of this definition appears, Olson wrote, in large, excited letters, "WOW," and, below the paragraph, "*history.*"[9]

Olson's marginalia are generally difficult to decipher, and the meaning, once the words themselves are made out, is not necessarily clear. The markings in the Corbin essay are, for the most part, no exception. It is apparent, however, that "Grammar—'a book'" (*Prose*, 27–31) was undertaken to explore the grammatical situation which is implicit in the *ta'wil*. Corbin reports Nasir Tusi's linguistic analysis in these terms: ". . . the aspect of action which we state in the infinitive, or the aspect of the event which we denote by an abstract noun, are by no means the true aspect of their reality, and . . . in the last analysis they refer back to the person of the *agent* who enacts the action of the event as the true reality of both."[10] Of course, this fact is by no means new to Olson. Summing up "Projective Verse," he writes:

> It comes to this: the use of a man, by himself and thus by others, lies in how he conceives his relation to nature, that force to which he owes his somewhat small existence. If he sprawl, he shall find little to sing but himself, and shall sing, nature has such paradoxical ways, by way of artificial forms outside himself. But if he stays inside himself, if he is contained within his nature as he is participant in the larger force, he will be able to listen, and his hearing through himself will give him secrets objects share. And by an inverse law his shapes will make their own way. (*Human*, 60)

[8]*Avicenna and the Visionary Recital*, trans. Willard R. Trask (New York, 1960), p. 29.

[9]"Cyclical Time in Ismailism and Mazdaism," in *Man and Time: Papers from the Eranos Yearbook*, ed. Joseph Campbell (New York, 1957), p. 150.

[10]*Ibid.*, p. 164.

Nasir, however, carries the analysis not one step forward but two.

First, he points out that "since the reality of the event, is thus reduced to the person who enacts it and understood as that person's mode of existence, every *verb* is mentally conjugated in the middle voice": i.e. "show me / myself." This possibility, too, has been perhaps hovering about, half-realized, through the first volume of the *Maximus*. In "Tyrian Businesses" Maximus speaks of "what musicians call / the middle voice, to command it / is to be in business" (*Maximus* I, 36), but it is not entirely clear what the reference is, and Olson's "explication" of the line in the reading at Berkeley (*Berkeley*, 35) is of little help. There is, in any case, a strong reflexive sense from the beginning of the *Maximus*, and it is intensified in "Maximus IV." It is the verb form of self-concept and self-birth. Corbin concludes this part of his discussion by saying: ". . . the person in whom his own action is incarnated is the *significatio passiva* of his action—that is to say, he is what his action makes him be."[11]

The greatest excitement which the Corbin essay occasioned for Olson is the next step which Nasir takes along this line of thought:

> But that implies that this person is an *agent* only in a superficial and metaphoric sense. More active than the person himself is the thought that is thought through him, the word that is spoken by him (and personified in him). And this thought of his thought is precisely what Nasir Tusi calls the Angel of this thought (or of this word or action). This Angel endows the soul with the aptitude for thinking it and rising by it; he is the Archetype, the finality without which a cause would never be a cause. He is the "destiny" of that soul. The subjective case becomes an instrumental.[12]

Again, Olson had anticipated this development. As we shall see in the discussion of "Later Tyrian Business," Olson had been aware of this more profound sense of action for almost a decade. It could almost be said, however, that the remainder of the *Maximus* is Olson's exegesis of this passage: Nasir provides the specific formal directive which allows the space of the poem to present itself. He seems to have suggested to Olson a sense of the *Maximus* as a whole. It is useful, at least, to think of the poem as passing from the subjective-genitive case

[11]*Ibid.*, p. 167.
[12]*Ibid.*, p. 166.

of the first volume ("I, Maximus of Gloucester"), to the instrumental case of the third (Maximus, *writing* a Republic), by way of the unstable mixture of objective and subjective implicit in the middle-voice verbs of the second.

In "Later Tyrian Business" (*Maximus* II, 36) Maximus recalls a cell of imagery which was left unexplored in the earlier Tyrian poem:

The seedling
of morning: to move, the problem (after the night's presences)
                                        the first hours of

    He had noticed,
    the cotton picks easiest

            As my flower,
            after rain, wears
            such diadem

                    As a man is a necklace
                    strung on his own teeth
                          (the caries
                of 'em
                    (*Maximus* I, 37)

In this earlier context the images define a certain quality of attention, in an attempt to establish a relationship between the dream sources of the poem ("the night's presences") and the possibilities for action which the morning offers. The freshness of morning is the sign and continuing energy of the dreams which, despite their obvious significance, leave the dreamer in his dream incapable of action. In the second volume Maximus attempts to approach the dream material directly, to bring it into the light of day. In "Later Tyrian Business" these other "dimensions" of reality, which have been occluded or, at best, enigmatic, begin to emerge as co-equal with space and history.

In the first volume Olson tries to cast his poem in Gloucester, to allow the city to be both the environment and the content of the poem, and, of course, he fails. Maximus overcomes his own estrangement from that which is most familiar only to find that "it's earth which / now is strange" (*Maximus* I, 149). In the unpublished piece "The principles of measure in composition by Field: Projective Verse II," Olson begins to prepare a way into the poem as both creation and ground for creation. He must find an environment in which the poem can occur. He writes: "Creation . . . itself awaits each novel advance men make as further evidence of her own primordial nature." The creation literally has an appetite for being known. In "Maximus VI" this urge will be identified with the primal hunger which, in Norse mythology, creates the world (see *Maximus* II, 164). As he goes on to say, however, ". . . all creation is also obstructive." For all of the force with which the creation puts itself forward for man's use, it also hides itself, insists upon its own character as the only useful context for any act of knowing. The poet does his work in the midst of the tensions which arise: "What the poem . . . has to do, is to keep the conditions of obstruction out of which it came—or it falls into the split between universal and particular, neither of which is any such thing. It cannot clear by throwing overboard the whistles and baggages of its own birth place. It has one law: it has to occur. And to occur it has to retain and create its own environment. Otherwise it lifts away, into culture."[13] Space and history as such begin to appear as the primordial reality which grounds the poem, keeps it inside a context which is neither cultural artifice nor egocentric. It is only in the "lucid" dimensions that man knows and acts.

These forms begin to make themselves manifest in Olson's prose long before they appear in the poem. Beginning from undigested possibilities in "The Discipline, and Area of, Totality" and "the mytho," they are carried through "Bibliography on America," "Projective Verse II," and come to full realization in *Causal Mythology* and the poems from the third volume which Olson reads in that lecture. Olson calls these new territories, swimming out of Pytheus's sludge in much the same manner as the North American continent in "On first Looking out through Juan de la Cosa's Eyes" (*Maximus* I, 78), the *imago mundi* and the *anima mundi*:

> Now, my argument would be, then, that the way that the Earth gets to be attained is that we are born, ourselves, with a picture of the world. That there is no world except one that we are the pictures of it. And by the world here I don't mean the Earth. I mean the whole of creation. And it seems to me that I, I don't know enough, but I think that the phrase *imago mundi* is as legitimate as the better known phrase the *anima mundi*. And I'd like to oppose that, really, to a condition of writing which is based on what I do or what others do, rather than comes from

[13]Copyright by the University of Connecticut Library.

the darkness of one's own initiation. Again I'm suggesting that even the overt spiritual exercise of initiation is initial in us. *We* are, *we* are, spiritual exercise, by having been born. (*Myth*, 15)

The appearance of the Ismaili angels in "Later Tyrian Business" (*Maximus* II, 36) is the beginning of Maximus's overt spiritual initiation. He has seen himself until now as existing in literal space and history. Beginning at this point, he gradually comes to exist in a world which has its being by virtue of his work *in* literal space and history.

Again, as in "Maximus, March 1961–2," the language, floating in the spatial field of the page, is not linear. The diadem from "Tyrian Businesses" returns as the emblem of the integrity which Maximus maintains in the face of the dualisms which appear, and the four images of the poem hang from it like the elements in a Calder mobile. In the balanced tensions the lucid and the obstructive components of the real are *both* simultaneous and agents of a recurring drama. The paradox is explained by the fact that the creation is final and complete, but it is perpetually re-experienced through the cosmic temporal cycles.

On the one hand, the world makes itself readily manifest:

> God the Dog,
> of the Ist
> Angel—who
> Adores. Only after
> was there a "Soul"
> of the World—*nafs*
> the Anima
> Mundi, Bred of a Dog's
> Admirer.

The passage is a paraphase of Corbin's redaction of an Iranian cosmology which he derives from the writings of Nasir-e Khosraw:

He describes the procession of the five primordial archangelical hypostases, the first two of which are the Intelligence ('*Aql*) and the Soul (*Nafs*). This eternal motion which moves the being of the first Intelligence or Archangel is an eternal movement of adoration of the Principle, which eternally activates it toward being. From this eternal movement of adoration, from this cosmic liturgy, the Soul of the World eternally takes its birth.[14]

[14]"Cyclical Time in Ismailism and Mazdaism," p. 150.

The first lines of the other half of the poem—"hangs / the 7 Angels of the 3rd Angel's Sleep—the 7 words"—are also from Corbin, but from a slightly different context:

> ... the third angel stops at himself: he remains motionless in a stupor which gives rise to a gap, a distance between himself and the world of eternal Existentiation from which he cuts himself off. There comes to be a "Time which passes" and creates a remoteness. ... When the Angel tears himself free from this stupor, he sees himself "retarded," surpassed ... , fallen behind himself. From third he has become tenth. To the Time of his stupor that he must redeem corresponds the emanation of the seven other Intelligences which are called the seven Cherubim or the seven Divine Words.[15]

The contradiction between the five angels of the first passage and the ten angels here results from the fact that Corbin bases his analysis on a composite of different sources. The outlines of the drama, however, should be clear.

The poem is, in one of its implications, a further exploration of the proposition "love is form." The Angel who adores forms himself in the primal image, but, as he becomes an image of potentiality as well as actuality, he extends beyond himself and issues in something which is not himself. The second angel in turn gives rise to the sleepy third, who is the cosmos itself. At this point, however, the process is obstructed, the third Angel, in his sleep, is surpassed, and, if the revelation of the creation is to continue, the process must "twist" back on itself and begin again.

In Olson's marginalia in the Corbin essay, especially toward the end, there is a running comparison of the Ismaili cosmology and Whitehead's. It might almost be said that, in the final image of "Later Tyrian Business," Alfred North Whitehead appears as an Angel in the celestial drama:

> as His Tongue
>   Hangs, dropping
> Eternal Events
>   the Salivarating
> Dog.

[15] *Ibid.*, p. 154.

The term "eternal events," at any rate, is Whitehead's, and it occurs here as a short-hand symbol for the obstructive fact of history. Eternal events resemble Platonic forms, as they are the determinants of the "real," given shape of things, but they are immediately knowable and local. Whitehead speaks of them as sense-data, "playing a complex relational role." As he says, "they connect the actual entities of the past with the actual entities of the contemporary world, and thereby effect objectifications of the contemporary things and of the past things."[16] The obstructive world, in other words, is not engaged in the drama: space, as an eternal, mathematical expanse, and history, in its eternal aspect, are objectified as a continuum of space-time and experienced as a totality. The limits of this possibility will be one of the prime concerns of the third volume.

"Later Tyrian Business" presents an image of the process of the *Maximus* in cross-section. Olson himself was not sure how to deal with it. In "A Later Note on Letter #15" Maximus says:

> the objective (example Thucidides, or
> the latest finest tape-recorder, or any form of record on the spot
>
> —live television or what—is a lie
>
> as against what we know went on, the dream: the dream being
>
> self-action with Whitehead's important corollary: that no event
>
> is not penetrated, in intersection or collision with, an eternal
>
> event.
>
> (*Maximus* II, 79)

But he adds, "The poetics of such a situation / are yet to be found out." The poem does, nevertheless, establish a set of relationships inside of which the *Maximus* can continue. The on-going drama of Maximus's research into the history and geography of Cape Ann plays continually against an eternal environment which is everywhere present but nowhere quite revealed.

The bulk of the remainder of "Maximus IV" is devoted to the geography and history of Dogtown and the earliest history of Gloucester. Like the involvement with Ferrini's magazine in "Maximus I," the subject seems at first hopelessly local and inconsequential. It will become apparent, however, as the *Maximus* continues that what we are witnessing in these poems is, in fact, the very beginnings

[16]*Process and Reality*, p. 78.

of human culture. Addressing Robert Duncan, Maximus says, "I walk you paths of lines I'd share with / you simply to make evident the world / is an eternal event" (*Maximus* I, 38). The central drama of "Maximus IV" turns on man's relationship to earth, which is played out fully in *every* revealed actual occasion. The smallest and the largest, the local and the cosmic, are joined in Maximus's embodiment of the growth principle of earth. He says: "I stand on Main Street like the Diorite / stone" (*Maximus* II, 51). Under the force of that vertical thrust, drawing everything to a point, the earth, too, is as local and as commonplace as the paths of Dogtown lives: "the arms / of Half Moon Beach, / the legs / of the cut" (*Maximus* II, 59). Cid Corman glosses these lines simply: "Mammy!" The Great Mother lies curled around Stage Head, where the first fishing stages were erected, and Blynman Canal, which connects Gloucester harbor to the Annisquam River, is her genitalia. So when Maximus adduces evidence in "My Carpenter's Son's Son's Will" (*Maximus* II, 69) that the original agreement on the management of the canal, which is quoted in "The Cut" (*Maximus* II, 67), has been betrayed by the pejorocrats, the enormity of the crime is obvious.

"Maximus, at the Harbor" (*Maximus* II, 70–71) stands at the end of the fourth book as the new beginning which Maximus demands of himself. It is in this poem that Maximus's intercourse with the Great Mother begins:

> love to sit in the ring
> of Okeanos love to lie in the spit
> of a woman a man to sit in her legs
>
> > (her hemispheres
> > loomed above me,
> > I went to work
> > like the horns of a snail.

The ego which Merry lost is transformed into a magnificent angel which is the manifesting soul, involved in the processive discovery of itself:

> apophainesthai: the soul
> in its progressive rise.

The source is again Nasir Tusi, by way of Corbin. Okeanos becomes the thought of Maximus's thought, an angel of the exegetical process, who goes forth, blessed or cursed, depending on the quality of the act from which it is impelled. It becomes the destiny: "it sends out / on the path ahead the Angel / it will meet." Maximus, however, secularizes Nasir Tusi, much as he does Jung. Corbin writes:

> To be in paradise, or to come into this world, designates above all different modes of being and understanding. It means either to exist in true Reality (*haququat*), or, on the contrary, to "come into this world"—that is to say, to pass into the plane of an existence which in relation to that other is merely a metaphoric existence (*majaz*). Measured time, too, is only a metaphor for absolute Time. Thus coming into this world has meaning only with a view to leading that which is metaphoric back to true being, and the external (exoteric, *zahir*) back to the internal (esoteric, *batin*), by means of an exegesis (*ta'wil*) which is also an exodus from existence.[17]

Maximus does not make the distinction: "Paradise is a person. Come into this world." Coming into this world is not to enter a metaphoric existence; it is rather to assume the full advantage of the paradise of personhood in one's self, to become the-man-with-his-house-on-his-head, to be born finally as "the perfect child" who at the end of the cosmic drama "leads back (*ta'wil*) to the Angel all those in the cycle who have belonged to his posterity—that is, who have borne his image and fought his battle."[18]

The line, "its accent is its own mirage," provides a typical instance of the way in which Olson uses (and abuses) his sources. The following passage is the source of the line: "The burgeoning and growth of the soul of the angelical or demoniacal virtuality is the measure of its ascent (*mi'raj*), or of its fall into the abyss."[19] "Ascent" suggests to Olson "accent," which carries here its etymological force of "song" or "chant," and *mi'raj*, ascent, is corrupted into mirage. The line might read then as either "its song is its own delusion," or "its song is its own ascent." Of course, the pun is so arcane that no reader can be reasonably expected to get it, and, as a matter of fact, he need not, because at this point in the process the song *is* delusion,

---

[17]"Cyclical Time in Ismailism and Mazdaism," p. 165.
[18]*Ibid.*, p. 169.
[19]*Ibid.*, p. 167.

for the same reason that the map which is to include Maximus's being is called "peloria," *both* monster and portent. As the "perfect child" which issues from the perfected *ta'wil* is still unborn, Maximus's condition is inevitably compounded of delusion and monstrousness, on one hand, and ascension and portentousness, on the other.

2

The first book of the *Maximus* and the fourth deal with methodology in the broadest sense of the term: publication, putting the body of the private experience into the public domain. Similarly, the fifth book parallels the second. Again the central concern is the westward movement of the cultural center. To this point, the connections back to Tyre and the Sumerian coherence which lies behind it have been realized only in occasional allusions. In "The Song and Dance of" Columbus appears as the link between the Mediterranean and the New World. And in "Letter, May 2, 1959" Maximus identifies the citizens of Gloucester with the barbaric "Peoples of the Sea," who swept "over the Eastern Mediterranean between 1225 & 1175 [B.C.], devastating the Hittite Empire and destroying Tyre and Phoenician power" (*Prose*, 34). The fifth book begins to recount this very large, and largely untold, story. At the same time, and through the same events, it also covers the period of Maximus's gestation. The migration of Indo-European culture to Gloucester is literally Maximus's prenatal experience. The Phoenicians, the builders of cromlechs and menhirs, and the Algonquins, as well as, more specifically, Typhon, Pytheas, and Pausanias, are agents of Maximus's genetic constitution.

Time in the *Maximus* is intensive: everything which has happened *still* happens. An event, a place, a person may be forgotten, but the evidence of primordial reality is always, everywhere present, in the blank pages of "Maximus V," for example. The whole world rises vertically from the blank whiteness of the page, "the calm grey waters," the forgotten recesses of the organism.

Probably the most useful guides to "Maximus V" are three pieces in "Proprioception," which were written in 1961 and 1962: "the hinges of civilization to be put back on the door," "A Plausible 'Entry' for, like, man," and "A Work" (*Prose*, 25–26, 32–33). They establish a chronology and indicate something of Olson's thinking at the time

the poems were being written. In Olson's view of history the loss
which human culture suffered about 1200 B.C., when the occident
separated itself from the orient and the possibility for any concrete,
universal image of order disappeared, has never been repaired, but
there have been epochs when the old secular advantage was temporarily aroused. As we have seen in the discussion of the first volume,
the opening decades of the seventeenth century were such a time, as
was the thirteenth century of Anthony of Padua and Nasir Tusi, and
the first century A.D., the time of Maximus of Tyre and Apollonius of
Tyana. Of course, for Olson, the other great opportunity is the present. Unless the hinges of civilization are put back on the door, he
writes, "the present will lose what America is the inheritor of: a secu-
larization which not only loses nothing of the divine but by seeing
process in reality redeems all idealism fr[om] theocracy or mobocracy,
whether it is rational or superstitious, whether it is democratic or so-
cialism" (*Prose*, 26). Olson proposes to investigate the continuity of
a literature and a use of man by himself which was fully articulated
during the late pleistocene. If the self-action of the dream is to become
again a factor of the real, as Maximus insists it must in "A Later Note
on Letter # 15," it is necessary to generate the subconscious material
which corresponds to Maximus's very literal quest into the history of
Dogtown.

The past in the *Maximus* is without objective content. Olson
asks, "What did happen? Two alternatives: make it up; or try to find
out. Both are necessary. We inherit an either-or, from the split of fic-
tion and science" (*History*, 20). The evidence, though Maximus treats
it with profound respect, is never adequate to reveal what happened.
Both the processes of the imagination and the processes of scientific
investigation, when either is exercised alone, are estranged from the
coherence which is most familiar. The evidence of history is treated
not unlike a lay-out for a reading of the tarot cards or an astrological
chart. It is a transmission from the past which reveals a range of possible futures. If there is vague evidence of a lost city, where now unknown sciences offered men extraordinary powers, two possibilities
present themselves: it was either a city in the manifest world or a city
in the unknown of consciousness, if that somewhat awkward con-
struction can be used to suggest a concreteness which is not generally
allowed to dream and myth. By placing the imagination in a concrete

landscape, Maximus renders that distinction meaningless:

> These
> are the chronicles
> of an imaginary
> town
>
> placed as an island
> close to the shore.
>
> (*Maximus* II, 103)

In "Maximus V" Maximus maps the historic-genetic routes by which the connections between topos and tropos are made.

There is, however, another more familiar history which must also be dealt with, moved aside, before man can enter into unconstricted familiarity with the spatial fact of his own existence. In "Human Universe" Olson writes: "We stay unaware how two means of discourse the Greeks appear to have invented hugely interdict our participation in our experience, and so prevent discovery. They are what followed from Socrates' readiness to generalize, his willingness (from his own bias) to make a 'universe' out of discourse instead of letting it rest in its most serviceable place" (*Human*, 4). The two means are, of course, logic and classification, which describe a cosmos in and of language, and allow a political order *only* in language, so the postlogical fact of any made thing, in its senseless and powerful particularity, is excluded. In "The Songs of Maximus" Maximus says:

> No eyes or ears left
> to do their own doings (all
>
> invaded, appropriated, outraged, all senses
>
> including the mind, that worker on what is
>
> And that other sense
>
> made to give even the most wretched, or any of us, wretched,
>
> that consolation (greased
> lulled.
>
> (*Maximus* I, 13)

In "Maximus V" the invader is identified as Alexander the Great:

> 128 a mole
> to get at Tyre.
>
> (*Maximus* II, 80)

The reference is to U.S. Highway 128, which is carried onto Cape Ann by the A. Piatt Andrews Bridge (see *Maximus* I, 148–50), and the mole Alexander built to Tyre, the one city which gave serious opposition to the universalization of his empire. As "Maximus V" begins, then, Gloucester-Tyre is under seige by the westerners, Bostonians-Macedonians.

It will be significant to recall in "Aristotle & Augustine" (*Maximus* II, 113) that Alexander was Aristotle's student. For Maximus, Alexandrian politics is an inevitable result of the misplacement of man in Aristotelian metaphysics. The Persian and Milesian thinkers were the last to retain even a trace of the ancient mystery which the polis properly manifests. Maximus says:

> Aristotle & Augustine
>
> clearly misunderstood Anaximander
>
> And in doing so beta'd
>
> themselves.

Anaximander argued that there is no first principle or cause of the infinite. What he calls "the One" is pure unlimited energy; it is neither one of the elements as Thales and Heraclitus maintain nor some abstract quality such as mind or friendship or love. Anaximander's One is clearly Maximus's Okeanos, the energy by which every event is "penetrated, in intersection or collision with, an eternal / event" (*Maximus* II, 79). It is the nameless, undefinable principle which allows Maximus to be transformed into all of the figures of the history which is told in "Maximus V."

The upheaval which took place about the time recorded history began was the result of one of those inexplicable failures of cultural nerve of the kind Olson defines in "The Kingfishers":

> When the attentions change / the jungle
> leaps in
>   even the stones are split
>   they rive.
>
>   (*Archaeologist*, 45)

The will to cohere suddenly gave way, and the cultures of the ancient Near East, which were, as Maximus says in "*'View':fr the Orontes*" (*Maximus* II, 81),

> the Ist to navigate
> those waters
> thus to define
> the limits
> of the land,

were no longer the informants of the genetic, feminine energy. The defeat of the Trojans by the Achians was the decisive engagement in a conflict which began in 1540 B.C., when "Zeus / as an immaculate / white bull with one / black stripe down him / . . . caught Europe / up on to his back" (*Maximus* II, 102), and carried her from Tyre to Crete. The cultural center began to move outward, along "those extending lines," west and north, into the Atlantic, toward the unformed Thule. In "*View*" the cultural migrations, from the fall of Troy to the Christianization of England, appear as a single spatio-temporal landscape. It is almost impossible, however, to give a linear account of the migrations. The action of "Maximus V" is cast in a space which is half geographic-historical and half dream. This "dream," unlike the dream material in "Maximus II," has some apparent archetypal content, but it is a very personal account of world history which Maximus gives "*My* memory," he says, "is the history of time" (*Maximus* II, 86, my italics), and, for the time being, he must depend upon the force of a vision which is largely personal.

The great migration is, at once, in objective, horizontal space and also fully contained in the vertical dimension. The ancient coherence has *always* been in Gloucester, as it has been everywhere, and what we witness in the *Maximus* is the process of that primal presence coming to consciousness. The "view" is, in other words, reversible. Later in "Maximus V" Maximus will note, in reference to Fitz Hugh Lane, the nineteenth-century painter of Gloucester:

> Lane's eye-view of Gloucester
> Phoenician eye-view.
>
> (*Maximus* II, 100)

In fact, the two are precisely equivalent. Lane is a Phoenician painter, exactly as Maximus is Typhon, "the blue monster," the last of the chthonic heroes to oppose the Olympian gods. His battle with Zeus, which will be detailed in "Maximus, from Dogtown-IV" (*Maximus* II, 163–72), is the divine equivalent to the Tyrians' battle with Alexander: both are engagements of local, "earthy" forces against universalism.

Typhon's name means "stupifying smoke,"[20] according to Robert Graves, who is Olson's source for the Typhon story as well as much of the other Greek material, and he is traditionally associated with volcanoes, especially Mt. Aetna, which Zeus is said to have hurled upon him. In the third volume Maximus will say, "Heaven is / Mind (drawn to Gloucester" (*Maximus* III, 86), and Typhon's quest, his effort to "shake off his cave-life / and open an opening / big enough for himself," is served by Maximus's drawing power. In his journey, which leads to Gloucester and Typhon's transformation into the young Maximus as a letter-carrier, Waddell's Many and Pytheas appear as his agents (see *Maximus* II, 94–97). Like the Mother Goddess, whose westward course is traced in "Cyprus" (*Maximus* II, 93) and "the coast goes from Hurrian Hazzi to Tyre" (*Maximus* II, 98), they are all being drawn to Gloucester.

Typhon is fairly obviously the volcanic unconscious, which both hides itself and delivers the mail. Because his journey is underway, Maximus can say, in the notes for a poem which he cannot yet write, "I want that sense / here, of this fellow going home" (*Maximus* II, 107). Maximus has been, to this point, ranging wider and wider, becoming ever more dispersed, in his search for a reliable source of his being; now the process begins to twist back on itself.

As a consciousness, however, Maximus seems for the first time in "Maximus V" somewhat tentative. "The Young Ladies," "Bk ii chapter 37," and "the rocks in Settlement Cove" (*Maximus* II, 82, 84–85) all involve in one way or another the kind of ironic mythicizing to which Olson so vigorously objects in Joyce and Eliot. For the present, it is only in the dream poem, "Peloria the dog's upper lip" (*Maximus* II, 87), that Maximus can fully anticipate the coincidence of Gloucester and Tyre.

The birth of the redeemed self is associated in the *Maximus* with rites of spring and alchemical transformation. Beginning in "Maximus VI," the myth of Horus and Osiris and their annual rites will become an informing presence. In "Peloria," however, the immediate reference is to the ancient Thessalian celebration of Zeus Peloros who, according to Jane Harrison, is a serpentine manifestation of Cronus. The vernal festival is a re-enactment of the Cronean Golden Age and, as such, it recalls the legend of the man with his house on his head.

[20]*The Greek Myths* (Middlesex, 1960), I, 135.

The androgynous Maximus who appears here is another figure of that consummate integrity, and now it is seen in a specific relationship to Maximus himself. The other cell of imagery, which is recalled in the poem, is the flower festival from "Maximus, to Gloucester, Sunday, July 19" (*Maximus* I, 152–54), where Gloucester's memorial service for the lost fishermen leads to at least a suggestion of an alchemical rebirth. The Earth, which is presented as the lapis in the earlier poem, is here internalized, and Maximus appears as the androgynous Mercurius or Hermaphroditus or, as the myriad-named philosopher's stone is sometimes called, the blue, dog-like woman, the "puppy of celestial hue."[21] In the non-Euclidean dream-space of the poem, the opposite ends of the migration route—like all other oppositions—are united in the alchemical marriage: Tyre is literally Gloucester. Maximus begins his journey in Tyre-Gloucester and travels to Gloucester-Tyre. Olson writes: "What is measure when the universe flips and no part is discrete from another part except by the flow of creation itself, in and out, intensive where it seemed before qualitative, and the extensive exactly the widest, which we also have the powers to include?" (*Human*, 119). The poet's measure of the process, rather than the measure of miles or years from Gloucester to Tyre, has become the element of control.

Maximus may seem at times nostalgic for the second millennium B.C., but it must always be recalled that the past which he conjectures is the form of the *future*. The break-up of the Sumerian coherence is a fortunate, perhaps inevitable, event, if the archaic forms are to be fully revealed. The world which the Phoenician sailors defined was itself partial. Maximus locates a cultural past which gathers its authority from the coherence of the continents themselves. The Sumerian culture, he suggests, was only a late, decadent form of an image of order which had prevailed in Gondwanaland (see the map on the cover of *Maximus IV, V, VI*). The "black-haired" previous people of the Ubaidian culture (*Maximus* II, 105), who were originally uplanders, moved into the riverine sights about the beginning of the fourth millennium B.C. and built the first cities. The second-millennium invaders were possibly

> Gondwannan creatures
> who swung off,

[21]Jung, *Alchemical Studies*, p. 232.

         for market
         from the eastern edge.

(Maximus II, 104)

In "off-upland" (*Maximus* II, 116) Maximus identifies Dogtown, which was also an upland culture, with the Ubaid, and the Norse, whose mythology will become significant in "Maximus VI," appear as the Gondwannan invaders who conqueor the original, Algonquin inhabitants. In Maximus's nontemporal history, there is a world-wide conquest of indigenous peoples by roving bands of sailors, who carry the word of the world's profound unity.

3

Maximus's success in "Maximus VI" balances his failure in "Maximus III." The book begins with the vision of the city which the two previous books make possible:

         The earth with a city in her hair
         entangled of trees.

(Maximus II, 119)

The city as an extension of the natural, rather than as a willful intrusion *on* the natural, can potentially rest in such intimacy with the Great Mother. Maximus has managed to regain the vantage with which he began the poem: "polis / is eyes" (*Maximus* I, 26). What has changed is that the city of the second volume is no more the casual Gloucester, where Olson happened to live, than the Mycenaean age which Homer describes was Homer's own. It is a visionary city, and, though it is like the literal Gloucester in remarkable detail, it is *also* an aesthetic fact of the poem.

Olson's strategy is Homeric. It is typical of Olson's process that he frequently understands himself—or at least reinterprets himself— after the fact. In 1963, after the second volume was finished, Olson found in Eric Havelock's *Preface to Plato* a terminology for what he had just done, and it would carry him into his continuing work. Homer was the first poet confronted with the cultural dissolution which followed the Trojan war, and it no doubt pleased Olson enormously when he recognized that his solution to the problem was not unlike Homer's. Havelock writes:

The problem faced by the migrating Greeks who left the mainland in mass formation and placed water barriers between themselves and their previous homes and institutions was in the first
place to resist absorption by their new neighbours and conserve
their group consciousness as Greeks. Political institutions were in
fact destined to change during these obscure centuries. The answer to *diaspora* and decentralisation was to invent the *polis*, an
adaptation and enlargement of the Mycenaean palace complex
which converted it into something new. But the tradition, the continuity of law, custom and usage must be maintained, or the scattered groups would disintegrate and their common tongue be
lost. The essential vehicle of continuity was supplied by a fresh
and elaborate development of the oral style, whereby a whole
way of life, and not simply the deeds of heroes, was to be held
together and so rendered transmissible between the generations.[22]

Maximus's visionary Gloucester refers to a present which is absolutely
immediate but which *retains* all of the advantages the present had
lost; and its purpose, like Homer's Mycenae, is essentially educa-
tional.

By the end of the first volume, however, the City as a context in
which a teachable way of life is preserved has disappeared. Maximus
calls out to the few who must "have the polis / in their eye" (*Maximus*
I, 28), and they fail to respond. Olson had the precedent of Pound to
learn from: the dead city is no more meaningful and useful as an image of order than a dead *Kulchur*. Again Olson found his own solution to the problem confirmed by Havelock: "The conservation of
Mycenaean memories in Homer is not a symptom of romantic nostalgia. Rather it provided a setting in which to preserve the group identity of the Greek-speaking peoples. It was a matrix within which or-
ally to contain and preserve their *nomoi* and *ethe*."[23]

The second volume provides, in other words, the *type* of a city.
Defining *typos* in the Beloit lectures, Olson makes reference to print-
ing type. The whole of the useful world, through this passage of the
process, is contained in the fragile pages on which the poem stands. It
carries the imprint of a topos which is, in the third volume, to be
published. In "The Advantage of Literacy is that Words Can Be on

[22]*Preface to Plato*, p. 119.
[23]*Ibid.*, p. 118–19.

the Page," Olson writes: "One wants phenomenology in place, in order that event may re-arise. There are only two facts about mythology which count: that they are made up of tales and personages, in place. Words then are naming and logography is writing as though each word is physical and that objects are originally motivating. This is the doctrine of the earth" (*Prose*, 51). In the sixth book Maximus is born to the word (*Maximus* II, 129) and of earth (*Maximus* II, 160); he joins earth and hades (*Maximus* II, 163–72); and phenomena are placed, so event may genuinely rearise. The whole of the second volume might be considered as investigation into a part of the structure first located in "I, Maximus of Gloucester, to You":

> the underpart is, though stemmed, uncertain
> is, as sex is, as monies are, facts!
> facts, to be dealt with, as the sea is . . .
>
> (*Maximus* I, 2)

The unknown interior, the unconscious perhaps, the literal cavity of the body as an "organ of novelty," as Whitehead calls it, is revealed as the agent in the creation of a redeemed world in which experience is itself a value and a sufficiency.

The formal movement of "And now let all the ships come in" (*Maximus* II, 120) is directly parallel to the movement ("in is out") which was established in "I, Maximus to Gloucester," but now Maximus's skin, the surface at which the objective world darts toward the subjective, is coterminous not only with the City but also with the Great Mother herself, who, in the Image of the World which the *Maximus* projects, lies along these same shores:

> And now let all the ships come in
>
> pity and love the Return the Flower
>
> the Gift and the Alligator catches
>
> -and the mind go forth to the end of the world

Olson's radical localism seems almost beyond comprehension. As Mircea Eliade observes, however, the archetypal creation myth does not impart form to the unfamiliar parts of the world. The cosmos, like the City, is *local*. For this reason, as Eliade goes on to demonstrate, "when possession is taken of a territory . . . rites are performed that symbolically repeat the action of Creation: the uncultivated zone is first 'cosmicized,' then inhabited."[24] In "Maximus VI" Maximus cosmicizes Dogtown. The ancient Indo-European coherence ("Veda upanishad edda," *Maximus* I, 128) is given a center for the first time since the great migrations began. The great primal serpent, this time in the form of the Algonquin Hepit Naga Atosis, is present in Gloucester (*Maximus* II, 121).

The sixth book begins slowly, retrospectively. There is still more Tyrian business:

> the diadem of the Dog
>
> which is morning
>
> rattles again.
>
> (*Maximus* II, 123)

Maximus is again at the limits of the created world. If in "Maximus V" he snatches a history from the mouth of the dog, now he must likewise find a cosmos. The Tyrian hero, however, begins to merge—as will become fully evident in the third volume—with Tyr, the Norse god of battle, who loses his hand in a bargain which leads to the shackling of Feniswolf, the Norse figure of cosmic disorder and dissolution. The hero is literally maimed in his effort to bring forth a cosmic shape, and it is perhaps for that reason that a certain reluctance seems to impel the backward glance which Maximus takes in these opening pieces. There are two poems directly or indirectly involved with John Winthrop. The letter which forms the major part of "They brawled in the streets" (*Maximus* II, 124–25) is addressed to him in his role as magistrate. And in "J[ohn] W[inthrop] (from the Danelaw) says" (*Maximus* II, 135) his restoration to the status of a hero of magnitude comparable to John Smith begins. "out over the land skope view" (*Maximus* II, 126) is a revision of Maximus's consideration of "undone business" in "Maximus, to himself" (*Maximus* I, 52–53). Maximus takes his stance between heaven and earth only to realize that he must join himself to "our father who is also in / Tartaros," as he will say in "Maximus, from Dogtown-IV" (*Maximus* II, 163).

Maximus has a pagan view of the underworld. It is an extreme

---

[24]*The Myth of the Eternal Return*, trans. Willard Trask (New York, 1954), pp. 9–10.

place, and therefore fearful, but as Odysseus's example indicates, it is better to brave it than to wander forever lost on earth. In "Part of the Flower of Gloucester" (*Maximus* II, 127) Maximus is reminded by the stench rising from "the rubbish on the Harbor bottom" that it is a putrifying Circe that he is bedded with, not his true Penelope.

Maximus, like any hero, is multiply born, and in preparation for his birth as the Perfect Child, he recalls his birth as a poet:

> Wrote my first poems
> and an essay on myth
> at Kent Circle
> at Kunt Circle.
>
> (*Maximus* II, 129)

Kent Circle where Olson lived during the winter of 1939–40, the year of the Valentine Day's storm, is the first north-south street west of Blynman Canal. The pun on "Kent," in light of the anatomical geography of "Maximus IV," "the legs of the Cut" (*Maximus* II, 55), is drawn directly from the mythic landscape of the poem. It is the example Olson gives in *Causal Mythology* of the inevitable dipolarity of the "accidental" associations which are the fabric of myth. Tearing the caul from his own head, Maximus is active, the working poet who is at least partially responsible for his own birth:

> Went off to New York
> by the Boston boat
> as soon as the work
> was over wearing
> going through the Canal
> an Arctic cold weather
> completely smothering
> upholstery fabric
> hair mattress
> headgear with eyes only
> protruding
>
> until I couldn't stand
> the god damn thing and went out
> on deck
> with my head
> itself.
>
> (*Maximus* II, 129)

150

Charles Olson's *Maximus*

In the remainder of the "Maximus VI" Maximus must take possession of his ship of birth. The Boston boat must be transformed into
the box upon the sea in which he sets out at the end of the volume.
The vision of the philosopher's stone which recurs in "I am the Gold
Machine" (*Maximus* II, 131) must imprint the literal landscape.

The decisive turn in "Maximus VI" comes in "The Frontlet"
(*Maximus* II, 145). It introduces a series of poems, running through
"at the boundary of the mighty world" (*Maximus* II, 160–62), which
grow more or less directly from Olson's reading of Henri Frankfort's
Kingship and the Gods, especially his explication of Memphite theology. In Frankfort, Olson finds important evidence relevant to both of
the major problems which he must face as the second volume moves
toward its conclusion:

> If we now consider the Memphite Theology as a whole, the
> most remarkable feature, besides its spiritual view of creation, is
> the manner in which reality and mythology are intermingled. It
> is true that all the personages are gods. . . . The locale of the ac-
> tion is, in fact, not mythological but real. It is Memphis, and,
> more precisely, the royal castle, the newly established seat of au-
> thority for the united country, which is the place where Osiris is
> interred; and the figure of Osiris is not exclusively at home in
> mythology either. Each king, at death, becomes Osiris . . . , just
> as each king, in life, appears "on the throne of Horus"; each king
> *is* Horus. . . . It is then possible that the Horus who appears at
> the end of the text [the Memphite theology on which Frankfort's
> discussion is keyed] as king of Egypt in the arms of his father
> Osiris (though the latter is dead and buried) is not only the god
> but also the king. . . .[25]

In framing his discussion, Frankfort addresses himself to precisely the two matters which, at this juncture in the process of Olson's
poem, occasion the most energy: the still uncertain relationship between the historical matter of the fourth book and the mythological
material of the fifth, and the knotty problem of the son's relationship
to the father. These two concerns, which appear unrelated, emerge in
Frankfort as factors of a single mythological context.

Maximus's attention has been directed to the *genetic* energies of
earth. He has attempted to put himself into some useful relationship

[25]*Kingship and the Gods: A Study of Ancient Near Eastern Religion as
the Integration of Society and Nature* (Chicago, 1948), p. 32.

to the Mother: "the Genetic is Ma," as he says in "Maximus, from Dogtown-II" (*Maximus* II, 9). From his invocation of Our Lady in "I, Maximus of Gloucester," to his birth from Blynman's Canal in "Wrote my first poems," Maximus seeks to answer a question which Olson posed to himself at least by 1948, in "Troilus":

> Why should love live
> when all that should enforce it fails
> this side of meaning
>   tearing off
> what love alone is key to, form
> that feature nature wore
> before man turned her, woman, whore.
>
> (*Archaeologist*, 3)

With the restoration of the feminine, those forms *do* begin to appear. Somewhat unexpectedly, there is a poem in "Maximus VI" entitled "*proem*" (*Maximus* II, 136–37): the *Maximus* at last has a beginning. The informing fact of the landscape becomes both Maximus's limitation and his responsibility:

>   —this is a precis
>   of land I am shod in,
>   my father's shoes.

As will become apparent in the following poems, Maximus is Horus, with Osiris in his arms. In the Egyptian conception of kingly succession there are only two generations: the father and the son. "Osiris," Frankfort tells us, "was life caught in the spell of death. Hence he was not a 'dying god' but—if the paradox be permitted, a dead god."[26] And it is his form which Horus both realizes and creates: "the Morphic / is Pa" (*Maximus* II, 9). As Horus, he is the local source of all order; as a potential Osiris, he is the *principle* of all order, which is revealed only in his death. Osiris is, in terms which are familiar to readers of the *Maximus*, the inertial force of creation, and his living son is an instance of it.

In the sequence of poems from "The Frontlet" (*Maximus* II, 145) through "at the boundary of the mighty world (*Maximus* II, 160–62), Maximus arrives at a vantage from which he can see his condition in terms of a single, coherent image of cosmic order. They represent a

[26]*Ibid.*, p. 185.

coming together toward which Olson had been reaching for thirteen
or fourteen years:

> All night long
> I was a Eumolpidae
> As I slept
> putting things together
> which had not previously
> fit.

(Maximus II, 157)

The feminine energy which has impelled the poem is suddenly embodied in the form of Ptah, the Egyptian creator god, the Primeval Hill or
"the Risen Land," who appears in the *Maximus* as Dogtown Hill. He
wears Our Lady of Good Voyage, who is now identified with Nut, as
a phylactery:

> Our Lady of Good Voyage sitting down on the front of the
> unnoticed head and body of Dogtown secretely come to
> overlook the City.

In "The Frontlet," however, she is still an ambiguous figure. As "the
Virgin / held up / on the Bull's horns," she is at once "The Great Goddess Tauroplus"—the manifestation of the eternal feminine by which
Merry sought to manifest his soul in "Maximus, from Dogtown-I"—
and Europa on the back of Zeus, their journey from Tyre to Crete
having extended itself to Gloucester (see *Maximus* II, 102), where
more Phoenician persons, like Minos, Rhadamanthys, and Sarpedon,
are to be born. Although "neither the exaction of sacrifice nor domination over the world of plants and animals, the instinctual world of
unconscious, is the central concern of the Great Goddess,"[27] as Neumann writes, she still appears in Gloucester in her most repressive
form, and Ptah is still passive, "Dogtown's / secret / head / & shoulder."

In "Homo Anthropos" (*Maximus* II, 146) Maximus looks to the
more ancient forms of the Eternal Feminine, in hopes of arousing her
in her obedience to "the Law of Transformation in which she subli-
mates all life and raises it to a development where, without losing its

---

[27]*The Great Mother*, p. 280.

bond with the root and foundation, it achieves the highest forms of psychic reality."[28] Behind Our Lady stands the Potniae, the powerful one, as the ancient triple goddess Hecate was called by the Greeks. There is an unfinished poem among Olson's papers, written about the same time as "Homo Anthropos," which celebrates "a goddess / of earth and heaven and sea."[29] She is not held up "into the light / of Portuguese / hill," like the Virgin, but, rather, "this is the goddess / on the *other side* of the light" (my italics). In "The Cow of Dogtown" (*Maximus* II, 148–50) Maximus recognizes that her force is literally the weather (*ta metarsia*), the shaping energy which pushed the pleistocene ice sheets down on Cape Ann, and formed the manifest body of Ptah:

> Nut is over you
> Ptah has replaced the Earth
> the Primeval Hill
> has gone directly
> from the waters
> and the mud
> to the Cow of Heaven
> the Hill stands
> free.

Like the Memphite theologians on whom he draws, Maximus runs the risk of paradox in accounting for the absolute primodiality of *both* Ptah and Nut. In their mutual primacy they are the "Homo Anthropos," the redeemed man of alchemy, and Sophia, who, as Neumann says, "not only forms the earth and heaven of the retort [i.e. the alchemical vessel, the womb, "the vault of heaven" (*Maximus* II, 158)] we call life, and is not only the whirling wheel revolving within it, but is also the supreme essence and distillation to which life in this world can be transformed."[30]

Ptah is the earth as obstructive fact, space and history, the earth manifest as external form. Nut is the world as experienced and lived, the *imago mundi* and the *anima mundi*, the earth manifest as internal energy:

[28]*Ibid.*
[29]"There is a goddess / of earth and heaven and sea," in *Olson: The Journal of the Charles Olson Archives*, 4 (Fall, 1975), 23–28.
[30]*The Great Mother*, p. 231.

> She leans
> from toe to tip of hands
> over the earth,
> making the Cow-sign
> with the earth.

Her force is downward, as Maximus evidences in "Stage Fort Park" (*Maximus* II, 151), and it is she who opens the way for the hero's direct encounter with the underworld in "Maximus, from Dogtown-IV." Ptah's force is upward. He is an avatar of the Diorite Stone, the growth principle of earth. In the third volume he will be transformed again into Enyalion, going forth to do battle.

The Egyptian account is confirmed by the Norse in "Licked man (as such) out of the ice" and "Gylfaginning VI" (*Maximus* II, 154–55), as it will be confirmed by the Vedic in "The Festival Aspect" (*Maximus* III, 73–75) and the other poems which arise from Heinrich Zimmer's *Myths and Symbols in Indian Art and Civilization*. Ptah and Nut become Shiva and Shakti. The ancient Indo-European culture had spread world-wide sometime aeons prior to the beginnings of the largely Romantic, post-Renaissance traditions which Pound traces in the *Cantos* and which have been the dominant concerns of western education. Maximus's City is grounded in a cosmology which the Norse brought to the Algonquins (see *Maximus* III, 23). It is therefore utterly unsullied by the energy-destroying generality and the paternalistic egotism of the more familiar history.

The cosmic conditions figured forth in Ptah and Nut are recapitulated in a more practical, political context in the story of Horus, Osiris, and Iris. These concerns will come to the fore in the third volume, when Maximus begins "to write a Republic," but Maximus is always a man of the City as well as, as he is so obviously in "Maximus VI," a man of the cosmos. The first lines of the poem—which begins "to enter into their bodies / which also / had grown out of / Earth" (*Maximus* II,147)—were first written in Olson's copy of Frankfort, in connection with this passage:

> It is argued that everything that exists found its origin in the conception of Ptah's mind ("heart"), which were objictified by being pronounced by his "tongue." In this process of creation, one god after another came into being; and through them Ptah evolved the visible and invisible universe and all living creatures, as well as justice, the arts, etc. This account imparts, at the same time,

the character of an established order, valid for all time, to the phenomenal world. The cities and sanctuaries of Egypt are part of this order. And the final phrase of the section [in the Memphite theology] closes the circle: while it had started by stating that the gods came forth from Ptah, objectified conceptions of his mind, it ends by making those gods "enter into their bodies" (statues) of all kinds of material—stone, metal, or wood—which had grown out of the earth, that is, out of Ptah.[31]

The specific reference in "to enter into their bodies" is to the recovery of Osiris from the flood by Horus, Isis, and Nepththys. Horus-Maximus himself draws the primal parents in his own conception. It is Horus, the god entered into his body, in the literal person of the king, who prevents Osiris from becoming a merely transcendent principle:

> he was as dust
> in the water
> the Monogene
> was in the water, he was floating
> away
>
> > oh I wouldn't let my Father
> > get away.

By calling to his mother, Isis, who retrieves Osiris from the water, he is re-embodied, and the process which, in its origins is obviously cyclical and seasonal, is renewed. In "Stage Fort Park" Maximus says, "I have eaten my father / piece by piece I loved my cannibalism" (*Maximus* II, 151).

Maximus is, in other words, literally "at the boundary of the mighty world," the point of contact between earthly, practical life and cosmic principles of energy. The line which Olson takes as his title or epigraph, in the poem which he sometimes called "Gravelly Hill" (*Maximus* II, 160–62), is from Hesiod's *Theogony*. In its original context it introduces the story of Typhon's battle with Zeus—the event which, in Maximus's reading of history, marks Osiris's escape, the loss of the intimate relationship between the cosmic principles and the chthonic and earthly embodiment of those principles. "Gravelly Hill" brings the *Maximus* to its first major conclusion. The earth has been made strange, as Maximus discovers in "Letter, May 2, 1959," but now, in Maximus's careful mapping, its familiarity and coherence

---

[31]*Kingship and the Gods*, pp. 27–28.

coherence are recovered. The earth can be known as precisely as any plot of a few acres. The very familiarity of Gravelly Hill may cause it to seem an insignificant location or merely an elaborate figure of speech. As a matter of fact, however, it *is* the cosmos in which Maximus defines himself. He merges with landscape, which appears as the motive force of both his biological processes and his poem.

The energy, which Maximus recognizes in "I, Maximus of Gloucester" only as a simple "crowding in" of perception, is revealed as the upward thrust of earth itself:

> Gravelly hill was 'the source and end (or boundary' of
> D'town on the way that leads from the town to Smallmans
> now Dwelling house, the Lower
> Road gravelly, how the hill was, not the modern usableness
> of any thing but leaving it as an adverb as though the Earth herself
> was active, she had her own characteristics, she could
> stick her head up out of the earth at a stop
> and say, to Athena I'm stuck here, all I can show
> is my head but please, do something about
> this person I am putting up out of the ground into your hands.

The image of Earth putting a person into the hands of Athena is a rendering of an archaic terracotta which Olson saw in Jane Ellen Harrison's *Themis*.[32] It show Cecrops, the most ancient of the Athenian heroes, pictured as a man with a serpent's tail, attending the birth of Erechtonius:

> My point is, the end of myself,
> happens, on the east side (Erechtonius)
> to be the beginning of another set
> of circumstance.

Like Hermes, Erechtonius is a god of boundary lines, the emanation of those zones between the known and the unknown, the familiar and the strange. Both Erechtonius and Hermes, as well as Cecrops, Harrison tells us, are *daimons*, and they are prior to Olympian gods and the "rationalistic" Homeric heroes. The complexity of such figures, the *daimons* who are represented in phallic and serpentine forms, is that they are associated with both fertility rites and funeral rites. She resolves this paradox by the fact that the *daimon* is "the representa-

[32]*Themis*, p. 263.

tion of collective emotion," and, though he is "a life-*daimon*, a spirit of generation, even of immortality," he becomes associated with funeral rites because he embodies "the immortality of the race, the people of a locale, rather than personal immortality."[33] The daimonic hero is the incarnation of a transpersonal condition of life as both temporal and spatial. He is *both* Horus and Osiris.

The world which Maximus defines is intensely private. It is difficult to say that he has himself become the *daimon* of Gloucester. His world does, however, *border* two other conditions; it is not locked into the rigidity of ego-privacy. It stands next to the underworld, on one side, and the city, on the other:

> It is Hell's mouth
> where Dogtown ends
> (on the lower
> of the two roads into
> the woods.
> I am the beginning
> on this side
> nearest the town
> and it—this paved hole in the earth
> is the end (boundary
> Disappear.

Gloucester is, for the time being, utterly obliterated. Its limitation is not that its institutions have gone astray or that its moral fiber has disintegrated but that it is world-less, it is no *place*. If Maximus is to become hero to the City, it is by virtue of the world which he has internalized, the fact that he knows where he is.

The vertical, in all of the forms which it has appeared—"the mast! the mast! the tender mast!," the volcanic unconscious, the Diorite Stone, Ptah—has had reference to the horizontal spaces. It has drawn to the Center, it has informed surrounding space, but it has had no content of its own. Maximus has dealt in a world in which, as Whitehead says, *statistical* probability applies. The process has been inductive and, potentially, within broad limits, predictable, or, at least, the possibilities for novelty and creativity have been played out inside an arena which is determined. The laws of statistical proba-

[33]*Ibid.*, p. 271.

bility which prevail in cases of radioactive decay, in the dynamics of human communities, or on actuarial charts are, Whitehead says, the product of a *social* environment in which both man and the physical world are mutually interacting constituents. The *Maximus*, however, takes its rise at a place and time in which that sense of participation in one's own experience has been lost. It seemed to Olson, when he was conceiving his master work, that for three millennia men had been ceaselessly attempting to interpose a concept of self-between themselves and that continuity of creative reality. All language, all knowledge, and all action had been so infected that men were largely ignorant both of themselves and the world they lived in. The poem to this point has been a reclamation of possibilities which any animal so complexly organized as man should claim simply by being alive, to know completely a statistical world inside and outside its physical organism. In "at the boundary of the mighty world," Maximus is able to realize *for himself* those advantages of which the Algonquin tale of the man-with-his-house-on-his-head told.

Beginning in "Maximus, from Dogtown-IV" (*Maximus* II, 163–72), Maximus begins to investigate the vertical dimension as sheer verticality, without any reference to horizontal space. The reality which begins to open, even though it continues to "involve" matters of geography and history, is defined strictly as Maximus's desire. In a very late piece, "The Animate versus the Mechanical, and Thought," Olson writes, ". . . man as love (plant, heliogeotropic) grows up and down, man as separateness (animal) disposes of himself by *sitio*" (*Prose*, 76). Maximus is no sooner *situated* than he begins to explore the heliogeotropic axis.

He may have been thinking of a passage in Harrison: ". . . in primitive communities this collective emotion [of which the *daimon* is the representative] focuses around and includes food interests and especially food-animals and fruit-trees. In consequence of this the daimon is conceived in animal and plant-form, as therimoph or phytomorph. Dionysos grows out of the sacrifice of the bull or the goat, or out of the sanctification of the tree."[34] The daimonic animal as creator of boundaries—laws and property lines, as well as cosmic boundaries—brings into existence regularities which are statistical laws of nature. That is, animal consciousness creates a world which is *know-*

[34]*Ibid.*, p. 261.

able but which, by its very advantage, limits the novelty which will, given a statistical order, probably occur. The animal condition tends toward mechanism precisely because it is a realization of genetic priorities. Mere plant-like animation, however, as the primordial instance of activity, is motion toward not "knowing" but "valuing."

Whitehead speaks of another principle of probability which is nonstatistical. The passage is worth quoting at some length both because of its specific relevance to "Maximus, from Dogtown-IV" and its bearing on the *Maximus* as a secular comedy as a whole:

> This principle expresses the prehension by every creature of the graduated order of appetitions constituting the primordial nature of God. There can thus be an intuition of an intrinsic suitability of some definite outcome from a presupposed situation. There will be nothing statistical in this suitability. It depends upon the fundamental graduation of appetitions which lies at the base of things, and which solves all indeterminations of transition.
>
> In this way, there can be an intuition of probability respecting the origination of some novelty. It is evident that the statistical theory entirely fails to provide any basis for such judgments.
>
> It must not be thought that these nonstatistical judgments are in any sense religious. They lie at a far lower level of experience than do the religious emotions. The secularization of the concept of God's functions in the world is at least as urgent a requisite of thought as is the secularization of other elements in experience.[35]

It is to experience of this nonstatistical kind which Maximus addresses himself in "Maximus, from Dogtown-IV." In his lecture at Beloit Olson says that it "was first published, deliberately, in the *Psychedelic Review*," and, although he does not say specifically why, it is evident that the poem represents one of those leaps into a reality in which appetite, rather than induction, was the motive force. ". . . I wanted it as an evidence of the process of poetry," he goes on to say, "as approaching truth with no other guise than itself" (*Beloit,* 14–15). Maximus takes the leap into a poetic in which, as he said in "A Later Note on Letter # 15," "no event / is not penetrated in intersection with, an eternal event" (*Maximus* II, 79). It is a poetic impelled not by the need to know but by love; it is not a process but an exercise of sheer intensity.

[35]*Process and Reality*, pp. 238–39.

In the narrative sequence the action of "Maximus, from Dog-town-IV" is prior to the events of "Maximus V." The poem is a re-working of Hesiod's *Theogony*, lines 620 through 880, the stories of the battle of the Olympians against the Titans, the birth of Typhon, and his last-ditch assault on Zeus. It is, as Olson says, the history of a period which saw the cosmic ascendance of "a curious mixed evil set who trouble thereafter all the established edicts of heaven and con-fuse the general cosmology" (*Prose*, 34).

The confusion which entered with the triumph of the Olympian gods was the intrusion of a purely human society on the all-inclusive cosmic society. "I find the contemporary substitution of society for the cosmos captive and deathly" (*Human*, 97), Olson writes, and that sense of "society" to which he objects appears with the ascendancy of Zeus. According to Norman O. Brown, "Zeus adds nothing to the physical cosmos; his divine cosmos is essentially a new order imposed on the human cosmos. . . . This new order for the human cosmos can be called civil society or political organization."[36] The organization which Zeus imposes in his victory over Cronus is reflected in the social order of the city states. The later Greeks took their stand against mor-tality in the suprapersonal order of the city. Because of the subsequent diminution of the political, we miss the force of Aristotle's definition of man as *zōon politikons*. Only in the public realm, where life could be conducted in terms of rational discourse, could man share the god's freedom from the necessities of biological life. The dualism un-der which men suffered in the Cronean age—said by tradition to be both a Golden Age and an age in which the law of the jungle pre-vailed—was internalized. Man was divided against himself, and genu-inely coherent action was rendered impossible. Cronus was bound in the underworld when it became possible to substitute the abstract time of political chronicles for the temporal fact of the human orga-nism. The public man potentially gained immortality through fame. Man as world-creating appetite was distinguished as private and thor-oughly mortal.

"Maximus, from Dogtown-IV" is an attempt to reawaken the hero as world-creating appetite. It is the third poem of Maximus's birth: he is born of earth as a poet in "Wrote my first poems"; he is born of earth as the earth's outward form in "at the boundary"; and

---

[36]"Introduction," in *Hesiod's Theogony* (New York, 1953), p. 25.

he is here born of Earth and Tartaros as Typhon. In one of the lectures at Beloit Olson says to his audience, ". . . think of yourself as an impediment of creation" (*Poetry*, 43), that is, as a social being who inhabits a world in which all hunger is only social, contained by the discourse of the city. The remainder of the *Maximus* is devoted to the removal of this impediment.

In "Fort Point Section" (*Maximus* II, 183–203) Maximus returns from Dogtown to the City and particularly to the neighborhood in which Olson lived. Maximus says:

> you drew the space in
> reticule
> now spread the iron net,
> Enyalion.
>
> (*Maximus* II, 184)

Maximus is, as a hero, no more than an adolescent. In "The Gate and the Center" Olson writes of a ritual among the Omaha in a passage which is relevant at this juncture: "A boy (or a girl, if she chose, though it was not required of the girl as it was of the boy) went out at 16, 17, alone into the woods, with nothing to take care of living, for three days of hunger & watch. The one end was, to woo a dream, and that dream, once it came, was, whatever its form, to be thereafter the SIGNATURE of that individual's life" (*Human*, 21). Atop Dogtown Hill, Maximus has his power dream, a vision of himself as the product of an earth so thoroughly known that its limits can be mapped in detail. In "Fort Point Section" he returns to a world of quotidien frustrations:

> So I console myself
> in the last spring discovering
> that down on the other side of the hill
> where Sam Novello who now owns the Federal Fort prop-
>   erty proper
> throws his rubbish up over the fence by the barking dogs
> who yell each time the city Fire Alarm goes off
> there is these days this peach tree bravely blooming
>
> (*Maximus* II, 185)

But Maximus must also give himself to practical concerns, such as the fortification of the City (see *Maximus* II, 185–87, 189).

Though Gloucester has had some experience with war (*Maximus*

II, 193–98), the City must prepare itself for a battle on a scale which it has never known. It is not sufficient to defend the City; it must prepare to carry its image of order forth into the whole of space:

> the heavens above
> do declare
> the handiwork
> of the orbits,
>
> and the axis
> of earth's day,
> and the sun's year on earth,
> are more important
> than the parietal
>
> the social
> is an undeclared war
> which, if there are damages
> no matter that the Congress
> will not support the President
> the problem then is whether
> a Federal organization
> or organization at all except it comes
> directly in the form of
> the War of the World
> is anything.
>
> (*Maximus* II, 197–98)

The war of Typhon against the Olympians is still to be waged, if man's order and the world's order are to coincide. The internal order of man or of the City—"the parietal," what goes on within the walls—is empty and pointless except that it bring a world order to focus.

In "*The River Map* and we're done" (*Maximus* II, 201–2) Maximus-Enyalion begins to "spread the iron net." The Annisquam River, which ebbs and flows with the tides, begins to carry the imprint of the blow of vision (typos) with which Maximus has been struck. According to tradition, "the river map" is the basis of the world order which the *I Ching* embodies. It is an image of the world as it is controlled by statistical probability. In its flowing the river tends to choke itself with the sand which its force carries along—"inspissate river / times repeated"—much as man becomes an impediment to his own creation, falls asleep, like the third Angel of the Ismaili cosmology, and is caught in the statistics of cyclical time. It is also, however, the river which flows "Between Heaven and Earth," and, despite the probabilities, it must be kept open. Maximus's journey up the river will be a dominant concern of the opening section of the third volume. As soon as he sets out "in a box upon the sea" (*Maximus* II, 203), he leaves the genetic, statistical cosmos of volume two behind. He has become the product of his own awareness. He has arrived at a point beyond which he can continue only as the product of his desire.

Chapter V

The Maximus Poems, Volume III

The third volume of the *Maximus* presents innumerable textual problems, and it always will. In a prefatory note Charles Boer and George Butterick, the men whom Olson chose as his editors, write:

> These poems were edited at Charles Olson's request from among his papers, now at the University of Connecticut Library. Some were published in periodicals before his death in 1970; the remainder were identified by the editors for inclusion.
>
> The arrangement is chronological (Spring of 1963 through November of 1969), following the precedent of the two previous volumes. The first and the last poems were designated as such by the author. (*Maximus* III, 5)

Other than the designation of the first and last poems, the editors apparently had few guidelines. The "manuscript" was an incredible jumble. Especially during the last years of his life, after the death of his wife, Betty, in March, 1964, Olson's time was filled with reading and writing. He gave up his teaching position at the State University of New York at Buffalo and devoted himself to the completion of the *Maximus*, but much of the material is obviously fragmentary. Poems would begin in the margins of a book or any scrap of paper at hand. Several of the poems are written on the backs of envelopes, and there are poems on paper placemats, apparently from a diner, even on the cardboard packaging for a Bic pen. Some of the poems exist in more than one version; only a few are in typed, fair manuscript or published versions.

For Olson, the making of a book was an extension of the process of making a poem. ". . . in composing," he says in "Projective Verse," "one lets-it-rip." The play of the mind among the syllables is the pure anarchy of creation. ". . . it is the LINE that's the baby that gets, as the poem is getting made, the attention, the control, that it is right here, in the line, that the shaping takes place, each moment of the going" (*Human*, 55). Similarly, from poem to poem Olson lets it rip, and it is in the volume that the shaping of the larger structures of the sequence takes place. *Maximus IV, V, VI* is a carefully made book, the juxta-position of poem to poem sweeping the fragments into a dynamic form. The meaning is often in the interstices. Even blank pages be-come elements of the design. Of course, we have no way to know what Olson would have done had the time arrived for him to edit the volume himself. His intention is always to bring into existence a new mind, and he has nothing but the present mind to guide him. The engagement with the poem, therefore, inevitably takes place in a blind-spot. The poem is a place of action rather than expression or rhetoric. Dwelling in that condition of intense, and blind, engagement with the written word is what Olson calls, in his later work, "logog-raphy": "Word writing. Instead of 'idea-writing' (ideogram, etc.). That would seem to be it" (*Prose*, 20). For Olson, thinking and writ-ing are one. To construct a book is retrospective work, a sorting through of the work done, to see what has accrued.

Boer and Butterick have faced this difficult situation, as far as I can tell, with care and responsibility. I doubt that Olson could have placed his manuscript in more reliable hands. They have rigorously followed Olson's precedent in the first two volumes, and, if it is not Olson's book, it has a great deal of Olson in it. Olson would have made, I imagine, a more challenging, perhaps a more surprising, book, but he would not have been required to be responsible to him-self in precisely the same sense his editors were. Boer and Butterick have clearly given us a beautiful text, at least for a beginning, one which includes the bulk of the finished and appropriate material. Their task was more to present the evidence of a poem than the poem itself, and so completeness seems more important than shapeliness. The inevitable textual problems can only be solved in the light of a firm understanding of the continuing form.

The third volume provides a conclusion to the *Maximus* only in the sense that it is an end. The process of the poem and the process of the life had so completely merged that it is difficult to imagine any other ending. Death is, after all, final but seldom conclusive. "I really wanted 10 years more," Olson told a visiting friend, during his final illness, "to look and listen and write."[1] To look, to listen, and to write were the three imperatives in which his life had declared itself. With a vision of what the eye and ear might be, he had understood that men were largely oblivious to their possibilities. Had he been given that additional decade, it is likely that Maximus would have seemed still to be on the brink of another momentous discovery. There would have been, one would guess, another volume or more. The process of the poem is an ever-expanding exploration of its own complexities. The subterranean lake which appears near the end of volume three (*Maximus* III, 191) is bottomless, and the forms which are hidden in its depths are self-creating shapes of what a man is as an engagement with archaic experience.

Inevitably, the reader of *The Maximus Poems, Volume Three*, like the editors, becomes involved in the making of the poem. Olson's characteristic tempo, his own special uses of his sources, the ground rules of the poem, are known. It is tempting to argue, when confronted with a piece which does not seem to fit, that it is not "true" Maximus, or even to feel that here or there there is a hole, something missing.

The tripartite divison of the third volume which I propose in this chapter is tentative and, admittedly, arbitrary. For Olson himself, the tripartite structure of the poem did not seem important enough, when he collected the first two books (*The Maximus Poems 1–10* and *The Maximus Poems 11–22*) and a new group of poems for the 1960 edition of *The Maximus Poems*, to mark the divisions. When he collected the second volume, however, he was sufficiently impressed by the significance and density of that structure not only to mark it but also to emphasize it in the title, *Maximus IV, V, VI*. Butterick and Boer tell us that on one occasion Olson referred to the third volume as "Books VII and After" (*Maximus* III, 5). The importance of the divisions is not so much to determine their limits with absolute accuracy as to preserve the continuing sense of a non-Euclidean three-in-one, one-in-three structure which is recapitulated again and again throughout the field of the poem, from the smallest structures to the largest.

[1]Quoted in Paul Kenyon, "Town's Own Poet, Charles Olson Dead," *Gloucester Daily Times*, Jan. 12, 1970, p. 1.

1

The seventh book of *Maximus* (I would suggest *Maximus* III, 9–65) develops concerns which are characteristic of the first and fourth: publication, the relationship of interior and exterior, methodology. In the third volume, however, these matters are not focused in their relationship to topology or typology but to tropology. Maximus is now "to write a Republic" (*Maximus* III, 9), to create the shared reality.

Paul Metcalf rightly points to Olson's assurance in the first volume that the poem can extend itself outward, "as political weapon." Maximus's confident address to the citizens of Gloucester is, without doubt, striking, and the cogency of the early Maximus is rooted in that persistent, and perhaps naive, belief that the poet is a man of power. "It is this political faith, this faith in the possible political power of the poem, that gives Volume One its early buoyancy," Metcalf goes on to say. "And the passage, through Volume One, Two and Three, is a record, among other things, of the gradual loss of that faith."[2]

It is true the third volume presents a somewhat diminished figure of the poet. He is neither the civic gadfly of the first volume nor the lord of creation, marking off the boundaries of the cosmos, of the second. Maximus/Olson appears more frequently as a lonely, sometimes almost pathetic, figure, haunting Gloucester at night, being watched by the police cruisers. The role of the poet as democratic bard, which Olson had tried to shed in "The Praises," has disappeared completely. His situation in the final volume is Homeric. It must be recalled that blind Homer may have been himself a somewhat pathetic character. He *is* pathetic in Maximus's account of him dying "on the road-side ruts from / having spent too long watching / & eating too little" (*Maximus* III, 211). Maximus's relationship to his material is Homeric in the sense which Eric Havelock defines it: "The Romantics sought to revive the conception of the poet as prophet and seer possessed of a unique vision of reality and a unique insight into things temporal. These powers, however, were conceived in a sense quite alien to those wielded by the Homeric poet. . . . They aspired but they did not inform."[3] The process is either utterly compelling, or it is not.

[2] "A Seismic Rift," *Parnassus: Poetry in Review*, 4, 2 (1976), p. 263.
[3] *Preface to Plato*, p. 145.

The poetry of the third volume is without device. There is not the slightest room for rhetoric or for any excitement but that which the poems themselves occasion. Havelock goes on to say: "The prince wields political power; he therefore is Zeus' child. The minstrel wields power over words; he therefore is the child of Apollo and the Muses. But the two kinds of power are somehow coeval, linked together."[4] The problem which Maximus faces is the failure of his political co-evals, who, like "the bewildered mob," are victims of "The Big False Humanism / Now on" (*Maximus* III, 11).

Yet in the third volume of *Maximus* the poem becomes for the first time *genuinely* political. It is no longer a "political weapon" or a mode of protest but the creation of a grounds on which politics can be, once again, practiced.

In the first book Maximus is a worker in space (topos), carrying *in* the bits and pieces of evidence which fit the design. As a political force, however, he is only a voice of right-mindedness, and though it is a true and beautiful voice, he demands a religious devotion to the City which his fellow citizens cannot or will not assume. He understands the problem, of course: as he says to Ferrini, "I . . . hark back to an older polis" (*Maximus* I, 20). But to hark back is not enough; Maximus must embody that older polis, to be it fully, and so he must give himself up entirely. In the fourth book space assumes a more active role in the process. The telluric forces which should be focused in the polis are focused in Maximus alone. The typological fact of experience—the way it strikes one—becomes more apparent: Maximus speaks of "the geography / which leans in / on me" (*Maximus* II, 15). Although it should be remembered that these are relative terms—topos, typos, and tropos are elements of structure which inform the entire poem—Maximus of volume two is receptive, still very much an Ishmaelian character, and the box in which he sets out upon the sea (*Maximus* II, 203) is, in a sense, Queequeg's coffin. It is in the third volume that he is to provide an image of a man as forceful as Ahab but who is not compromised by his infernal pact or driven by his relentless will. Melville, Olson says, "lived intensely his people's wrong, their guilt" (*Ishmael*, 15). The third volume of the *Maximus* is an attempt to provide a space for man in which the City can be a *sacred* place, without loss of its full secular advantage.

[4]*Ibid.*, p. 110.

The three stages of feeling which Olson derives from Whitehead in *The Special View of History* can be usefully recalled. The poem is taking its turn into the third stage. He says: "The first is that in which the multiples of anything crowd in on the individual; the second is that most individual stage when he or she seeks to impose his or her own order on the multiples; and the third is the stage called satisfaction, in which the true order is seen to be the confrontation of two interchanging forces which can be called God and the World" (*History*, 50). The first and second stages of feeling are obviously the dominant modes of experience in the first and second volumes respectively. The paradox of the third volume is that the end of the personal process is a denial of the personal. The form which begins to emerge excludes every perfection but its own. *The Maximus Poems, Volume III* is perhaps the first religious poem to have been written since the seventeenth century. Of course, an abundance of poetry has been cast in the dilemma of belief or has asserted a belief which the poet wished he had, but no one has so successfully established himself in his own being that he becomes an agent of "two interchanging forces which can be called God and the World." "I believe in religion," Maximus says, "not magic or science I believe in / society as religious both man and society as religious" (*Maximus* III, 55). The God which appears in the *Maximus*, however, is "fully physical" (*Maximus* III, 13). It is the God which Whitehead describes "as the lure for feeling, the eternal urge of desire."[5] He is not a final cause or creator but a principle of continuation which is no sooner manifest than it becomes the basis for a new beginning.

Like all American writers before him, Olson was obsessed with beginnings, with being the source, the Adam, with the Edenic landscape, or with returning to the source. These notions dominate our most overblown rhetoric and our highest poetry. How to begin what has *already* begun? How to return to the source that has disappeared utterly into the lost past? Olson's application to these paradoxes is radical, and he solved them, or he could have. In *The Maximus Poems, Volume Three*, American literature finds its beginning. This is not to judge Olson in relation to Pound or Whitman or Melville, only to recognize that after Olson we are no longer required to go back to anything, or to begin something anew with much self-consciousness

[5]*Process and Reality*, p. 406.

and braggadocio. We are not released from history, but we no longer need to "recover" it. It is *there*, as a commonplace fact. We need not again re-enact the mythos of the lost innocence or retrieve the lost Eden. The Olson-Maximus who appears in this volume is no longer a beginner, but he has *just* begun. Although the cost has been considerable, the light for which Maximus has waited begins to shine:

> Imbued
> with the light
>
> the flower
> grows down
>
> the air
> of heaven.
>
> (*Maximus* III, 18)

Butterick annotates this poem with a passage from *The Secret of the Golden Flower* which proves to be crucial throughout the remainder of the poem:

> Master Lu Tzu said: that which exists through itself is called meaning (*tao*). Meaning has neither name nor force. It is the one essence, the primordial spirit. Essence and life cannot be seen. It is contained in the light of Heaven. The light of Heaven cannot be seen. . . .
> The Golden Flower is light. What colour has the light? One uses the Golden Flower as an image. It is the true power of the transcendent one.[6]

A complex clot of cognate images and isomorphic forms arises from this passage, all of which are directly related to the nasturtium of "Tyrian Businesses" (*Maximus* I, 36) and the radically secular implications with which it is freighted.

Olson's presence, as apart from Maximus, is felt strongly in the third volume, but he is just an inhabitant of the world he has created. Although Maximus still appears as a colossal figure astride the halves of the world (*Maximus* III, 37), Olson-as-Maximus is seldom associated very directly or closely with the larger action of the poem. The tone has changed: Maximus now writes "in gloom." Both "the Big False Humanism / Now on" and the death of Betty—an event which

---

[6]C. G. Jung and Richard Wilhelm, *The Secret of the Golden Flower*, trans. Cary F. Baynes (Princeton, N.J., 1967), p. 23.

nowhere appears but which continually haunts all of these poems—
occasion a sadness, a sense of Maximus as vulnerable, that is new to
the poem. As a historian, finding out for himself the evidence of what
is said, he now appears, when he questions Mrs. Tarantino, perhaps
about the ghosts of Fort Point (see *Maximus* II, 177), as a busybody:

> You have a long nose, meaning
> you stick it into every other person's
> business, do you not? And I couldn't
> say anything
> but that I
> do.

(*Maximus* III, 10)

He is a tour guide, pointing out sights of interest in Gloucester, as in
"I told the woman" (*Maximus* III, 14), for example. He is an idler,
"overlooking creation" (*Maximus* III, 15). He obviously identifies
with the condylura cristata which he finds

> on Atlantic
> Street West
> Gloucester
> spinning on its
> star-wheel
> nose,
> in the middle of the
> tarvia.

(*Maximus* III, 26)

In order to end the ravages of the chaos, Maximus himself has been
maimed:

> the demon
> the canine
>
> head piercing
> right through the letter carrier
>
> trousers and into the
> bone, the teeth of Fenris
>
> craves and locks
> directly
>
> into
> the flesh, there isn't

> any room
> except for
>
> pieces, holes
> are left.

(Maximus III, 33–34)

The story to which Maximus alludes here is a dream which is confirmed by the story of Fenriswolf and Tyr. The tenous balance which prevails in Norse mythology is also the common condition of Maximus's world. Murray Fowler, on whom Olson depends for much of his Norse material, writes:

> The world of duration is seen as the constant battle ground of conflicting forces, both of which are necessary for existence. The armed truce is characteristic. One of the finest qualities of this religion, therefore, is the natural result of its most typical one—that is, the sense of tense alertness everywhere; the gods preserve themselves only by constant watchfulness; the universe exists only in perilous balance between growth and decay; and all things that are: gods, men, animals, plants, rocks—are doomed to eventual disintegration and return to chaos.[7]

Or, as Maximus says:

> the Alligator,
> clapping at my balls
>
> the Soul
> rushing before.

(Maximus III, 48)

In his lexicon he marked the etymology of "chaos": "the gaping jaws of the crocodile."

Although personal life in this cosmos is tenuous and difficult, it is conducted in a realm where ecstatic insight and moments of beautiful, alert restfulness are possible. The effective form of the third volume, to the extent that it emerges, is prismatic or radial. The light of heaven *does* begin to show its secular colors. In the non-Euclidean geometry of the poem the Poles of Bond's Hill (see *Maximus* II, 16) and the North Pole, which is for Maximus also the "novo siberskie slovo," begin to coincide. The center, which Gloucester has become,

[7]"Norse Religion," in *Forgotten Religions*, ed. Vergilius Ferm (New York, 1950), pp. 245–46.

is also a center in the unformed sludge of the cosmos—Pytheas's Ultima Thule. The vertical axis on which the action of the poem has turned begins to refract the light of heaven across the face of the earth.

The somewhat enigmatic figures of the Bulgar and his sons appear in the radial torque of this new coincidence (*Maximus* III, 35–36). "The twist," both as a methodological feature and as an image of the poem's central mystery, is reintroduced as the literal turning of the sun through the seasons, the turning of the earth's crust, the turning of the rose of the world, and the widdershins confusion which both Maximus and the condylura cristata suffer. The Bulgar, like Enyalion, is a complex figure. He is associated with the Rainbow Bridge which passes from heaven to earth (Bifrost of Norse mythology; see *Maximus* II, 169), and he shares something with Horus, who "hides in his father's brother's thighs / his own four sons." Although it would be possible to speculate further, it is clear that he is a superterrestrial equivalent of the subterranean Typhon. In a note among the unpublished papers Olson writes,

> to the t[op] of the w[orld] (wholly opposite to
> e[nd] of the w[orld]—actually *outside*)
> & t[op] is the same as Bulgar's—or colorful sides of.[8]

Existing "actually outside" of the world, the Bulgar is in the realm of the imaginary. Heaven does not have a location, as Hades does. It is the future, the always receding potentiality, and until it is realized— and, so, becomes something else—it can only be seen reflected in the philosopher's stone, the Golden Flower, the figures of the imagination.

"The Bulgar emerges," Maximus says, "to take anything / up in his arms," and his appearance here is auspicious. As Maximus begins to "spread the iron net" (*Maximus* II, 184), to include the Republic in the coherence which appeared to him in "Gravelly Hill," the Bulgar is the first sign of the more inclusive coherence which the third volume proposes. In "Astride," "rages," "7 years & you cld carry cinders in yr hand" (*Maximus* III, 37–42), and in a fourth poem which I believe should be included here, "The Song of Ullikummi" (*Archaeologist*, 236–37), Maximus arrives at a second definitive statement of his mappemunde. In *Causal Mythology* Olson reads these four poems and identifies them all as "from the *Maximus*" (*Myth*, 3), and he says, "I mean I'm excited by this series of four poems. They represent for

[8]Copyright by the University of Connecticut Library.

me an out break of much that the *Maximus* had been approaching for me for the ten, fifteen previous years" (*Myth*, 19). The lecture itself is, without doubt, the most useful commentary on them to be found. The four poems represent a fuller analysis of the components of "the Divine Inert," from "Some Good News" (*Maximus* I, 122), which begins in "Later Tyrian Business" (*Maximus* II, 36). Finally, that mode of perception which Whitehead calls "causal efficacy" becomes fully operative. Whitehead writes:

> To take an example, the slight eye-strain in the act of sight is an instance of regional definition by presentational immediacy. But in itself it is no more to be correlated with projected sight than is a contemporary stomach-ache, or a throb in the foot. The obvious correlation of the eye-strain with sight arises from the perception, in the other mode, of the *eye* as efficacious in sight. This correlation takes place in virtue of the identity of the two regions, the region of the eye-strain is so immeasurably the superior in its power of regional definition that, as usual, we depend upon it for explicit geometrical correlations with other parts of the body. In this way, the animal body is the great central ground underlying all symbolic reference. In respect to bodily perceptions the two modes achieve the maximus of symbolic reference, and pool their feelings referent to identical regions. Every statement about the geometrical relationships of physical bodies in the world is ultimately referable to certain definite human bodies as origins of reference. A traveller, who has lost his way, should not ask, Where am I? What he really wants to know is, Where are the other places? He has got his own body, but he has lost them.[9]

The reason for Olson's excitement in these four poems is that he has not only located himself but that, henceforth, he also knows where the other places are. On the one hand, Maximus is utterly dispersed, as an active geography which is simultaneously the whole of earth and history, existing through themselves, and, on the other, he exists through *himself* as an *imago mundi* and an *anima mundi*.

In "Astride the Cabot fault" the energy of "the volcano anyone of as does sit upon" (*Maximus* II, 1) is re-envisioned as the literal movement of the earth's shifting crust, and Maximus is the center holding the halves of the world together. He is both the victim of that power and evidence of it. As "the Diorite Stone / to be lopped off the

[9]*Process and Reality*, pp. 197–98.

left shoulder" and as Tyr, he is maimed in his effort to bring earth to coherence. As an *imago mundi*, however, Maximus-Enyalion is an image of possibility. In this dimension he can grow; he can become an image of the perfections of the earth which coincide absolutely with his own.

A similar relationship obtains between "7 years & you cld carry cinders in yr hand" and "The Song of Ullikummi," but they define conditions which are transpersonal and political rather than individual. The *imago mundi* is masculine and morphological; the *anima mundi* is feminine and genetic. The *imago mundi* is the form of the landscape; the *anima mundi* is the energy which is revealed in and through the landscape as history.

"7 years & you cld carry cinders in yr hand" is a revision of "Some Good News," "Stiffening, in the Master Founders' Wills," and "Capt Christopher Levett" (*Maximus* I, 120–35). John Winthrop, who is dismissed in the first volume as a sign of Cartesian rigidity, is restored. He appears now as an avatar of the maimed hero:

> he was broken
> on the wheel   his measure
>   was broken   Winthrop's
> vision was broken he was broken the country
> has walked away.

(Maximus III, 41)

Although Winthrop's restoration begins in "JW (from the Danelaw) says" (*Maximus* II, 135), he is now John Wanax, the High King of the Mycenaeans and the carrier of the archaic vision. He can be heard again precisely because the resurgence of the archaic in the figure of Maximus allows him a language which had not been available. "Hesiod," according to Havelock, speaks "of the Muse 'consorting' with the prince: this symbolizes the minstrel standing by his side, attendant to his words which he is to reframe in *epe* for the audience."[10] The wanax does not rule by virtue of the petty tyranny of Charles II, whom William Stevens refuses to obey, or the tyranny of bureaucracy, such as ground Olson's father down (see *Maximus* III, 30–34); his power rests solely in the image of the polis and its relationship to the earth as it is bodied forth in his speech.

[10]*Preface to Plato*, p. 110.

The "realer" condition, Olson says, however, is not the literal, compromised City but the causal myth which informs the city as an image of possibility. The story which is told in "The Song of Ulli-kummi" concerns the conception of the Diorite Stone itself. In a sense, it adds nothing which is not present in the second volume of the *Maximus*. Ullikummi is a Hurrian-Hittite cousin of Typhon, whose conception is told in "Maximus, from Dogtown-IV," but the Hurrian-Hittite version of the tale is more ancient and so, for Olson, closer to the source. He has not yet been driven so deeply into the underground, and, like the Bulgar and Enyalion, he is a dimension of the unconscious brought directly into the light of heaven. In the context of the four poems of this group, moreover, the largely personal unconscious of the second volume comes directly into a relationship with the City as public fact. The cosmic vision which Maximus comes to possess is abstract, without its full content, until it is realized in the Republic.

The *Maximus* never comes to a more conclusive statement of its process than is contained in these four poems. The remainder of "Maximus VII" is a ritual celebration of Maximus's success. The form that is love is now a fact of the geography:

> To have the bright body of sex and love
> back in the world—the moon
> has her legs up.
> in the sky of Egypt.
>
> (*Maximus* III, 52)

Nut and Geb are figured forth in Gloucester as a simple "view":

> the sky,
>
> of Gloucester
>
> perfect bowl
>
> of land and sea.
>
> (*Maximus* III, 57)

And Maximus is initiated as the Perfect Child, not of the Ocean, as he is in the second volume, but of the City:

> I am the
> Child, Jupiter
> *furens* — Ocean's
> Child; I am
> Round Rock Shoal

> I am the one from whom the Kouretes
> bang their platters.
>
> (*Maximus* III, 58)

The reason for Maximus's birth as Jupiter is not immediately clear. Jupiter is, after all, one of the "bosses" of the patriarchal pantheon whom Maximus and Olson consistently oppose. The situation is not so mystifying, however, when we begin to inquire into the ritualistic sources of the political-religious order which the birth of Jupiter *furens* initiates.

Olson's source in this passage is Jane Ellen Harrison. She explains that "the Kouretes are armed and orgiastic dancers" whose function it is to defend the new-born hero, but the original context of these rites is not, in the familiar modern sense, "religious." The celebration of death and resurrection which is associated with the traditional rites of passage bears much more directly on the social life of the group than on the spiritual life of the individual. She writes: "At and through his initiation the boy is brought into close communion with his tribal ancestors: he becomes socialized, part of the body politic. Henceforth he belongs to something bigger, more potent, more lasting, than his own individual existence: he is part of the stream of the life, one with the generations before and yet to come." [11] At last Maximus comes into a sense of being in which he is the embodiment of the City as both political and sacred, a context in which one is both saved and made a citizen by the same rite. In his notes from the Vancouver Poetry Conference in 1965, Clark Coolidge reports Olson as saying, "Supreme Court knocks out Lord's Prayer just at the moment when it becomes valid again." [12] It is once again possible to live the images of the sacred and the images of the social without separating either from the cosmic. Olson's revision of Whitmanian democracy is to propose a ritualistic practice in which *everyone* is reborn as Jupiter.

In "Maximus, from Dogtown-II" Maximus speaks of himself as gnostic figure of the monogene, "the only begotten," as Jung tells us, who dwells in the monad, which is *also* "the Mother-City." [13] The

[11]*Themis*, p. 19.

[12]"Notes Taken in Classes Conducted by Charles Olson at Vancouver, August, 1963," *Olson: The Journal of the Charles Olson Archives*, 4 (Fall, 1975), 118.

[13]*Psychology and Alchemy*, trans. R. F. C. Hull (New York, 1953), p. 104.

monogene, however, is dispersed in time. He is uncreated, and Maximus's task is to

> brang that thing out,
> the Monogene
>
> the original unit
> survives in the salt.

(Maximus II, 72)

In "to enter into their bodies" (*Maximus* II, 147) Maximus as Horus, the son, manages to prevent the Monogene (i.e. the father, Osiris), "who comes to the skirt / of the City," from floating away, but he must invoke the aid of his mother. In "Maximus VII" Maximus tells us, in a poem which I take to be the conclusion of the book, "There was a salt-works at Stage Fort" (*Maximus* III, 64–65). The implication is obvious: Maximus has brought out "the original unit" which "survives in the salt."

2

Through the first two volumes Maximus is obedient to a genetic design. Seeking to realize the primal parents in himself, he lives out the forms of a history and a geography which are known or knowable. In "Maximus VIII" he reaches that point in the familiar story at which, it seems to him, some horrible confusion or grotesque mutation begins to grasp the genetic dialectic. In terms of Greek mythic chronology, he is in that shadowy time of transition from the second to the third divine generation. In the emerging order, another dialectic generates itself inside the organic: images are divorced from things, words from objects, language from memory, the City from the world—all together producing an abstract parody of the evolutionary process which has prevailed.

The attraction is, of course, power, personal power. If it is possible to become utterly subjective, to withdraw totally into a rational universe of discourse, one enters a realm of eternal essences, where it is possible to overcome the uncertainties and dangers to which mere flesh is liable. In "The New Empire" (*Maximus* III, 66–67) Maximus paraphrases Otto Rank's assessment of the development of the Self: "there is Mother (family), father (heir)—& Self. Self, he says (hero, poet, psychoanalyst, in that / order (!)." The knowledge of self is transformed from a concrete, visible form to an abstract form which requires professional interpretation. One mystery of the self is exchanged for another which is less immediate, conjectural rather than absolute, and only apparently more powerful, because it locates the source of power *in* man. Maximus assesses Rank's theory in unequivocal terms: "boo, Rank." The New Empire cannot be grounded on the endless recapitulation of ever more abstract heroic postures. "Procreation," Maximus says, is "a secondary function of man." He speaks of a man who, rather, spills "out his being," who has "the axis, unwearingly revolving in the act of *initial* creation" (my italics). Maximus must engage in the process of myth-making at a point beyond which the ritual and repetition that has successfully carried him this far is of no further use.

The eighth book (*Maximus* III, 65–176), like the second and the fourth, deals with the great migration, but it is no longer a prenatal condition. Maximus now confronts it as the determining factor of his adulthood. The hero-father can know only the earth, the body which is, for him, the center of earth, and the City, which is an organization of men and women, each, likewise, centers to themselves. Walking with his son on Cole's Island, however, Maximus has his first encounter with Death himself:

> My impression is we did—
> that is, Death and myself, regard each other. And
> there wasn't anything more than that, only that he had appeared,
> and we did recognize each other—or I did, him, and he seemed
> to have no question
> about my presence there, even though I was uncomfortable.
>
> (*Maximus* III, 69)

The old estrangement temporarily returns, and Maximus is athwart precisely that experience which first fed the intuition that some *other* world, in which this discomfort is avoidable, is possible: the self need only become to itself an image of transcendent reality to avoid the encounter with death.

Those who would be pleased to find only a complex revelation of the archetype of the self in the *Maximus* will find support in both "Maximus VII" and "The Secret of the Black Chrysanthemum" (*Olson*, III, 64–92), the piece which Olson wrote on the deathbed, but that is only half of Maximus's story and interesting only because of the other half, which, in effect, denies it. The usefulness of Olson's work is that it proposes the impossible and dwells in it. We are of the world, in its space, history, gravity, the field of whatever gods shape and energize the world, and it is, as we know it, of us, as percept, dream, and the public dreaming called "myth." For better or worse the two halves of the world never completely coincide. We are, despite all of our stratagems, finite, and, if the world is not infinite, it is larger than we. In the *Maximus* these two forms play against one another, alternately reinforcing and frustrating one another. At the moment when they appear to be moving toward congruence, some irreducible surd manifests itself, or some wholly unexpected dimension obtrudes, and what is gained is an expansion of the space in which life is conducted. The two—they might be called "the genetic" and "the morphological," to be in keeping with Olson's usage—are everywhere in touch with one another, but only in death and transcendentalism do they coincide.

"Maximus VIII" is a radical, pragmatic investigation of what can be called perhaps "the gates of transcendentalism." Maximus undertakes to determine where his own world joins the transcendental nonspace, much as, in the second volume, he locates its jointure with the underworld. In the lectures at Beloit, delivered about two years after most of the poems in "Maximus VIII" were written, Olson incidentally summarizes the movement through this section. The material which was, in the earlier volumes, more or less unrealized dream is now a specific and identifiable migration of the mind and soul through its own possibilities:

> I think it may be Gerhard Dorn that argues it as closely as I am going to. That, as a creature of, as creatures of organism, the original difficulty is that of the soul having its chance to realize its separateness from the body; but that only the mind can free it from its fetters to the body. . . . There're three things that are going on at the same time, as these three parts of you are seeking to reach a fourth: that you have to pass through composite nature, things of composite nature, things of dispersed nature, and you arrive at a point where the mind refuses the soul any further progress, will *not* let the soul into the heaven of itself. And at that gate . . . you suddenly have nothing but matter. (*Poetry*, 57–58)

"The soul, / in its progressive rise," which begins in "Maximus, at the Harbor" (*Maximus* II, 70–71), here reaches its limit. It cannot extend itself beyond because, as he says, quoting Al'Jabir, the Ismaili alchemist, "in natural things, there is a *veritas efficaciae*" (*Poetry*, 56). The soul can migrate through the natural to the limits of its efficacious truth, to the very gates of the transcendental paradise, but it can never enter. The mind, however, conceives of a further possibility, of a paradise which might be, like the City, fully secular. Olson speaks of "the world which prevents, but once felt, enables your being to have its heaven" (*Poetry*, 58). Maximus begins to confront the paradox with which Ludwig Wittgenstein is concerned in the closing pages of the *Tractatus*: "If the good or bad exercise of the will does alter the world, it can alter only the limits of the world, not the facts—not what can be expressed by means of language."[14] In the third volume the limits of the world are so expanded that they at least approach the total revelation of the Real, in one dimension, and death, in another.

The somewhat unlikely context for these considerations is not the *Theogony*, as may seem appropriate, considering Olson's insistence that it is one of the earliest documents of western culture's wrong turn, but the so-called Vinland map, which was published in 1965.[15] It seems to prove that the Norse had settlements in North America by or before the end of the first millennium A.D., and in "*The Vinland Map* Review" Olson proposes that this new evidence adds significantly to the sense of history developed by Brooks Adams in *The New Empire* (see *Maximus* III, 66–67), a book to which Pound had called his attention in the 1940s. In 1954 Olson wrote a short note on Adams, whose overview of history he summarizes in these terms: ". . . in civilization nothing is at rest, the movement is trade, the necessity is metals, and the consequent centralization of power also moves" (*Human*, 135). The important fact which the Vinland map adds to Adams's picture is that the twelfth-century shift from land travel as the basis of the economic system put the Norse squarely in the vanguard of the cultural advance: ". . . Norse *sea* abilities of the 10th century by the end of the *12th* had in fact become the *virtue* of Europe itself. Thenceforth, the withdrawal or conversion of all Norsemen on all three sides including their own center to the 'new system' (out of which, in the 13th arose the mindedness of which generally our own

---

[14]*Tractatus Logico-Philosophicus*, trans. D. F. Pears and B. F. McGuinness (London and New York, 1961), p. 147.

[15]R. A. Skelton, Thomas E. Marston, and George Painter, eds., *The Vinland Map and The Tartar Relation* (New Haven, Conn., 1965).

power and acculturation is still a weakening instance" (*Prose*, 60). The Norse, in other words, not the Renaissance Europeans, are the archaic instance of modernity and are, for that reason, crucial if the inherited paradise of the New World is to be revealed. The Norse retained something of the ancient Indo-European sense of the world as a totality and brought an image of man as equal to that totality to the New World:

Norse are

able to

travel

to America

to Russia

to all but China

in the 2nd half

of the Christian

Era they travelled

as Greeks Vedic Indians Irish travelled likewise

in the 2nd

B.C.

(*Maximus* III, 77)

From Maximus's point of view the harsh Norse theology is, for the westerner, the most immediate instance of the ancient coherence which is otherwise developed by Vedic transcendentalism. "The care anyway, in any of this, is to improve, or re-gain an attention, which off-hand would seem to have been lost, for Europe and, subsequently, for the West sometime around 1225 AD and certainly decisively by 1250" (*Prose*, 67–68). In an attempt to rejoin that ancient tradition, Maximus turns to Hindu mythology, to find in Shiva a figure who rimes with and enlarges Enyalion.

"Sweet Salmon" (*Maximus* III, 72) seems to stand almost as a ritual preparation for the poems which follow—like a prayer one repeats when he is about to invoke some magic which he knows to be dangerous. Maximus assures himself that he has tasted the salmon whose flesh confers wisdom and that he has "A home / for life." The task at hand is to bring an even more commodious home into the secular world.

The ultimate truths of the transcendental absolute cannot, of course, be spoken. Heinrich Zimmer, whose *Myths and Symbols in*

Indian Art and Civilization is the source of "The Festival Aspect"
(*Maximus* III, 73–75), writes, "Brahman-Atman, the All in all of us,
surpasses human reason, cannot be conceived of by the human imagination, and cannot be described; yet It can be experienced as the very
Life within us (*atman*), or intuited as the Life of the cosmos (*brah-
man*)." [16] Maximus has said what can be said; he is now faced with
the problem of making a reality directly manifest. Taken as discourse,
which it first appears to be ("The World / has become divided / from
the Universe," etc.), "The Festival Aspect" is literally non-sense. The
story of the Three Town to which it refers is told by Zimmer, but in
large measure the narrative is only the melody for an improvisation
which adds paradox to paradox. In a later poem Maximus will say:

> Here in the Fort my heart doth
>
> harden,
>
> Or my will does, and my
>
> heart
>
> goes
>
> far far
>
> farther
>
> Into the Diagram.

(Maximus III, 103)

Although the forms of the absolute can be neither visualized nor spoken, they can be witness. The "Diagram" is Zimmer's generic term for
all of those self-destroying forms which endeavor to make the invis-
ible and unspeakable manifest, the parables, the *yantras*, the paradoxical phenomena which reveal the paradoxical realities.

Zimmer writes of the sense of "growing, or expanding, form" in
certain works of Hindu art—the form which extends beyond itself
and involves the transcendental space in its dynamics. Of one sculp-
tural monument, he says:

> While Brahma and Vishnu speed in opposite directions, the sub-
> stance of the stone correspondingly expands outmeasuring their
> movement. The solid rock is apparently animated by an energy
> of growth. The niche-like split in its side seems actually to be
> widening, unfolding, to disclose the anthropomorphic apparition

[16] Joseph Campbell, ed. (New York, 1946), pp. 142–43.

within. The solid, static mass of the stone, by a subtle artifice of the craftsman, has been converted into a dynamomorphic, multiple event.[17]

In a sense the whole of the *Maximus* is an expanding form. Olson's insistence upon stance as one of the three (with fact and space) "locations" in the Real is required by the need to find a solid, stone-like, *and* responsive point of rest between two dynamic processes. "The Festival Aspect," however, appears to be a specific attempt to establish an expanding form, a "balance between the dynamism of manifestation—process—constant evolution, and the serene, static repose of eternal being."[18]

The Three Town, which again recall the triune form of the *Maximus*, are the earth, the middle space or atmosphere, and the firmament or sky. As the story goes, they are captured by a tyrant named Maya who, through his yoga, consolidates the Three Towns as his fortress, "a single, prodigious center of demonchaos and world-tyranny."[19] He is obviously the ultimate instance of what Maximus would call a "pejorocrat." Only Shiva, of all of the gods in the pantheon, has the necessary strength to recapture the world. He is the God as conqueror and liberator of the world, a figure whose power, like Enyalion's, is in the image of his own perfect proportions. When his arrow pierces the fortress of Maya, Zimmer says, "The tyrannies of the fearful yet fearsome ego, brutal with inconsequential ambitions and lusts, are dissolved at a stroke. The energies of universal existence, freely pouring again from the transcendental sources, break through all the worlds, and the cosmos sings with the tingle of regenerated life."[20]

In "The Festival Aspect," however, that fortunate time has not appeared, or, more accurately, it has appeared again and again—and the regenerated life is embodied in the expanding form of the poem— but it stands in no immediate relationship to the on-going processes of the *Maximus* as a whole. Through roughly the first half of "Maximus VIII," Maximus bends himself to the task of bringing the Third Town into existence and, as the demand seems to be, simultaneously

[17]*Ibid.*, p. 131.
[18]*Ibid.*, p. 136.
[19]*Ibid.*, p. 185.
[20]*Ibid.*, p. 187.

to destroy it. The migrations, which have been the persistent linear force of history, have been, in effect, a search for the third town, and at Gloucester it reaches its goal:

> Migration in fact (which is probably
> as constant in history as any *one* thing: migration
>
> is the pursuit by animals, plants & men of a suitable
> —and gods as well—& preferable
>
> environment; and leads always to a new center.
>
> (Maximus III, 176)

The center is, of course, where the Three Towns are captured and consolidated by Maya, as well as where they are destroyed by Shiva: "The War / of the World / is endlessly / poised" (*Maximus* III, 99). It is at this point of tense engagement that the tropos begins to appear. In a poem which begins "Physically, I am home"—that is, simply and comfortably an occupant of space—Maximus says:

> Heaven is,
> mental. No Viewpoint,
> from within. No "height" (no Face
> of God, no clogging
> in the light. Night
> is solely
> an elipse
> by the Earth
> of the Sun. Night is solely
> not day.
>   Heaven
> is a condition,
> likewise. Heaven is
>   Mind (drawn to
> Gloucester.
>
> (Maximus III, 86)

If there is a release from the War of the World, other than cosmic dissolution, it arises not from a *denial* of the soul's space-time—by some exaggeration of man's place in the order of things—but from man's achievement of a reality which is completely and brutally physical. Heaven is not—like Hades—a geography which man embodies:

there is "No Viewpoint, / *from within*." In *The Special View of History* Olson recalls the passage in Keats concerning "negative capability." He says:

> To stay in mysteries, uncertainties, doubts, then, is Keats' way of talking about staying in process in order to realize the ontogenetic in the face of the phylogenetic, not to slip into the error of trying to fix things by an irritable reaching after fact and reason. The emphasis here is irritable, which is man's tease to know by stopping. . . . And he can't: if he stops it he gets a half, which will turn out to be only his proper self or his ego or Character, an imposition, POWER. (*History*, 42)

The heaven which begins to appear in the third volume is achieved by precisely such negativity. Maximus must go *through* everything, beyond himself, beyond any power of himself, all the way through both life and death, and the ultimate trop—whatever it is—emerges only as he comes out on the other side. Maximus stakes his paradise on perhaps the most fundamental intuition of Indo-European culture: that the absolute is to be known only through the endless process of resurrection and death which is imaged in the turning of the seasons. Those gods whose rituals involve the seasonal fertility of the earth are the only legitimate counterparts to the Great Mother which presides over the second volume. Maximus says:

> There are 70 odd "forms", there are 70 chances at
> revealing
>
> the Real. The Real
>
> renews itself each year, the Real
>
> is solar, life is not, life is 13 months long each years. Minus
>
> one day (the day the sun turns). The Sun
>
> is in pursuit of itself. A year
>
> is the possibility, the Real
>
> goes on forever.
>
> (*Maximus* III, 90)

The expansion in the durations which Maximus proposes to grasp is immense. In "I, Maximus of Gloucester" he seeks to respond instant by instant to the measure of the breath. The cycle from one turning of the sun to next, however, is the totality of time, as the literal, graspable earth is the totality of space. Maximus's measure is now what seems almost the breath or the rhythm of the earth.

Maximus begins to see himself as a monk of his process, sacrificing everything, including "sex and woman . . . to this attempt to acquire complete concentration" (*Maximus* III, 101). He must locate the point at which the whole continues to turn and, at the same time, reveals its own completion:

> Half Moon beach ("the arms of her")
> my balls rich as Buddha's
> sitting in her like the Padma
> —and Gloucester, foreshortened
> in front of me. It is not I,
> even if the life appeared
> biographical. The only interesting thing
> is if one can be
> an image
> of man, "The nobleness, and the arete."

In his reach for that perfection the very words on the page begin to revolve around the Center, making "the rose" which "is the rose is the rose of the World" (*Maximus* III, 104). In "The winter the *Gen. Starks* was stuck" (*Maximus* III, 105–6), written on December 2, 1965, the winter solstice, Maximus seems to speak in full confidence that this is the year in which the Real will finally be revealed:

> if I twist West I curl into the tightest Rose, if right
> into the Color of the East, and North and South are
> then the Sun's half-handling of the Earth. These aspects,
> annular-Eternal—the tightest Rose is the World, the Vision
> is the Face of God—in this aspect the Nation
> turns now to its Perfection. Its furthest or its highest
> Point, its Limit now reached, the Imagination of it
> here or anywhere men in duress or need in thought which taken
> is belief, go on the frozen being and do take the marks and
> bearings.

And Maximus himself is the year-god, preparing for this fresh opportunity:

> The whole thing has run so fast away it breaks my heart
> Winter's brilliance with the sun new-made from living south
> I also re-arisen another numbered year from December's
> threat. Love all new within me ready too to go abroad.
>
> (*Maximus* III, 108)

Maximus also confronts the dark aspects of his new identity, however. He asks, "Has March now been added so I have to live a 2nd month of fear & Hell each year? / And is it therefore possible that a Year of Man wld end in 12 such months of livid Hell?" (*Maximus* III, 112). The cosmic economy is cannibalistic, always extracting a death for the new rebirth.

"a 3rd morning it's beautiful" (*Maximus* III, 114–16) is a retrospective poem, looking back over the work which had accrued during the previous year, since "The Festival Aspect." It had been a difficult year for Olson. It is perhaps unfortunate that the editors chose not to include some of the poems concerning the death of his wife. Although he consistently rejected what he called "affective poetry," Betty's death left both him and Maximus disoriented. In October, 1964, he wrote a sequence of poems addressed to her, and they would have added resonance to the poems which followed:

> I went full tilt
> and then she was killed
> in her automobile
>
> > I need every bleeding minute now
> > I don't have any time for any new life.[21]

And in another poem, which seems to have the characteristic movement of the *Maximus*, he says:

> Her skin
> covered me, let light into me, held
> my nature, kept me
> for myself, and I wasn't Sorry
> to be closer. In the horrors and transparent
> policy
> of the present.[22]

[21]Copyright by the University of Connecticut Library.
[22]Copyright by the University of Connecticut Library.

In the *Maximus* of 1964 and 1965 it seems that the hero—to the extent that he is distinct from Olson himself—is at once most hopeful and most desperate. In "Human Universe" Olson says, "Plato may be a honey-head, as Melville called him, but he is precisely that—treacherous to all ants, and where, increasingly, my contemporaries die, or drown the best of themselves" (*Human*, 5). Maximus is never in greater danger of falling into the honey-head himself than he is during these years.

In "a 3rd morning" (*Maximus* II, 114–16) Maximus recognizes that he has reached another limit of his world, that he can go no further in the direction the poem has been moving. In "Gravelly Hill" he stands at one "boundary of the mighty world," and now he stands at the other:

> And I heard the soul, I had successfully walked
> round the Three Heavens—the Three Towns, the
> trimurta
> And was, in this last month and this
> winter seeking
> another step (or objecting, in my soul & to my soul
> at fate, I was indeed planning
> to walk around the higher world, to go as my cormorant flies
> if such a short distance   when those words
> of the soul—how could the heaven of the soul itself say
> 'That is no way for thee' how could I
> be left
> as the cormorant
> with no more flight than
> our own Rock?

The *Maximus* was well into the second volume before it was begun, and in this passage it does not conclude, but it arrives at a condition which is eternal:

> and what is the 'prison' the soul says
> you shall stay in?
> It is none, my Island
> has taught me.

The poem goes on, of course, but the process has arrived at a point beyond which Maximus' future is no longer bound to his history. It will become apparent in "As of Parsonses" (*Maximus* III, 130–31) that Maximus has assumed his own destiny, and though he will cele-brate "Events long past," they are no longer determinants.

Maximus recognizes that the perfect image of man, which he has sought, leads only to another mechanical and, so, unredeemed, future. He says:

> I have been an ability—a machine—up to
> now. An act of "history," my own, and my father's,
> together, a <u>queer</u> [Gloucester Sense] combination
> of completing something both visionary—or illusions
> (projection? literally
> lantern-slides, on the sheet, in the front-room Worcester,
> on the wall, and the lantern always getting too hot
> and I burning my fingers—& burning my
> nerves. . . .

> (*Maximus* III, 117)

From the beginning of the *Maximus*, what is known is only a skin between two knowable but largely occluded landscapes. The outer landscape is the province of the hero as son, the inner landscape the province of the hero as father. Until the middle of the third volume, the interchange between inward and outward has been controlled by the geometry which is established in "I, Maximus of Gloucester." It has demanded a conscious realization of genetic reality. Once it is achieved, however, the world which appears is a simple, literal land-scape, existing completely through itself. Maximus has established himself in a space which is nowhere broken or confused by abstrac-tion or generality: "This is the rose is the rose is the rose of the World" (*Maximus* III, 176).

Not since "Letter, May 2, 1959" has such a definitive break in the movement of the poem occurred. The self-questioning is pro-found:

> all does rhyme   like is the measure of
>   producing like, the Guardian
>   does <u>dictate</u> correctly the <u>message</u>
>   is a discrete & continuous conduction
>   of the life from a sequence of event measurable
>   in time   none of this <u>is</u> contestable
>   there <u>is</u> no measure without it or

with anything but <u>this</u> measure:

—it <u>does</u>, my Beloved's head grows to Heaven,

does my Life grow

out of my "life" Likewise—likewise?

is the <u>Modus</u>

absolute?

(*Maximus* III, 124–25)

It seems an inevitable problem for anyone so thoroughly mindful of process as Olson was: the process is clear, the relationship of the process to all else is not. Maximus never gives a definitive answer to his question.

In the remainder of "Maximus VIII" Maximus seems to be at loose ends. Although there are some interesting individual poems— "Essay on Queen Tiy" (*Maximus* III, 139–44), "Oceania" (*Maximus* III, 155–61), and "An Art Called Gothonic" (*Maximus* III, 168–72)— they are not fully engaged with the unexpected stasis which has appeared. Something in these poems recalls "Letter 29" and "King's Mountain"—two of the pieces which Olson wrote between 1953 and 1957, when, he says, he got off the "proper track" (*Origin*, 128). There is a strong sense that the poem is over; Maximus is summing up:

Sunday

night June 19th with some hope my own daughter

as well as 3 year old Ella may

live in a world on an Earth like this one we

few American poets have

carved out of Nature and of God.

(*Maximus* III, 173–74)

In some of the longer poems Maximus becomes "talky," the tension is gone. The excitement which any reader of the *Maximus* who has managed to get to the third volume has come to expect appears only in shorter passages:

This town

works at

dawn because

fishermen do—it makes therefore a
> very different
> City, a hippocampus of a
> City   halfish set & halfish land &
> day is riverine: when men
> are washed as gods in the Basin of Morning.

                              (*Maximus* III, 175)

In "An Art Called Gothonic" he begins to work out the demands which the poetic of this new situation makes on him, but it is never clearly enough established to carry the poem on.

3

I cannot believe, as the blurb on volume three insists, that "the Republic is successfully constructed, the Golden Flower attained, and Gloucester stands revealed, a perfect 'monstrance forever.'" The triumph of the *Maximus* is very real and important, but to exaggerate serves only to confuse and possibly to obscure what Olson does genuinely manage to accomplish.

The final book of *Maximus* (which I assume begins at *Maximus* III, 177, only because "Migration in fact," *Maximus* III, 176, seems to conclude the typical concerns of "Maximus VIII") opens with a passage from Keats's "Lines Written in The Manuscript of *The Cap and Bells*":

> This living hand, now warm, now capable
> of earnest grasping . . .

                              (*Maximus* III, 177)

Although there must be some question as to whether these lines which Olson copied out in his notes were intended as part of the *Maximus*, they are, without doubt, appropriate. Since Whitman, American poetry has tried to get in *touch* with its subject or to find objects in its subjects. Although Maximus as Tyr has lost one hand, the other now reaches out, as the eye reaches out. In the *Maximus* the hand and the eye have been closely associated since "Letter 7" (*Maximus* I, 33–34); both, in those verbs which are perhaps most characteristic of Olson, grasp or seize their objects. Commenting on this aspect of the *Maximus*, Robert Duncan writes: "The hand is intimate to the measuring of the eye. Michael McClure in an early poem refers to the hand: 'Opposable, . . . in the way, . . . dumb' and again 'This eye my thumb.' A rule of thumb. McClure refers to the role of the hand in perception; the hand & eye which never appears to share precisely the space we daily inhabit."[23] In "Human Universe" Olson speaks of the need to grasp our knowledge in such a way that experience is "returned to the only two universes which count, the two phenomenal ones, the two a man has need to bear on because they bear on him: that of himself, as organism, and that of his environment, the earth and planets" (*Human*, 4). The *Maximus* offers some measure of how completely one might be located in a place where all knowledge is completely local, completely graspable, completely and immediately relevant to the inner workings of the self.

The grasp which Maximus exercises is in no sense Faustian or Ahabian; it need not be. The Romantic will must strike with incredible force, because its objects are occluded by the whole of the physical cosmos. Maximus is almost passive:

> I bend my ear, as,
> if I were Amoghasiddi and,
> here on this plain where
> like my mole I have
> been knocked flat, attend,
> to turn & turn within
> the steady stream & collect which
> within me ends as in her hall and I
>
> hear all, the new moon new in all
> the ancient sky.

(*Maximus* III, 183)

He has learned to dance sitting down. He is, he says elsewhere, like Genji and Lady Murasaka; even they could not "in that far distant & more heightened time / have been more relaxed in their hands and / fingers or more alert to morning's beginning" (*Maximus* III, 207). At once relaxed and alert, Maximus has managed to *possess* the present as it can be possessed only by those who have the whole of the world inside themselves. He is, therefore, as he says,

> Wholly absorbed
> into my own conduits to

[23]"Notes on Poetics Regarding Olson's *Maximus*," pp. 189–92.

an inner nature or subterranean lake
the depths or bounds of which I more and more
explore and know more
of.

(*Maximus* III, 191)

The closing pages of the *Maximus* are obviously fragmentary, without any apparent direction. The images and insights are frequently contradictory in tone, but they are juxtaposed without that urgent sense that they must be harmonized. He can write:

The sea's

boiling   the land's

boiling   all the winds

of the earth are turning

the snow into sand—and

hiss, the land into

desert sands   the place

into hell. snow wild

snow and hissing

waters.

(*Maximus* III, 186)

But immediately thereafter he can say:

the salmon of
wisdom   when,
ecstatically, one
leaps into the Beloved's
love. And feels the air
        enter into
strike into one's previously breathing
system.

(*Maximus* III, 187)

Maximus is alert to the energies of the instant. The moments of power arise spontaneously from sight, to a placement in his world. It is that simplicity which he had sought from the beginning. In "Maximus, to himself" (*Maximus* I, 52–53) he says:

I have had to learn the simplest things
last. Which made for difficulties.

> Even at sea I slow, to get the hand out, or to cross
> a wet deck.

The striking fact about the collection of fragments with which the
poem concludes is the simple and perfect gestures of which Maximus
is now capable:

> the left hand is the calyx of the Flower
> can cup all things within itself, nothing else
> there, itself, alone limb of being, acting
> in the beneficent air, holding all tenderness
> as though it were the soul itself, the Soul's
> limb.
>
> (*Maximus* III, 208)

Early on, Maximus warns, "People / don't change. They only stand /
more revealed" (*Maximus* I, 5), and nothing *does* change in the almost six hundred pages of the poem. Olson begins with three abstract
terms: space, fact, and stance. The *Maximus* drives them back to their
specific and concrete meaning:

> the Blow is Creation
> & the Twist   the Nasturtium
> is any one of Ourselves
> And the Place of it All?
>   Mother   Earth   Alone.
>
> (*Maximus* III, 226)

It may not seem like a great deal to achieve in a lifetime, to begin to
have a full and useful sense of the meaning of three words. It is however, a beginning, a reality which can be shared, the grounds for a
possible City—something we have never had before.

In the tradition of western culture it is assumed that one speaks of knowledge or, in art, radiance when one is satisfied that the multiplicity of the thing is understood in terms of a single principle, a logos or theme. Otherwise, one is "incoherent." The same term is used for intellectual and artistic failure as for madness. Consequently, it is necessary to limit the perspective or, as Olson would have said early in his career, close the field. Information, bound by unifying disciplines, and works of art, themselves seamless self-enclosing forms, become inert, unless reference is made to totalizing chains of larger abstract unities which reach finally to some absolute, the Beautiful and the Good, the unmoved mover, God, or some surrogate absolute, the state or culture itself.

During the nineteenth century the development of technology allowed an opportunity finally to put theory into practice. The industrial revolution was a test not only of the scientific information which had accrued but also habits of mind which organized knowledge in a hierarchy of increasingly inclusive timeless forms. In practice, these beautifully coherent theoretical precepts resulted in cruel, destructive chaos. The eternal verities—necessarily true in logical space—served to make life in time even more treacherous than before, and, as they worked out so badly applied to practical life, people began with good reason to doubt their value, if not their absolute truth.

Olson's perception of this problem was not unique. He was anticipated by Melville, Nietzsche, Charles Sanders Peirce, Rimbaud, Oswald Spengler, Whitehead, Jung, and others. His work is addressed to the central cultural and intellectual problem of the past century. What does one *do* with the massive accumulation of information when the structure which seemed the source of its ultimate meaning and use suddenly collapses? Piecemeal repair of the structure is impossible. It is an all or nothing situation: the structure depends upon its absolute coherence. The liberal response, therefore, is disallowed on logical grounds. At best, it results in drift, in vagueness of thought and indecisiveness in action. When Olson was beginning his career the options were clearly determined: there was a choice between totalitarianism (in thought, in the broadest cultural sense) or radical reform of the institutions of artistic and intellectual production. These were the terms in which the *political* situation presented itself to Olson. The lack of political vitality was only a symptom.

In his radical vision Olson undertakes to demonstrate how fact relates immediately to fact and how factual complexes relate immediately to life, without resort to abstract forms. He takes unity to be the final, achieved condition, when everything is counted, not something which is assumed at the outset.

The process of the *Maximus* is the enumeration of emergent forms. In "I, Maximus of Gloucester, to You" he disallows allegiance to any absolute but the immediate present. With that entry into time, the logical unity produces a duality, and the duality produces a trinity. These three—space, fact, and stance, as Olson initially calls them—discover an identity with the mother, the father, and the son, the figures of the family drama. Olson's account of the family, however, though it derives from Freud, is not Freudian. Three is no more final than two. Freud's narrative of repressive fathers, fickle mothers, and murderous sons allows for individual adjustment to the chaos of the family and to the chaos of a social, temporal order which cannot reconcile itself with the timeless structure of the knowledge which it uses. In *Maximus* the son does not *replace* the father, he becomes a citizen. In the poem in which the circle—father to father—begins to close, Maximus literally, typographically, breaks out, and he prays, "rest Beloved Father as Your Son / goes forth to create Paradise / Upon this earth" (*Maximus* III, 121; see text for typography). The three generates a four, a political reality.

At this point the *Maximus*, which is a creation from an almost endless array of voices, can no longer contain the process in a single voice. The relevant information no longer bears on a single person. The world of the poem is no longer specific to the poem. It becomes the task of others. In "Letter 6" Maximus says,

> so few
> have the polis
> in their eye
>
> . . .
>
> so few need to
> to make the many
> share (to have it,
> too)

The few who make the city do not share a program or a belief, only a sharpness of eye which keeps them so close to the physical demands of their lives and jobs that a shared place appears, so

> that one suddenly is walking
>
> in Tartarian-Erojan, Geaan-Ouranian
> time and life love space
>   time & exact
> analogy time & intellect   time & mind   time & time
> spirit
>
>   the initiation
>
>   of another kind of nation.

(*Maximus* III, 228)

Index

in God," 169; "I believe in religion," 169; "I have been an ability," 190; "I live underneath," 109, 198; "I told the woman," 171; "I was bold, I had courage," 167; "IF THE DEATHS DO NOT STOP," 188; "Imbued/with light," 170; "the left hand is the calyx of the Flower," 195; "Main Street," 171; "Maximus of Gloucester," 187; "migration in fact," 190; "the Mountain of no difference," 190–91; "My beloved Father," 197; "The New Empire," 178–79; "The Ocean," 186; "Oceania," 191; "Physically, I am home," 143, 185; "rages/strains," 173; "Said Mrs Tarantino," 171; "the salmon of/wisdom," 194; "The sea's/boiling," 194; "7 years & you could carry cinders in yr hand," 173–75; "the sky,/of Gloucester," 176; "Stevens Song," 172, 175; "Sweet Salmon," 182; "There was a salt-works at Stage Fort," 178; "a 3rd morning," 189; "This town," 192; "to get the rituals straight," 191; "To have the bright body," 176; "West Gloucester," 171; "Wholly absorbed," 166, 194; "The winter the *Gen. Starks* was stuck," 187–88
—Writings, prose: "The Advantage of Literacy Is that Words Can Be on the Page," 28, 146–47; "Against Wisdom as Such," 6; "The Antimate versus the Mechanical, and Thought," 158; "Apollonius of Tyana," 65–66, 67; "The Area and Discipline, of Totality," 32, 54–55, 96; "Bibliography on America for Ed Dorn," 132; *Call Me Ishmael*, 5, 8–9, 17, 56, 59, 65–66, 168; "Captain John Smith," 90; *Causal Mythology*, 26, 31, 46, 61, 92, 124, 132, 149, 173–74; *Charles Olson & Ezra Pound*, 4, 6, 118; "Conditio," 27; "David Young, David Old," 116; "Equal, That Is,

to the Real Itself," 15–16, 28, 60, 66, 93, 104–5; "The Escaped Cock," 38–39, 94; "Experience and Measure," 126–27; "A Foot Is to Kick With," 38; "The Gate and the Center," 11, 119–22, 161; "Grammar—a 'book,'" 33, 64; "The hinges of civilization to be put back on the door," 102, 138–39; "Human Universe," 16, 27, 31, 49, 52, 74–75, 140, 189, 193; "Letter to Elaine Feinstein," 34, 57, 160; *Letters for Origin*, 7, 28, 33, 91, 96, 127; "Logography," 165; "The Materials and Weights of Herman Melville," 127; "Mayan Letters," 52, 74, 85, 86, 100; "On Poets and Poetry," 31; "A Plausible 'Entry' for, like, man," 138–39; *Pleistocene Man*, 109; *Poetry and Truth*, 60–61, 161, 180–81; "The principles of measure in composition by Field: Projective Verse II," 131–32; "Projective Verse," 5, 16, 17, 22, 32, 34–35, 38, 62–63; "Proprioception," 51, 71, 117; "Quantity in Verse, and Shakespeare's Late Plays," 29–31, 48, 102; *Reading at Berkeley*, 130; "The Resistance," 19, 47, 68; "Review of Eric Havelock's *Preface to Plato*," 34, 39; "The Secret of the Black Chrysanthemum," 179; *The Special View of History*, 10, 40, 48–53, 88, 139, 169, 186; "A Syllabary for a Dance," 84; "*The Vinland Map* Review," 181–82; "A Work," 138–39
Olson, Betty (wife), 164, 188, 170

Paracelsus, 57
Paul, Sherman, xii
Peirce, Charles Sanders, 196
Perse, St. John, 3
Pindar, 18
Plato, 35–37, 189
Plutarch, 10
Poe, Edgar Allan, 71
Polis, 92, 124–25, 145–46, 160, 168

204

Charles Olson's *Maximus*

Pound, Ezra, xiv, 4–6, 7, 9, 16, 25,
  31, 38, 61, 69, 72, 98, 100, 102,
  125, 154, 169, 181
Pythagoras, 19
Pytheas, 91, 113, 126, 138, 143,
  173

Rank, Otto, 178
Rimbaud, Arthur, 9, 196
Rose-Troup, Francis, 109

St. Augustine, 141
Sapir, Edward, 33, 64
Schrodinger, Irwin, 50
The Secret of the Golden Flower,
  170
Shakespeare, William, 29–31, 48,
  81, 89, 102
Shaler, N. S., 115
Smith, John, 68, 102, 104–5
Snell, Bruno, 17
Snyder, Gary, 84
Space: and the vertical dimension,
  26, 66; and language, 62, 64; and
  open form, 73; and objectivity,
  77; and history, 89; mentioned,
  xiv, 8–15, 24, 54, 58, 110–11,
  168
Spengler, Oswald, 196
Spirit of the world. *See Anima
  mundi*
Stance (as poet), xiv, 22–26, 54, 59
Standish, Miles, 90
Stefansson, Vilhjalmar, 125–26

Stevens, William, ix, 175
Surrealism, 71, 97

Tarot cards, 21, 139
Thales, 141
Thomson, J. A. K., 36, 100
Topos, 110–11, 140, 168. *See also*
  Space
Tropos, 110–11, 140. *See also* Fact
Tusi, Nasir, 129–30, 137, 139
Typos, 110–11, 146. *See also* Stance
Tyre, 55–57, 141, 144. *See also* Ol-
  son, Charles, writings: "Tyrian
  Businesses," "Later Tyrian Busi-
  ness"

Vashi, Natarja, 83
von Hallberg, Robert, 20

Waddell, L. A., 118, 143
Whitehead, Alfred North, 25, 27,
  41, 46, 48–53, 101, 102–3,
  113–14, 135, 147, 157, 159, 169,
  174, 196
Whitman, Walt, xiv, 41, 62, 169,
  192
Whorf, Benjamin L., 26
Williams, William Carlos, xiv, 3,
  6–7, 16, 25, 31, 38, 63, 64, 98,
  102
Winthrop, John, 60, 106
Wittgenstein, Ludwig, 181

Zimmer, Heinrich, 154, 182–84